COUNTING DAYS

By Brenda Lindsey

Brenda Lindsey

For my sweet Annie,
I love you,
Mom

Leukemia

In the beginning, God created the heavens and the earth. When God had finished making man, He looked at all He had created and said, "It is very good."

And the Enemy saw all that God had created, and he heard man speak of life being in the blood. He saw the Son of God come to earth as the Son of Man and give his life-blood in exchange for their lives, and the Enemy was very, very angry. He wanted the souls of men and he knew because of the blood of Christ, he had lost them. So, the Enemy hated God and man. And in particular, he hated the blood.

So the Enemy devised a plan. He decided to use the very essence of man, the life-giving blood, and turn the blessing into a curse. He formed a disease to enter the blood of man very quickly and quietly. So subtly would the disease enter, that man would walk around laughing, thinking he was healthy until it was almost too late to detect. Then he made the disease strike the ones man clung to closest of all – the children.

The Enemy made the disease to have many types and sub-types. He made the disease so complicated that the average man could barely comprehend what was being discussed and would need it explained to him many times. He made it necessary for man to devise difficult and painful tests and treatments that would need to be repeated in order to treat the disease. Tests so difficult to understand with decisions needed so quickly, that the average man would not know what was being done to the body of his own child. He forced parents to make decisions they did not understand and trust in people they did not know.

The Enemy made the cause of the disease to be hidden from man. And then he tricked man into thinking it was something the man had caused. The man would question what he had eaten, what he had smelled, or what he had rubbed or sprayed on his body. The Enemy caused good men to think they had caused the disease.

The Enemy made the disease so horrific, that the very mention of its name would strike a fear in the hearts of parents. When a day arrived that they heard their child had the disease, they would fall to their knees and cry out in despair thinking surely they had been forsaken by God. Because of the existence of the disease, the Enemy tried to make men question God and His love and grace.

When the Enemy had finished making the disease, he looked at all the suffering it had caused and said, "It is very evil."

And man called the disease "leukemia".

Caught Unaware

DAY -5 – Friday, October 10, 2014

It is Annie's 16th birthday! We are letting her go on her first real date alone with the boyfriend tonight. For us it seems like yesterday our little Tiger Lily (the Indian princess from Peter Pan) was being born. Her daddy brings the tiara he ordered from Amazon upstairs where I am getting ready. He wrapped it himself. We forgot a card! I remind him that we won't be seeing her tonight anyway. She and the boyfriend are leaving early (likely before I get home from work) and they have a big night planned. Tomorrow is her slumber party with all her BFFs. We can have her cake, ice cream and card then. We talk about plans for Sunday to go look at a new car for her. Well…new to her. We have a fleet of used cars in the driveway already. Another car will add to our skills of maneuvering around obstacles each morning. (The hubs' skills were a bit off last week as he backed in to our son's car while leaving for work. Nothing like wrecking two of your cars at once.) We talk about how our insurance agent will likely remodel his offices (as our orthodontist did), compliments of our family.

Her daddy leaves the gift and leaves for work with her sister in tow. The hubs is a teacher in the next town at the Jr. High and our eighth-grade baby girl, Red Bull (so named by her soccer coach because of her red hair and aggressiveness on the field), rides with her daddy to school. A while later, I hear Annie is up and my phone rings. It is my mom, her Granny. No one in the family can remember a birthday getting started without Granny singing "Happy Birthday." I track down Annie in the laundry room and hand her the phone. She listens to the singing, then talks to her Granny a minute...all smiles.

I finish getting ready and leave for work, wishing her a wonderful day on my way out. I remind her to wear the crown all day. She rolls her eyes and says, "Are you trying to get me beat up at school?"

I leave work early that day, go to happy hour with friends, come home and watch a movie with the hubs and Red Bull. My daughter-in-law is there with my ten-month-old adorable grandson (aka cutest baby in the world!). Annie comes in with the boyfriend. We are surprised to see them back early. She wants money (of course she does) so she can go to Walmart and buy supplies for her upcoming slumber party. I remind her to take it easy. Walmart charges $100 just for walking in the door. She comes home with enough junk food to clog the arteries of a dozen teenage girls. The hubs and I are exhausted. We go to bed. Life is good!

DAY -4 – Saturday, October 11, 2014

Red Bull normally plays soccer every Saturday, but it's raining today so soccer games are cancelled. Even though I know this means make-up games later, just like snow days during the school year, rained-out Saturday soccer games make everyone happy. Red Bull and I go to Walmart to pick up a cake and ice cream for Annie's party tonight. She wants a vanilla cake. We select a flowery one and the lady behind the counter practices her penmanship while writing "Happy Birthday Annie" in red letters across the top. A tub of the cheap Neapolitan ice cream that leaves a film in your mouth and 16 candles later, we are checking out and ready to party.

When the guests arrive, we are all standing in the front yard looking at the jack-o-lanterns the girls cut out during the day. They made one to look like it was puking…teenage humor at its finest! After everyone arrives, we travel to Chili's for dinner. Though Annie and friends sit at a table on the other side of the restaurant, they have made it clear to give the bill to Daddy. Afterward, we go home to eat cake and ice cream and open presents. Annie wears her crown and her daddy talks to her about checking out the used car lots on Sunday to pick out a car. The hubs and I go to bed early leaving the girls to stay up all night. The boys used to run through the woods and have air-rifle wars for their parties. The girls have planned facials and mani/pedis. When I ask where they are all planning to sleep, Annie says "Wherever we end up!" Whatever. I go to bed exhausted and unaware.

DAY -3 – Sunday, October 12, 2014

I come downstairs for coffee and it looks like we have been vandalized during the night. Blankets, pillows, make-up bags, dishes and half-eaten snacks are everywhere. Mattresses have been pulled off the beds and put in my living room. Bodies are wrapped in blankets in several rooms. I am trying to creep through, but am in desperate need of coffee and making much more noise than intended. I hear a few sighs, but mostly the girls are all sound asleep.

I put a lasagna in the oven for lunch. The hubs and I leave for church, sans kids, which is unusual. We are late as usual, even though we don't have the girls to blame. It is a nice day to be praising the Lord with the Methodists.

We return home after church to find all the girls have gone home from the party. It is a hallelujah moment! At lunch, my oldest son and his wife are there with my adorable grandson. They have just moved back in to live with us while they go to college. My garage is full of their boxes that need to be cleaned out so I can park in the garage, and the house is still a mess. I tell Annie she needs to clean up the mess left from her friends. She isn't eating and says she doesn't feel good, but I'm not buying it. We talk about taking her driving test later in the week, and her daddy tells her they can go look at cars after the house is picked up. She agrees and I enlist her brother to help return the mattresses to the beds. I go take a nap, while they go look at cars.

When they get back, Annie goes to bed early. I remind her she has mid-term tests this week so she needs to quit texting early and get some rest. She agrees and goes upstairs to bed. I have planned a few days of vacation later in the week while the kids are on Fall Break, so we discuss traveling to see our parents. Looks like a fun week is in store.

DAY -2 – Monday, October 13, 2014

Annie wakes up complaining she doesn't feel good. She looks fine to me. After all, she got up out of bed and found me just to tell me this. I remind her she has tests the next couple of days and needs to be reviewing in class. She assures me she will do fine on the tests, but she just needs one more day off. She has shown me a sore on the side of her tongue that looks awful. I think maybe the sore is hurting (or infected) and making her sick. I make her an appointment with our pediatrician and ask her brother to take her later. I tell her if she stays home, she can't go anywhere else and she MUST go to school tomorrow. She agrees and goes back to bed. I go to work. It's a Monday.

The doctor gives her some medicine for the sore in her mouth and some anti-nausea medicine for her upset stomach, likely caused by a virus. Several viruses are going around. I make a mental note to get her a flu shot. When I get home from work, she says she feels better. She plays with my adorable grandson for a while and goes to bed early after planning what she will wear the next day.

I go to bed looking forward to only one more day before my mini-vacation.

DAY -1 – Tuesday, October 14, 2014

Annie wakes up crying and tells me she can't make it to school again today. I tell her there is no way she can miss because she won't be able to take all her tests tomorrow – the day before Fall Break. She assures me she can take all her tests in a day and will be fine. I am frustrated with her. She asks for a thermometer and I take her temperature. It's 100.9 and I decide to give her a pass for one more sick day. But I tell her this is it – no more missing school. She has to take her tests on Wednesday or she will never pass tenth grade (yes, I am a little dramatic, but she only has a little bug, right?).

When I get home from work, the house is quiet. The hubs and Red Bull have gone to a football game and Annie is already in bed. I check on her and she says her stomach hurts. I try to get her to eat and bring her some yogurt thinking her empty stomach might be the problem. I take her temperature. It's 100.9 again. I take my temperature just to see if it works. Mine is 100.6. I figure the darn thing doesn't even work. I fall asleep reading my Kindle.

I have a text from Annie that I don't even see until the next morning. Somewhere in the fog of my brain, I hear Red Bull saying her daddy is taking Annie to the ER. Apparently, Annie was putting on her shoes when they arrived home from the football game. She said her stomach hurt so badly that he could take her to the ER or she would drive herself. About 10 p.m. the phone rings and he asks about our insurance. He is at a hospital in our town that is known for its long wait. I tell him we have excellent insurance, and to take her to another hospital. Annie tells me later he was not convinced she was really sick either.

He calls me sometime later and says her blood count is very low. Our small regional hospital ruled out appendicitis as the cause of the stomach pain, but now wants to take her to St. Francis in Tulsa via ambulance for a blood transfusion. Having never experienced anything like this, I ask if I need to come along. He tells me one of us should get a good night's sleep so I can just see them in the morning.

GROUND ZERO – Wednesday, October 15, 2014

The hubs calls and they have admitted Annie to the hospital. Instead of taking a vacation day, I get dressed and head to see them. When I arrive, she is very pale. She has received one transfusion, but needs another. The doctor explains the myriad of tests they are running, and I don't understand much of it. I know they have checked for appendicitis and are doing a chest x-ray. I think they are still looking for an infection. I ask when he thinks we can go home and the doctor says we should plan on staying at least a few days. A few days? No one stays in the hospital overnight. Can't a blood transfusion be an outpatient procedure? If they give me some antibiotics, I can take care of her at home. He gives me a sad look which I did not recognize at the time. He asks Annie if she wants to be filled in on all the details as they find out what is wrong. She says yes, she likes to plan and wants to know details. We agree it is okay.

It's the afternoon and they have been up all night. I had stopped to get us breakfast from

McDonalds on the way in, not knowing it will be the last time I feel like eating for days. I am working on my laptop from the hospital room and am anxiously waiting on a diagnosis so we can get some medicine and go home. The hubs is sitting in another chair and Annie is lying on the bed watching TV. A different doctor we haven't seen before walks in. He again asks Annie if she wants to know all the details, and she says that she does. He then says the three words that will change our lives forever. "You have leukemia."

I immediately think he is confused who he is talking to. I ask "Are you sure you are in the right room? Because the other doctor didn't say that. We are looking for an infection. We aren't here for that." I am already feeling sorry for the poor souls in the next room who have to hear this horrific news. But he looks at me and says, "This is Annie, right?"

I feel like I have been kicked in the stomach. There isn't enough air in the room. I can't breathe. I will myself to breathe in and breathe out. No one speaks. I look at Annie. She is looking at me wide-eyed. The hubs is expressionless – staring like he is dead. The doctor asks to sit down. I say, "Of course." Where are my manners? I look back at Annie wondering if she realizes what the doctor has just said. She bursts into tears. I move to the bed and sit beside her. We hold on to one another and cry and cry and cry. The hubs breaks down and we all cry and cry.

When things calm down again, the doctor asks Annie if she has any questions. She asks, "Will I lose my hair?" He says she most likely will. After another round of crying, she then asks, "Am I going to live?" He starts giving statistical information and from this point I have no idea what is being said. I feel like it is a bad dream and maybe I can shake myself awake. While I am holding her and we are rocking back and forth, Annie asks me "What are we going to do?" I tell her we will take one day at a time and we will get through it. It sounds good, but I have no idea what I am talking about. I just try to say the right thing.

We learn she has acute myeloid leukemia (AML). The doctor tells us not to look on the internet. We may receive misinformation and get discouraged. I cannot wait for him to leave so I can get online. We learn it is not the kind of leukemia most kids get – which has a 93% survival rate. It is less common in children and only has a 67% survival rate. We just went from bad news to worse.

My phone is going off with texts from my mom, her Granny, asking about Annie. How do you tell someone this news? Especially when you cannot speak. I give family and friends the news via text. Not exactly appropriate, but all I can manage. I am making myself keep breathing calmly. I keep telling myself, just breathe in and breathe out. It is a struggle to keep upright and not throw up. I take a Zofran and pray that I will not get sick so I can be strong for Annie. I don't remember the rest of the day.

DAY 1 – Thursday, October 16, 2014

I begin to wake up thinking about work, the things I need to do and the calls I need to make. I open my eyes and stare at a blue vinyl cushion that is way too close to my face. My disorientation is only a second and then I remember. It feels like someone just punched me in the stomach and I physically gasp. I roll over and see Annie lying in the bed. She's so pale, but beautiful. How can something so deadly be living inside her?

Red Bull is beside me sleeping in a recliner. They have never enjoyed spending that much time together, but now she doesn't want to leave her sister's side. I look out the window of the hospital room. We have a beautiful view of Tulsa and it is a beautiful morning. Why does that upset me? I feel like it should be raining. I want God to cry with me.

People are calling, texting and wanting to visit. Our pastor and Annie's youth pastor came by yesterday and prayed with us. Other people and friends start coming again. As people learn the news that we will be in the hospital for a lengthy stay, I am bone tired, but want Annie to see the support of her friends. Wondering how much time she has, I don't want to deny her anything.

They need to give Annie another blood transfusion, but she is running a fever. Her last transfusion only brought her hemoglobin count from a 5.4 to a 6.3. I don't even know what that means, but they tell us the low end of normal is 12. That puts it in perspective. My nurse friend tells me she has never seen someone with counts that low still standing. Great, I was making her clean the house! They don't want to start the transfusion until the fever comes down. Annie fights the fever all day and finally gets the needed blood that evening.

My sister calls the hubs and arranges for her to come and help us at home. As a teacher on Fall Break, she will come and stay the rest of the week to help with laundry and getting those boxes out of my garage. She will be here by the end of the day. She texts me "Call me she is approved for St Jude!"

I have heard of St. Jude, but I have no idea what my sister is talking about. I call her and she begins telling me a long story about a friend putting her in contact with a doctor at St. Jude. I ask "Where is St. Jude?" "Memphis." MEMPHIS? Annie overhears. She says she is not going to Memphis. She is not going to leave her friends. She says please tell my aunt not to come. Annie begins sobbing and I tell her we are not going anywhere. My sister follows up to text me the name and number of the doctor to call. I get another text, "Call this number and get her there ASAP. They can get her on a plane." I cannot make these decisions. I think I am going to be sick. There is not enough air in the room. I cannot breathe.

We speak to a doctor about the possibility of St. Jude. He tells us the protocol for her type of leukemia will be the same no matter where she is. He tells us this type of leukemia is not new or unusual, but very straightforward. They will treat her well at the hospital in Tulsa. They have access to the same information or research that the doctors at St. Jude have. I am convinced we should stay in Tulsa.

We switch and the hubs will stay the night at the hospital. I go home to meet my sister. My older sister calls. I begin to tell her I am not anxious to see our younger sister because I know she will start in on me about moving Annie to Memphis. My older sister starts in on me. She tells me Tulsa is not the best place for her to be. She starts talking about the best hospitals in the country. I tell her I have seen the rankings and it is only because St. Jude treats really complex cases that they are so highly valued. Annie's case is straightforward. The protocol is the same. I feel smart because I can repeat what the doctor said.

My older sister is not agreeing. She is trying to tell me what to do. Everyone is trying to tell me what to do. In my over-exhausted, over-loaded, stressed-out mind, I feel like everyone is telling me I am not smart enough or don't care enough to make smart decisions on behalf of my own daughter. I start yelling at my sister on the phone and hang up on her. I go into the other room and start screaming at my younger sister. I tell her to go home. I tell her it is my child who is dying and they need to leave me alone. I scream and act like a toddler while yelling how I know what's best for my own child. My sister doesn't even speak. I look over at Red Bull. She is sobbing. I feel like an idiot.

I call and talk to the hubs who gets upset because I am upset. We decide to keep Annie in Tulsa.

I go to bed and cannot sleep. I know my sisters love me and love our family. I don't want this to come between us. I send them a long text apologizing for my crazy behavior. I try to convince them via text that staying in Tulsa is best. My older sister responds no explanation is necessary. I don't hear anything from my younger sister. I get up and go into where my younger sister is sleeping – in Annie's bed. I wonder if Annie will ever sleep in her bed again. My sister is just reading my text. I sit on the bed with her and we hug and cry and cry and cry. I didn't think I had tears left. Just how many can a person shed in one lifetime? I think I read a Bible verse where God stores our tears? Where does He put them? Are they recycled? Because I am sure he will surely be running out of storage space with mine.

At last my sister says, "Just promise me one thing. You will not rule out St. Jude until you have had a chance to talk with the doctor from St. Jude." I tell her I promise and go to bed.

DAY 2 – Friday, October 17, 2014

I wake up early. I want to sleep, but can't. Goals for the day: Remain vertical, try to breathe normally, and don't throw up. Seems simple. I take a Zofran and get out of bed.

I call my right hand at work (who jokingly calls himself Captain Awesome) to tell him what is going on and to get someone to agree with me. He will not tell me what to do, but reassures me moving her to Memphis is a decision for Annie's dad and me to make. He says he knows we love our children and will make the best decision. He agrees with me that staying in Tulsa would be encouraging for Annie and having her friends beside her is important, but he admits he also knows nothing about St. Jude.

I arrive at the hospital and they are making arrangements for Annie to have a bone marrow biopsy. While they have her under sedation, they will also do a spinal tap and give a small dose of chemo. We have heard that if we start chemo in Tulsa, they will not take her at St. Jude. We decide to hold off on the spinal tap until we can speak to the doctor at St. Jude.

In the sedation room with Annie, the doctor comes in. He tells me he hates delivering the news that a child has leukemia. Over the years, he has had all types of responses. He has *never* had someone tell him he was in the wrong room. If only I had been right!

After the procedure, the doctor begins telling us about the pros and cons of St. Jude. My nurse friend has arrived and is helping me understand all the medical vernacular. She has worked at St. Francis and tells me the doctors are excellent. She plays the devil's advocate a bit with my younger sister just to help us make an intelligent decision. My younger sister insists we get the doctor at St. Jude on a conference call and speak with him together.

The doctor at St. Francis arranges the call, and we begin to pepper the St. Jude doctor on the line with our questions. The more he talks and explains that it is not necessarily the protocol (the combination of meds in the treatment plan) that makes St. Jude the best in the country, but the supportive care. He explains that children at St. Jude are less likely to have follow-up issues, particularly with infection, because you are staying close by and receiving so much support from their staff.

He tells us there is a research study currently going on at St. Jude for children with AML and we can be admitted. After a long round of questioning (for which I will later feel stupid), we thank the doctor. Our doctor at St. Francis won't tell us what to do, but says, "Whatever you decide, don't second guess yourself later." My nurse friend won't tell us what to do. My sisters have already told us what to do. We look at Annie and she knows what we need to do. She begins sobbing and says, "I won't get to see my friends."

We begin to make plans to head to Memphis.

Welcome to Memphis

DAY 3 – Saturday, October 18, 2014

I wake up crying. The hubs and I both went home last night to sleep. Our youngest son, an eighteen-year-old, stayed with Annie overnight so we could pack. They tell us to be at the hospital by 6:00 a.m. I feel like I have been drugged and cannot think what to pack or who to call or what needs to be done to take care of things at home. Two weeks ago, I was lamenting that my twenty-year-old son and his little family were moving back in with us. Now I am so glad that someone will be there. He volunteers to take care of things while we are gone. Fortunately, my brain is too foggy to focus on the possible implications of my twenty-year-old son "taking care of things." I don't need another meltdown.

We arrive at the hospital, but Annie needs another transfusion before she can travel. We learn they are taking her by ambulance. Something about the cabin pressure not allowing her to fly. I don't understand, but really don't care. We need to drive our car anyway and will follow the ambulance. It is a morning of waiting and waiting. Finally, we leave around 11:00. It is a long trip with lots of stops.

Stopping to get lunch, the gal at the fast food counter is extremely rude. Apparently, she is upset that we are making her take our order. I tell her this is the worst customer service I have ever seen. People are looking at me. My sister is shuffling me out the door, afraid I may pull the gun I am packing. Stressful!

Annie has to use the bedpan in the ambulance because she is hooked up to IV antibiotics and pain killers. She is freaking out. So am I, on the inside. Her boyfriend rides along with her until he gets motion sickness from the ambulance ride and has to get in the car. The EMT's give Annie something to make her sleep and we arrive at St. Jude Children's Research Hospital at night.

We enter through a gated wrought-iron fence which surrounds the campus. St. Jude is in downtown Memphis. On the outside of the campus it looks scary. Inside the gate is another world, another life, another kind of scary. Our new normal.

The hubs starts filling out paperwork at registration while I go to the room with Annie. There is a separate room beside her hospital room just for our family. It's so small my sister names it "The Kennel." We go through all the rules about the hospital room with the nurse. There is a sink just outside the room. We must wash our hands before entering and after leaving the room. Every time. Always wear shoes. (I think that one is just a subtle reminder of normal social etiquette, given the proximity to Arkansas.) No fresh flowers, no stuffed animals, no food or drink left exposed for more than an hour, no leftovers (no problem there), and no visitors with even a trace of the sniffles. Also, everyone needs their flu shot to visit.

Annie's boyfriend cannot stay, so she says she doesn't want company for the night. She later posts on Facebook how she has been left alone. Great. Now the whole world will think we are loser parents. The hubs, my sister, Red Bull and I go find our new "home" for the next couple of weeks. It's called Tri Delta Place. I always wanted to join a sorority. I'll pretend that's what it is. I unpack for our stay in the sorority house.

We all go to bed exhausted. I'm so cold I shiver. I snuggle next to the hubs in our too small bed. He reaches over for me and his hands begin to roam. Really? Now? Some habits die hard. I give him a look that says, "Touch me again and you're a dead man!" and fall instantly asleep.

DAY 4 – Sunday, October 19, 2014

I wake up crying. It's Sunday. I should be getting ready for church. I'm getting ready to be surrounded by the sick and dying. I think of how cruel this disease is. There are no stages. When cancer is in the blood, it is immediately in the whole body. There are only risks: low, standard or high. When we tell this to people, they ask, "Risk of what"? How do you say "Risk of death"? Awkward.

I write a story about leukemia and how it is evil. I cry as I write and it is therapeutic. I e-mail it to my sister, who is still sleeping in the next room. She comes out crying. "That was so true," she says, and heads off to the bathroom. I hear her crying more. The hubs gets up and wonders what's up. I pull what I have written up on my computer for him to read. He is totally breaking down and sobbing while reading it. I think that means it is good, but I didn't mean to make him start his day with crying.

Annie needs clothes. When we hurriedly left from Tulsa, she was wearing a hospital gown. She is sick of the gown, and though I packed for everyone else, I didn't think of the patient needing clothes. We

23

find a Walmart and find that parts of Memphis are a little scary – even in the daytime. We divide and conquer, grabbing everything on her list and receive a text from the boyfriend's dad (who flew in from Tulsa to pick him up) that the doctor is wanting to speak with us. We rush to the checkout line in record time only to find all Walmart's are created equally – 7 out of 33 lanes are open and it takes us another twenty minutes to get out of the store.

The weekend doctor (is it attending, resident, intern, kid playing doctor? – I have no idea) tells us things we have already heard in ways we already did not understand. I thank him for coming by to check on us. Minding my manners. The boyfriend leaves and it is very emotional for everyone. It's like another part of home is leaving when he does – another part of our old normal.

The nurse tells us once chemo starts Annie will likely be sick and may not feel like getting out. This may be her last chance for a while to wander around. We load her up in a wheelchair and roll her around the campus. My sister takes a picture of us in front of the Danny Thomas statue out front. I can't remember who Danny Thomas is, but there are statues of children looking at him like he has all the answers. I wish he was here to share those answers. We roll Annie to the sorority house to show her where we live. She stays a while and we pretend everything is fine before she says her back hurts and she's really tired. We roll her back to her hospital room.

Annie asks her daddy to spend the night. The rest of us go to the sorority house. I fall asleep crying.

DAY 5 – Monday, October 20, 2014

I wake up disoriented again. This time in the sorority house. My sister brings me coffee and a muffin from the café downstairs. They make really good coffee here. It hits the spot. I am ready to face the sick and dying. We get in my sister's SUV to drive back to the hospital. It's only about a block, but we like to drive. We drive around and around the parking lot looking for a spot. There isn't one. We decide to go back to the sorority house to park. Our spot is gone and there are no others. St. Jude on weekdays is nothing like the weekends. People are everywhere. It is like a little bustling city within the gates. My sister drops me off in front of the hospital and goes to find a parking spot. I wonder how long it will be before I see her again.

A doctor tells us they want to rerun all the tests that were performed in Tulsa. He says they want to confirm the diagnosis. I ask him not to confirm it, but instead to tell me it's all been a big mistake. I am holding on to that hope. They take her for two bone marrow biopsies and do the spinal tap test to see if the leukemia is in her spinal fluid. Just in case, they give her a small dose of chemo in the spinal column while she is under sedation from the test. We send out a prayer request for no cancer in the spinal fluid. They replace the IV in her arm (the PICC line) with an IV in her chest (a central line or Hickman). This way the medicine will go straight to the heart. So will an infection if it is not kept clean. No pressure.

Annie has different medicines being pumped through her Hickman all the time. She is allergic to one of the antibiotics she gets and to the blood platelets she receives. The allergies require even more medication. I have lost track. I trust in people I do not know.

We finally meet our primary doctor. I have heard the name Dr. Rubnitz for days, but there has been no sighting. I get a text from a co-worker who says a mutual friend of ours knows one of the doctors at St. Jude. They have been friends since childhood. The mutual friend has e-mailed the doctor asking him to locate our family and make sure we get extra special care. I ask the doctor's name so I can try to find him. My co-worker texts back, "Dr. Rubnitz." Wow! Maybe God does have my back after all. Too much to be a coincidence, I start believing again.

Dr. Rubnitz is a kind soul. He wants to know all about our family and Annie – not the medical history, but about our life before leukemia. He puts us at ease and tells us we did nothing to cause this. In our case, it is not hereditary, it is just bad luck. I make a mental note: Don't ever go to Vegas.

It's my turn to spend the night in the hospital room. My sister goes home. The hubs goes to the sorority house. I am exhausted, but a light sleeper. I lay awake listening to the sounds of the hospital room. I question, "Why can we put a man on the moon, but we cannot invent an IV pump that does not make an unbelievably irritating clicking noise?" (And why do we measure all other inventions against our ability to put man on the moon?) I am also very cold. Annie is comfortable and I don't want to upset that. The nurse comes in and I feel guilty asking for another blanket. She offers me a heated one. She is my new BFF. I don earplugs and fall asleep.

Annie is restless and has been running fever. She wakes up at 2:30 needing to go to the bathroom. She wants her sheets changed. I am thinking her voice has gotten remarkably weaker. I can barely hear what she is asking. Oh yeah – need to remove the earplugs. The nurses hop to change the sweaty sheets. I ask them if they ever say no. They look at me with a puzzled expression. Apparently not. We go back to sleep with clean sheets and heated blankets…and earplugs.

DAY 6 – Tuesday, October 21, 2014

Waking up early, I go in The Kennel to get dressed. I talk to Captain Awesome. We devise a plan for me to work remotely. After finding out about Annie, my work e-mail has been ominously silent. I begin to get paranoid that they will make me take a leave of absence. Hearing, "Take as much time off as you need" sounds great. Not getting paid for time off sounds like a plan for bankruptcy. I am afraid I will lose my job. I am not afraid of being fired, but just of being out of sight, out of mind so long that going back will never be the same. I feel guilty for worrying about my job. What kind of mother thinks of a job when her daughter is dying? Don't they say things like this put everything in perspective? Yet it puts nothing in perspective and everything in doubt.

The hubs and I plan to set up a portable remote office and schedule when we will be in Memphis versus Tulsa. Being told we will be here for at least the next six months, we decide we can trade off. The hubs' fellow teachers are volunteering to donate their PTO to him, but we are not certain what his employers will do either. We need a calendar. Back to Walmart for office supplies.

We choose a different Walmart. This time it is at night and Memphis is even scarier. I try not to make eye contact in the store fearing they will prey on me because I'm clearly a tourist. We get our supplies and go back to The Kennel. We map out the plan and I e-mail it to management at my office. I get one word back from the President – "Perfect." That felt like a hug.

The tests results come back from the spinal tap. They are positive for leukemia in the spinal fluid. This means weekly chemo via spine injections in addition to the "regularly scheduled" chemo. We put the news out on her Facebook page the hubs has set up called "Annie's Army." Everyone is very supportive and promises to continue praying. People post Bible verses and sweet messages of inspiration. My good friend in

Texas sends my favorite reply that sums up exactly how I feel, "Oh holy hell. Y'all just can't catch a break."

I go to bed anxious about what lies ahead.

DAY 7 – Wednesday, October 22, 2014

I wake up early and begin working on my laptop. After letting everyone at work know that I would work remotely, I receive e-mails until 10:00 p.m. that start again at 7:00 a.m. Be careful what you ask for.

Annie starts her chemo today. The medicines are pumped through her Hickman line. The first bag of medicine takes two hours to pump into her body. Then she has a two-hour break. The second medicine takes another two hours. With chemo, you either get sick or you get *really* sick.

While she is on her two-hour break, she wants to take a bath. I help her take a bath and wash her hair, being careful to keep the Hickman line dry. No easy task especially with her very long hair. We talk about cutting her hair short before it starts falling out. We talk about getting a wig, but she doesn't want a wig. She jokes about decorating her head – maybe making it look like a Christmas ornament around the holidays.

After the bath, she wraps in a towel and steps out of the tub. She sways and says, "I'm going to be sick" right before she turns and begins violently vomiting and retching. I try to stand by to help, but I start feeling sick and light-headed. I think I am going to pass out. I am no help. I walk out into the hospital room. Where is the nurse? I lay down on the recliner trying to keep breathing. I can do this...I can do this. I get back up to help her. She is in the honeymoon period right after throwing up. Quickly we get the hair in a bun, clothes back on and get her back in the bed. What kind of mother can't help her own daughter when she is sick? Mental note: Be stronger.

Annie goes to sleep while the second bag of medicine is pumping into her Hickman line. My sweet aunt has sent some money via Walmart and we need to go pick it up. Since I am working remotely, I need a second monitor and a printer. We find a Best Buy and Google Map our way to it. There is a Walmart close by. We are in a much nicer part of Memphis. Mental note: When looking for the good side of town, google Best Buy, not Walmart. We buy a printer and order a monitor. My remote office is looking promising. We pick up the money at Walmart. Enough to turn around and spend at Walmart. Nice.

Red Bull tells us she is ready to go home. She has been extremely helpful doing laundry for us at the sorority house and running back to the room when we forget things. She has never been away from both of us for more than a night. But she wants to go back to school, sleep in her own bed, and get some of her normal back again. We call the boyfriend's dad with the plane and ask if he can take her home. If the weather is good, she will go home Saturday.

The line nurse comes by and teaches us how to flush a Hickman line. Every day something must run through the line to keep it from clogging. After cleaning like we are scrubbing for surgery, we will put a syringe of Heparin into the Hickman line. The end of the syringe twists into the end of the Hickman line. I have trouble getting the pieces together. The line nurse tells me one part is male and the other part female and they screw together. Focusing intently on the problem at hand, I say I have always had problems doing this. The hubs and Red Bull have clearly spent too much time at the Jr. High. They are turning red from trying not to laugh. I shoot them a look that says "Stop being stupid!" We finish the lesson and I'm hoping the line nurse will think we are mature enough to flush a Hickman.

Annie wants company for the night. It's my turn. I grab a blanket and earplugs and settle in.

DAY 8 – Thursday, October 23, 2014

I wake up crying. Lying in the recliner next to Annie's bed is not a good place for a meltdown. Get it together. Annie is still sleeping. I creep to The Kennel and start answering e-mails from work. I text the hubs to ask for makeup and a flat iron. I wonder if anyone will notice I am wearing the same clothes from yesterday.

The e-mails and calls from work keep coming and my morning is spent working. I had thought it would be a nice diversion. I feel guilty that I am not sitting with Annie more. The hubs tells me not to worry. There is nothing we can do for her. Her body is the only one that can fight the cancer.

All day we are receiving calls and texts from friends who want to help by offering to walk, run or wear an armband in Annie's honor, sell T-shirts to raise money, set up accounts for donations, etc. They question her favorite color, her motto, our schedule. The support of all our friends and family, not to mention complete strangers, is much appreciated, but it is a bit overwhelming. I am thankful to have the hubs here. He becomes Annie's agent.

During this second day of chemo, Annie is so sick she cannot eat. She prefers the lights out, and she sleeps all day. The doctors say this is normal. She will probably not eat for days, but not to worry. Good advice, but hard to follow.

While she is sleeping, we run some errands. Seems we never get everything we need while we are out. Since Red Bull is returning home, she will need some things we had previously shared. We go to Target for supplies. I get Target popcorn for lunch. Things feel normal for a bit.

Another nurse comes by to visit with us. I cannot remember her title. So far I have met the head nurse, day nurse, night nurse, line nurse, nurse practitioner, nurse coordinator, and a kid playing nurse. This nurse tells us she will teach us to administer antibiotics through Annie's Hickman. Ah, time to toughen up again. We ask if we can learn tomorrow. It's late. Brain is closed-down for the night. She says sure. She knows just how we feel. I am thinking she doesn't. Then she tells us her son had AML when he was eighteen. "Not ALL, but AML?" I ask. Not that any type of leukemia isn't devastating, but I am still angry that we didn't at least get the lighter devastation. She says, "AML." She does know just how we feel. I ask a question, but I am not sure I want to know the answer. "How old is he now?" She answers, "32 and cancer free." I have a total meltdown. But it is a good meltdown for a change. She hugs me and holds onto me and tells me she usually doesn't share that, but felt it might help. She has no idea.

The hubs is spending the night with Annie. Around seven, Red Bull and I go to the cafeteria for dinner. The hubs has no appetite. The cafeteria has just closed for the night. Is this a senior citizen's home? Why is dinner over at seven? Red Bull tells me we eat late compared to all her friends. I thought everyone ate at seven. How did I not know this about our culture? We walk back to our room at the sorority house. As we walk in the door, I see a sign that says "How about pizza for dinner?" I walk up and say "Pizza for dinner would be great." Dominos offers a pizza deal at the sorority house.

In order to get the coupon for the deal, the lady at the counter asks for my room card. She cannot get my room card to show we are a guest at St. Jude. She is rude to us. It is the first rude person I have encountered since arriving at St. Jude. Fortunately for her, I am way too weary to give her a lecture in customer service.

We get our pizza and watch *Pirates of the Caribbean*. Red Bull is upset because when she went to borrow the movie downstairs, the attendant wasn't going to let her have it since she was only 13. For that movie you are supposed to be 14 to borrow it. She offered to go get her mom, who is tired from staying with her sick sister all day. He let her borrow the movie. Go Red Bull!

We have pizza, coke and M&M's. Though Johnny Depp is cute, the movie is filmed in the dark and cannot be clearly seen. I need subtitles because I cannot understand what they are saying. Red Bull begs me to watch the whole movie with her. But about an hour into it, I cannot hold my eyes open. I drag myself into the next room to bed, and I go to sleep crying.

DAY 9 – Friday, October 24, 2014

I wake up crying. I decide to sit and do some writing. Before I know it, a couple of hours have passed and I need to get to the hospital to see how the hubs and Annie made it through the night. I pack up my laptop so I can work in The Kennel, grab a third cup of coffee and take off walking across the campus. I call in to work to tell them I will be late for our morning staff call. The hubs looks bone tired when I arrive and he takes off for breakfast in the cafeteria. I feel guilty for having a good night's sleep.

Annie wakes up feeling good and eats an entire blueberry muffin. Since it's the first thing she has eaten in days, the nurse and I are clapping and cheering. This is her third day of chemo. She gets her first medicine and still feels good for a while. But in the break between medicines, she gets sick. The muffin reappears, ruining blueberry muffins for her forever. Her blood counts are low, so they give her a blood transfusion before her chemo and another one after.

I work all day answering e-mails, taking calls and trying to be normal. The United Way campaign is wrapping up at our office in Tulsa and I get a break when they all leave to celebrate. The hubs works all day being Annie's agent. Many fundraisers are being planned. Pictures of Annie are being put on T-shirts. The hubs is a good agent. We receive a video from Annie's high school showing where the students have made a wall in her honor. One of the teachers reads a poem to her in front of the wall. Many of the students are cheering her on to "Fight like a girl!" (a cancer awareness motto). They have left her seat vacant in one of her classes, waiting for her to return. We cry while watching the video. I am overwhelmed at their thoughtfulness. We watch it over and over, though it makes us miss home even more.

Another nurse comes around to show us how to administer antibiotics through the Hickman line. There is an acronym, SASH, to help us remember the steps. Saline, Antibiotic, Saline, Heparin. I practice putting the male and female parts together on each one. Red Bull and her daddy practice being mature.

We have run errands nearly every day to pick up things we have forgotten. Today Annie is complaining that her bras we bought her are not comfortable. She wants a sports bra. I beg her not to ask us to go back to Walmart. Her daddy volunteers to go for her. He doesn't go back to the nice neighborhood next to Best Buy, but decides to go to one close by. He calls me, slightly anxious, saying the GPS took him through the middle of an even scarier part of town. He is driving while trying to hunker down in the seat so his white head cannot be clearly seen.

He finally makes it to Walmart and begins to look for bras. He calls me. He has found the sports bras. I tell him Annie has, certain specifications that must be met. He tells me to hurry and explain because he feels like a pervert shopping in girl's bras. I try to explain the difference between camisole versus racer-back, adjustable versus non-adjustable, spaghetti versus wide straps. He is lamenting that he volunteered to help. He says he has found what she wants. He comes back with the bra. Wrong kind of straps. We will try again tomorrow. Bra shopping is not for the faint of heart…and not for dads.

Annie finished her chemo and felt okay for a change. I go back to the sorority house to get my makeup bag. It's my turn at the hospital. While I am talking on the phone to a friend, she calls and tells her daddy she doesn't need us for the night. We don't argue. I get a reprieve. Another hallelujah moment! We get another Domino's pizza deal, watch some TV and go to bed.

DAY 10 – Saturday, October 25, 2014

I wake up crying. I know where I am, but I try pretending I am back in my own bed. The hubs is next to me and I will go downstairs and make coffee. We will sit on the back patio and read *The Power of Praying Parents* together and pray for the kids. This was our Saturday routine and I loved it. I love knowing what power those prayers have. Or do they? Did we not pray enough for healing? Did our prayers even matter? Were we fooling ourselves? I do the only thing I know to do and continue to pray. I know Satan has asked to sift me like wheat, so I pray that my faith will not fail. That's all I have.

We go to Target – back in the good neighborhood – to look for the perfect sports bra. After closely analyzing various styles and shapes, we make our purchase. We head back to the hospital and the hubs makes a wrong turn. His GPS re-routes, and we end up seeing even more of Memphis. Not exactly a good time for a tour, but at least we are on the good side of town. Finally making it back to the hospital, Annie is up and not feeling well. Her blood counts are still low, and they are giving her another transfusion.

She wants a bath. I help her into the bathtub with flashbacks of the last episode, hoping she won't get sick. This time, since blood is still being pumped into the Hickman, we have to manage the pole and lines while washing. Not an easy task. I help her out and she tries on the new bra. She hates it. She wants to put on one bought several days ago. We are still on the hunt for the perfect sports bra.

Annie gets back in bed just as the boyfriend arrives. The nurse has suggested since she feels better that we get her out of the room for a while. She hasn't been out of the hospital room since last Sunday and weekends are good for wandering around because the hospital is empty compared to the weekdays. She doesn't want to go. We talk her into going, but she doesn't want to walk. She wants to go in a wheelchair. We convince her if she will walk as far as the elevator, we will wheel her around after that. She agrees. The nurse tells her she has to wear a mask. She balks. Not going. We beg her to wear the mask. She cries, but puts it on. She says it's hot and she can't breathe. We ignore her. She starts speed-walking down the hall to the elevator with the boyfriend struggling to keep the pole next to her and not let the line pull out of her Hickman. But in the maze of hallways, she realizes she doesn't know where she is going. She slows down and lets us direct her to the elevator and then collapses in the wheelchair. We wheel her outside and leave her to sit with the boyfriend for a while. My heart breaks watching them sit together.

We come back to the room, but receive a call in a short while that she is tired and wants to go back to her bed. We go get her and wheel her back. We all eat lunch together and it's time to start her chemo. She is really tired. The boyfriend has to go back home. That means it's time for Red Bull to leave too. Red Bull says goodbye to Annie and we go back to the sorority house to get her things. While we are loading her in the SUV, we are trying to be strong, but I break down and cry. Another part of normal is leaving us.

Red Bull sends us pictures from the small four-seater plane. We were afraid she would get sick. Instead, she says it's awesome!

Thankfully, they have an uneventful flight and drive her home. She sends us a text when she gets home. I ask her what the house looks like. She texts "Dirty. Nasty. Gross." So much for the twenty-year-olds "taking care of things." I ask if the boyfriend and his dad came into the house and saw the mess. "Yes," she texts back. Nice.

Annie feels okay after her chemo finishes. She got a new blanket from the boyfriend's mom. It's a Vera Bradley. I'm glad she knows how to pick a good boyfriend. Annie wants the blanket washed tonight. I tell her to wait until tomorrow. No one is going to do her laundry tonight. Her daddy volunteers. When I ask him if he will ever tell her no again, he gives me that familiar puzzled expression. Apparently not.

It's my turn to spend the night in the hospital. I build a nest in the recliner with three blankets wrapped around me like a cocoon. I'm getting used to the creaking and tapping sounds of the pump. I'm getting used to nurses coming in to check on things throughout the night. I fall asleep without the earplugs and sleep all night.

DAY 11 – Sunday, October 26, 2014

I wake up to the sound of Annie moaning. She says she hurts all over. The nurse says it will be two hours before she can get more pain medication. I get dressed in The Kennel and get her some water. She asks me to hand her the barf bag and leave. She is going to throw up and doesn't want a crowd. I tell her one person is not a crowd. She asks me again to leave. I'm sent back to The Kennel.

She's having another allergic reaction to the medication and has a slight fever. Her face is red and blotchy. The nurse gives her Benadryl and puts heat packs on her aching joints. She has so many syringes and medicine bags going through her pump that I am not sure what else she is getting. I continue to trust people I don't know. The nurse stays with us for quite a while. She tells funny stories. I feel guilty laughing, but feel good that Annie still can.

The hubs brings coffee and a muffin to me. We go for a walk to talk. We find a quiet place on the indoor bridge connecting the hospital to the Chili's Care Center. It's a beautiful Memphis day. We talk and cry and share encouraging e-mails and texts from our friends. I let him know, as Annie's agent, he needs to contact a few more people who are asking about ways to help. We talk about what good may come from this nightmare we're living. I think about Joseph in the Bible and how God turned every curse into a blessing for him. I don't want to be like Joseph. I want to be like Eve, pre-bad apple experience.

If all goes well, Annie comes "home" tomorrow. While Annie gets her final round of chemo through her

Hickman, her daddy and I go to look for a charger with a longer cord for her iPhone. Buying things for an iPhone 4 in an iPhone 6 world is like trying to buy VCR tapes. So yesterday. We start at Target and I have a Target popcorn lunch. We strike out there and go to Best Buy. Strike two. As we are standing there lamenting not being able to redeem ourselves as good parents and provide this very important necessity for our daughter, I wonder out loud why we don't just get a long extension cord and plug the phone's short-cord charger into it. We stare at each other for a second, and then we bust out laughing. Our distress and lack of sleep has affected our ability to figure out the least of problems. No redemption for us as parents. We return to Target and get a long extension cord. Annie can use the phone while it's charging. Crisis averted.

We return to the room and Annie is feeling better. She says she doesn't need us for the night. We both get a night in a real bed. Today was a better day. I fall asleep looking forward to Annie leaving the hospital.

DAY 12 – Monday, October 27, 2014

I wake up anxious. Today is the day Annie is supposed to come "home" from the hospital to the sorority house with us. What if I give the medicine wrong? What if she gets sick? What if, what if, what if? The hubs and I go to see her. They need to give her another round of chemo in her spine, but her blood counts are too low. After another transfusion (I have lost count how many she has had), they take her for the injection. I start packing up the things we have accumulated in her room and in The Kennel during the eight days we have been here. The hubs and I load a wagon (the mode of transportation preferred by most of the younger kids at St. Jude) and we move all our things to the sorority house.

I stay at the sorority house and work until evening. I return to the hospital to find the nurse has loaded the hubs down with Annie's medications. I ask "Is this an annual supply?" No, only a few days. It is overwhelming. The nurse has gone over it with the hubs, but she goes over it again with me. There are eighteen different medications from as simple as eye drops and nose sprays to IV medications. We load up the wagon again with the meds and all the peripherals that go with them (e.g. alcohol pads, rubber gloves, syringes of saline and heparin, claves, dressing covers for bathing, line caps, face masks, thermometer and pill cutters).

We finally are released, load Annie in the wheelchair, and she puts a mask on her face. As her ANC and white blood cell count are both zero, she has no ability to fight infection. She will have to wear a mask everywhere except in the sorority house with us.

Running a slight fever will mean going back to the hospital. Though Annie is thrilled to be leaving and I want us all together again, I feel sick with the pressure and the hubs has one of his daily anxiety attacks where he breaks out in a cold sweat. She has lost eight pounds in eight days. She is pale and fragile, sick and irritable. We can do this. We can do this.

It is a nice evening and we walk the block to the sorority house. We wheel her inside and she smiles as she lays in a real bed. One of her few smiles since this whole ordeal began. (We have only heard her really laugh once when her daddy was wearing a blue rubber glove on his head.)

The hubs and I begin to sort medication and come up with a plan. He downloads an app on his phone, I make a spreadsheet on my laptop. Between the two of us, maybe she will get the right doses at the right time.

We have to get up in the night to give the IV medication. I feel drugged, and we bicker over whether or not we should read the instructions as we go. The hubs felt he needed no further instruction. We finally get the medication pumping. Two hours later when we are both near comatose, the hubs alarm goes off. Time to remove the eclipse (the manual, disposable pump) and flush the line with saline and heparin. My body will not leave the pillow and warm blankets. The hubs takes care of Annie.

DAY 13 – Tuesday, October 28, 2014

I wake up when my alarm goes off to call Red Bull to wake her up. Since oversleeping the first morning she was back at home, she wants me to be her alarm clock. I am exhausted. Annie wakes up saying she slept like a baby. I did too. Just like a newborn, I was up every few hours. We have to be at A Clinic at 8:00 a.m. On the ground floor of the hospital, it is where we will go for all outpatient appointments. The hubs and I get ready quickly. Annie cannot be rushed. We are late getting to the hospital. Nothing new there. Long lines await us. They finally call her name, take her blood and we wait on the results.

I have my morning staff meeting on the phone in the waiting room. I move to the corner where it is quieter. An Amish family comes in and sits close by. I am wondering what they are thinking as I talk on my phone about SEC filings and the quarterly report. I am thinking our worlds are so different. Yet, here we are all the same. We all have a child who has cancer. We are all trusting people we do not know. We all are desperate to save our children.

We find out Annie's hemoglobin is still above 8 (her target) and she has no fever. We are good to go. We come back to the sorority house just in time for the next round of medication. Annie and her daddy watch some TV. Then the hubs leaves to run a few errands. He is bored. I work all afternoon and into the night. I am stressed. I get a call from someone at work complaining about Captain Awesome. Really? Does she understand where I am? I don't need this stress. I can't lose Captain Awesome, a CPA/MBA who does the work of two people.

I call to talk to Captain Awesome about the situation, and he tells me he will take the high road and "play nice." I pray to win the lottery. Since I haven't even bought a ticket (does Tennessee play the lottery?), I get back to work.

Annie wants to take a shower. She has only had baths since the nightmare began. We tape the plastic dressing cover over her Hickman and tell her not to take too long. Almost time for more medicine. She has permission from the doctor to shave her legs today if she will be careful. She can only use a razor one time, then it gets trashed. I am mentally adding the cost of six months' worth of razors. As if disposable razors are a drop in the bucket compared to our costs.

After she spends twenty minutes in the shower, I yell at her to get out. Past time for medication. She screams. She has nicked herself shaving. She yells that it is my fault for rushing her. I yell that it is not my fault. Mature. Blood is running down her leg. I wipe it off. It is a small nick, but bleeding a lot. I get an alcohol wipe and apply pressure. The hubs is frantically looking for a Band-Aid. A wagon load of medication and no Band-Aid to be found. He runs downstairs and comes back with a couple. We prop up her leg and put a Band-Aid on it. It stops bleeding and we pray she won't get an infection.

She finishes her IV medication at 1:00 a.m. and we go to bed exhausted.

DAY 14 – Wednesday, October 29, 2014

I wake up to call Red Bull 4 ½ hours later. I go back to sleep until 7:30.

Two weeks. We have been living the nightmare for two weeks. It seems like two years. We are just getting started. Will we still be on the prayer lists at two months or six months? Will people grow weary of hearing about Annie? Should we stop talking about it? Are we making everyone else uncomfortable? What is the protocol for cancer-patient socialization?

Annie doesn't have to be at A Clinic until 9:00. We give Annie all her 8:00 meds and start getting ready for the day. I go to work. My commute is two steps away. I sit down at 8:30 and don't quit working until 7:30 when I walk across the street to take Annie her meds at A Clinic.

Annie and her daddy are at A Clinic off and on all day. They started with a visit to the line nurse to learn how to change her dressing. I have to go for a make-up class on Friday. I'm feeling guilty because I worked instead of going with them to the doctor. The hubs says for me just to keep my job. One thing I have learned about the hubs. When times are tough, he is super kind to me. When I was pregnant with each of the kids, I could do no wrong. Now that we are in the fight of our life, he is patient and extremely kind. I make a mental note to be nice.

They return from A Clinic with more disappointment. Annie needs another blood transfusion and more platelets. The doctor tells them she is also moved from low risk to standard risk. Weren't we supposed to wait for more test results? He wants her siblings to get their blood tested to check for a bone marrow match. He says the leukemia is in her MYC gene and they have never seen that before. We don't understand what the doctor is telling us and we wonder what he is not telling us.

We find out we are being moved from the sorority house to the Ronald McDonald House on

Friday. Not looking forward to another move in another tiny set of rooms. Not sure they will have cleaning service either. I am spoiled by my cleaning lady at home. Wednesday is her cleaning day. I left her a check on the desk before I left town, so I text her to make sure she is coming. She calls. She says she refuses to charge me for cleaning until we come home with Annie. I tell her it is going to be a long time. She asks me to please let her do this for me. I agree and then I cry. Once again I am overwhelmed at everyone's acts of kindness.

Annie enrolls in school here. She starts next week at St. Jude. Because of the hundreds of patients on any given day, they have thought of everything. They will get her records from her high school in Oklahoma and allow her to continue her classes three days a week. Maybe that will bring some normal back to her. Maybe we can forbid watching TV until her homework is done. Maybe we can have some normal things to say.

We put the word out asking if anyone knows anyone in Memphis who will come by and cut Annie's hair. It's very long. She wants to cut it before it starts to fall out. But she cannot be in a crowd, and she has to wear a mask outside our room. Hard to have a haircut while wearing a mask. I just want someone to arrange it for us. We receive texts and Facebook messages with salons to call. Not helpful. Just send me someone. I don't want to make appointments. I don't want to explain our needs. I don't want to plan another thing. I don't want to think. I don't want to be here. I hate cancer. Annie finishes her IV meds. I go to bed upset.

DAY 15 – Thursday, October 30, 2014

I wake up and call Red Bull at 5:30. She doesn't pick up the first time, so I call again. I smile when I hear her sleepy, sweet voice say hello. "Time for school. I love you, baby. Have a wonderful day." It's my morning mantra. I have always said this to the kids as they leave for school. Even if we are running late, arguing, whatever. I can be rushing through the carpool line and screaming at them to get out of the car, but the last words they will hear are, "I love you, baby. Have a wonderful day."

I cannot make myself move from the bed. I doze until 7:00 when the hubs gets up to take Annie's meds out of the mini-fridge. We don't have any appointments today. I still cannot make myself get up. I lay there until time to go to work, then go to the computer in my jammies. It is the first day that I don't get dressed all day. I look like hell and I don't care.

We are wrapping up the quarter at work and the accounting department is in crisis mode. Schedules aren't tying out, cash flows don't work, variance analysis not making sense. Next year's budget needs work. At least this is normal. At least we will find answers to these problems.

Annie sleeps most of the day. Her daddy is stir-crazy. I don't know where he goes for a good part of the day. Wandering around campus. He brings in a package. It is a box of T-shirts for Annie's Army that says "Fight Like a Girl." Someone sent us all one. Her Texas cousins are sending bracelets that say "Pray for Annie" on one side and "Proverbs 31:25" on the other side. I ask how they came up with the verse. The hubs says Annie picked out the verse herself. Her daddy is doing a good job as her agent.

Red Bull calls. Her normal evening call to tell me about her day. Normal conversations are good. Having them over the phone is hard. She turned in all her make-up schoolwork today. The teachers are impressed. She is a smart girl. She tells me she is getting extra attention from the students and the teachers are extra nice. She is milking it. Red Bull is a very smart girl.

Annie's sense of smell is on overdrive. We buy every fragrance and brand of air freshener on the market, searching for the right smell. The boyfriend's mom sends a gift bag full of air fresheners. Earlier we smelled like cinnamon pumpkin. Tonight we are tropical.

Annie finishes her meds and I go to bed pretending I'm in the Caribbean.

Home of the Blues

DAY 16 – Friday, October 31, 2014

I call to wake up Red Bull and wait for the alarm at 7:00 to take Annie's meds out of the mini-fridge. Need to get moving. Need to pack to move to Ronald McDonald House today. We have to be out by noon. Can't check in to the new place until 2:30. We pack everything we have accumulated in the last two weeks into my Chevy Sonic (Annie has always called it the clown car because it is so small. Fitting. The clown car going to the clown house.) We pack so much in the car there is barely room to sit. I can't see Annie in the back seat and her daddy can't see out the back windows.

We have an appointment at the hospital first. I am taking my make-up class with the line nurse. I am learning how to change the claves and the dressing covering Annie's Hickman line. I am feeling smart that I am becoming a medical professional. We pick up a kit for the hubs to take home to the other kids to have their blood tested for a bone marrow match.

I get a Facebook message from someone who works for a blood bank. She tells me siblings are rarely a perfect match unless they are twins. Thank you. I wanted to hear depressing news. I haven't had enough lately. I take a Zofran and try not to be sick.

It's Halloween. The cold air outside takes our breath away. Winter is coming. Annie doesn't even have a jacket. Packing up again. Moving again. In the cold. We enter the hospital and everyone is dressed in Halloween costumes. I look scary enough. They are letting all the kids trick-or-treat around the hospital. A girl smiles at me and asks if we want to trick-or-treat. I don't smile. I say I don't think so. We are tired. The hubs and I start to bicker. He says I'm being hateful. He is right. I am. But I say he started it. Mature. He calls bulls__t. Annie starts to cry. She says this is all her fault for getting cancer. Not too proud of myself at this moment.

We take care of our errands at the hospital early and head to the clown house. They say we can start orientation early. We go inside the gates after getting the rules for entering and exiting and security guard hours. We meet one of the managers in a nice living area. We sit at a table while she goes over pages and pages of rules. She gives us a key to the bedroom. Our bedroom? Doesn't she mean our apartment? Everything besides our bedroom is a common area. Common family room, common kitchen. Communal living at its best. She tells us we do all our own cleaning and laundry, even the linens. I miss my cleaning lady back home. She tells us there should be only light snacks eaten in the room. No meals in the room. No microwave, coffee pot or toaster in the room. No alcohol. No fun. There will be room inspections. The clown house manager will enter at random times to inspect and the room must be neat and clean. I get that with a lot of people under one roof, there must be rules. But I feel like I've entered a half-way house from prison and try not to cry.

We get a tour. Our bedroom is upstairs, but all the common rooms are downstairs. We are taken to the kitchen and shown the stove, microwave, sink and dishwasher we will share with five other families.

Similar sets align the walls. Our oven handle is broken and our stove top has a greasy pan sitting on it. Dirty dishes are in the sink. Clearly, there should be random kitchen inspections. Of course, they would have to interrogate six families to find out who is to blame. We are shown the refrigerators. We are allotted one shelf. We are shown the freezer. We are allotted half a shelf. We have a small pantry with our very own key. Nice. I may want to put some midnight snacks under lock and key...at the end of the hall...downstairs. We are shown the two shared coffee pots for our side of the building. I wonder what caffeine withdrawal is going to feel like. We are shown the laundry room with the community iron and ironing board. We are shown the fitness room with a few items of workout equipment. You have to check out a key. I get a key. I will probably never work out in the fitness room, but I feel in better shape just having the key. We are told to note the dumpsters outside where we are to take our trash. This is not on my list of job responsibilities back home. I miss home.

We are taken to our bedroom upstairs. Our room is painted a bright lime green color. There are two double beds, two small sets of shelves, a closet, a small TV, a single sink with about a foot of counter space, a toilet and tub. This is our new home. Again, I try not to cry.

We go to the car and bring one load of stuff up. We go for the second load and sit in the car. I tell the hubs I don't think I can do this. We call the hospital and ask them how someone with no white blood cells or ability to fight infection can live in communal living. We are told to pick a time with the fewest people in the dining room to eat. We beg to get into Target House.

We have heard it is an apartment with its own kitchen and living room…luxuries I took for granted two weeks ago. Target House is full. They will put us on the list. We ask if we can stay on the list if we check into a hotel. They tell us not to check into a hotel…too many germs. Huh? They say the air in the clown house is HEPA filtered and there is no carpeting. It's the best place to be. Plus, they want us to stay close in case we need to get Annie back to the hospital fast. They nicely explain to me how everyone is in the same situation here. As if all the families here are enjoying themselves. They tell us to give it some time.

Has someone studied the needs of dislocated families with extremely sick children and determined it is best for us to share everything with each other? Is "misery loves company" a tried and true statement? Should I want to make new friends with people I have little in common with except a sick child? We have no success stories to share. We are all living the nightmare. Is it going to make me feel better hearing about their nightmare? Should we share stories of blood counts, chemo and hair loss? I am truly in foreign territory.

We look for a furnished apartment. As if we even know where to look. The least expensive one that we find close to downtown is $1,700 per month. Most places don't even consider month-to-month. You get what you pay for. Back to the clown house. I try to quit being a snob and be appreciative that it is free. We bring up the rest of our stuff. Annie says she can get used to it. If she can, I can. I don't need a kitchen.

We hang out in our room, follow the rules and eat only light snacks. Popcorn, Cheez-its, Chex mix, chips, and several small Haagen-Dazs ice-creams later, we feel better and get ready for bed. Annie finishes her evening meds and I go to bed crying.

DAY 17 – Saturday, November 1, 2014

I wake up to the sound of the hub's app telling us it is time to take Annie's eclipse out of the mini-fridge. Thank goodness for medicine that needs refrigeration, so we can have a mini-fridge in our room. It's bad enough popping my popcorn in the communal microwave…at the end of the hall…downstairs. At least I can keep cold drinks in the room.

An announcement comes over our phone (another thing to get used to…random messages over the speaker on our phone). Breakfast is being served in the dining room. Charitable groups come to the clown house from time to time to feed us – the homeless refugees. The hubs and I go check it out. Coffee first. Both coffee pots are empty. We make coffee and get a cup each. We get in line for breakfast. Lots of food. Biscuits and gravy. Unlimited bacon. I am liking the clown house.

The boyfriend and his dad show up. Today they will fly the hubs home and I will begin to fly solo with Annie. They stay awhile. We show them around the clown house. We sit in one of the common areas. A group of bikers walks by. They have come to visit with the refugee families. I feel like a monkey at the zoo.

Early afternoon is time for them to leave. I walk with the hubs to the parking lot and try not to think about him leaving. I hug him and hold onto him. I start to cry. I have to let go and watch them drive away. He leaves. I go back to the room where Annie is waiting.

She says, "And then there were two." I make myself keep it together and smile.

When Annie wants something, she will not drop the subject. She wants her hair cut short with red highlights. I look online for haircut places in the nice part of town. I find Supercuts. Super. I am so directionally challenged. I pray Google Map can lead us there and back.

Annie wears her mask and gets right in. We are there over two hours while they cut and highlight her hair. It looks terrific. I get mine trimmed too. They only charge me for the product and don't allow me to tip. Very Super! I pray she will not lose her hair.

We make it back with only two wrong turns. Fortunately, Google Map re-calculated before I ended up in a bad part of town. I work for a few hours. We have peanut butter crackers, cheese crackers, Kit-Kats and coke for dinner. I drink a two-ounce bottle of vodka someone slipped in one of our care packages from home. Since alcohol is taboo, I drink fast lest the warden show up. I hide the second bottle in my purse. Surely I won't have to empty it upon room inspection. I get a call at 10:00 from the front desk. Our visitors forgot to sign out this afternoon. Fortunately, since we are new to the system, I get a pass. We don't want to get kicked out of the clown house.

Daylight savings time begins so I turn the clock back. Just what I wanted. One extra hour in Memphis.

Annie's meds are finished for the night. I go to bed dreading the week ahead.

DAY 18 – SUNDAY, November 2, 2014

I wake up at 7:00 when the alarm goes off to take the meds out of the mini-fridge. Time to get started. Today is my first day as sole caregiver. I can do this.

We get ready for the appointment at 10:00 to check Annie's blood counts. Just as we are leaving, Annie says she feels "blah." I learn this is code for "I'm about to start violently puking." So we are late. But nothing new there. Annie's platelets are low. She gets Benadryl, then the platelets. We watch most of *Pirates of the Caribbean* (again) while they pump in the meds. I try to follow the plot (again). Maybe next time.

After the platelets, she feels good. Now she wants to go shopping. She says she needs clothes for the colder weather. I try to convince her we can have some sent from home. She wants to go shopping. I follow everyone else's lead. I cannot tell her no. We go to Target. She is all masked up and I scrub the cart like we are taking it into a surgical ward. She picks out winter clothes and a coat. I offer hand sanitizer every time she touches anything. I smell Target popcorn. But

I know she cannot eat food that others have prepared. Even though she says she doesn't mind, as a sacrificial act of kindness, I do not get Target popcorn.

On the way back, Annie says she is hungry. We stop at Kroger. Again, she is masked up and I am sanitizing the cart. We load up on junk food and microwavable meals. My kind of dinner. Back at the clown house, she eats her junk and falls asleep watching TV. I work on a cash flow projection for tomorrow's budget meeting. I get a call from Captain Awesome that he will not be in the office tomorrow because his son is puking. He will have to work from home. I feel his pain. Tomorrow will be crazy. I go to bed exhausted.

DAY 19 – Monday, November 3, 2014

I wake up at 5:30 when the alarm to wake Red Bull goes off. Her daddy is home with her now, but cannot be trusted to wake her. I call and hear her sleepy, sweet voice tell me she's up. I miss home. I wake again when the alarm goes off to take the meds from the mini-fridge. I get a text from Captain Awesome. I get up and get dressed for the work day.

Annie teases me and asks why I am getting ready as if I am going in to work every day. I explain I need normal. Getting ready for work is normal. All day pajamas are not. Some people at the clown house have given up normal altogether. I have seen enough bathrobes and slippers in the common areas to suggest street clothes are not welcome here. But I have never enjoyed slumber parties. I get dressed and go to get coffee….at the end of the hall…downstairs. The coffee pot is empty. Why am I not surprised? I make another pot and make my way back upstairs.

Annie tries to sleep while I talk for hours on conference calls with work. She gives up and starts playing music on her phone. The close quarters have us in each other's space. Hoping to move to Target House soon. I serve Pop Tarts for brunch and work until time to take her to see the line nurse in C Clinic. I have another lesson in changing her dressing. When I remove the old dressing and see the tube poking out of her chest, I have to take deep breaths and not get queasy. Annie teases me that my hands shake. The tape is like saran wrap and I get it all waded up and have to start over. Finally, I get it re-dressed. I have not yet passed this class. We will have another lesson on Wednesday.

We come back from the clinic and she texts all her friends while I work again. She reminds me our rooms are being inspected tomorrow. I need to take the trash out. Ugh! I haven't taken out trash since the boys got big enough to carry the bags. I did not take note of the location of the dumpster in our orientation and have to stop to ask two people for directions. Dumpster located. Breath held. Trash dumped. Have to pick up replacement bags at the office. They generously give you food, housing and even transportation via shuttle here. But trash bags? They need to be carefully monitored.

I get a call from the doctor. The lumbar puncture from last week showed no more leukemia in the spinal fluid. Finally, we have caught a break. A big hallelujah moment! Next blood test is on Wednesday, just to check the counts. One week from Wednesday, will have another bone marrow test. Level of treatment will be determined by how well Annie responded to Round One of chemo. I try not to be anxious. I try to have faith. God, please help my faith.

Annie masks up and we go to the communal kitchen to heat our microwavable dinners. Chicken enchiladas. Yum! Not as good as homemade, but we pretend. After her meds start at 8:00, she turns off the TV and falls asleep texting. I work a little more as I wait for the meds to finish. I update the hubs on the doctor's call and he says he will update Annie's Army – since I am Facebook challenged. The meds finish. I flush the Hickman and go to bed exhausted.

DAY 20 – Tuesday, November 4, 2014

I wake up at 5:30 and call Red Bull. Going back to sleep, I wake again in time to get the meds out of the mini-fridge and get the next round of pills ready. Thinking ahead. Won't have to get out of bed in thirty minutes. Getting smarter.

Finally at 8:00, I get up and dressed for work. By 8:30, I am making coffee…at the end of the hall…downstairs….in one of the two empty coffee pots that several dozen people share. Apparently, many people drink coffee, but no one knows how to actually make the coffee. Fortunately, it is pre-measured McDonald's coffee (of course) and it is good. I get two cups for myself and a couple of pop tarts for Annie and head back down the hall and upstairs.

No appointments today. I work at my computer all day. Annie is on Facebook and keeping up with the Kardashians on cable. Boring day for her. Nice.

I work through the evening. At 10:00, I check Annie's eclipse that has been in the IV line for two hours. It is still full. I call the hospital. They tell me to flush the line with Saline, try it again and call back if it still hasn't emptied. Line flushed. I forget to check again in an hour. I finish working at midnight and check the eclipse. Still full. Ugh! I call the hospital again to ask if I can just switch the eclipse for another. No. Too much risk that there might be a problem with the line. They want to check it. We get our coats and head to the car.

It is a very dark night and it is raining. Double ugh!! I have my glasses on instead of contacts and the prescription is slightly old. Night and raining and a driver with little depth-perception is not a good combination. We make it to the St. Jude gate. They call ahead to tell them we are coming at the hospital and the guard tells me it is okay to park right in front. They are waiting for us in the Medicine Room. They check Annie's line. The line is fine. The eclipse is faulty. Go back home and get another.

Back at the clown house we start the IV at 12:30. We are beat. We go to bed. I get up at 3:15 to take it out and flush the line. I get a couple hours sleep before waking Red Bull. Long day. I don't feel like I ever really went to bed.

DAY 21 – Wednesday, November 5, 2014

I wake up at 5:30 and call Red Bull. Did I sleep? I feel like I barely shut my eyes. I can sleep a little longer because I won't have to start the IV as early today. I get up and dressed for work at 8:00 because I have a call in an hour. I go to the end of the hall…downstairs…to one empty coffee pot and the other one being emptied by a smiling man. Sure he is smiling. He is taking the last cup. He walks away. Really? I am not smiling. I begin my morning routine of making coffee for the refugees. It is my contribution to the clown house.

I go back to work for a couple hours until it is time for Annie's appointment at the hospital at 10:30. It is still raining. We are still late. They take her blood for testing and we go sit to wait for the results. We sit and wait and wait. I work on my laptop and take calls in the hospital waiting room. Annoying, I'm sure, but not as annoying as the screaming kid next to us. Finally, we see the doctor.

He tells us Annie's kidneys are not functioning normally. They think she is probably just dehydrated from being so sick. We stay while they give her IV fluids. After one bag, they start another. I work from her room on my laptop. She plays on her phone. Finally, they say they are sending us home with a bag of fluids hooked up to the IV. We go for a lesson in what to do if the pump stops. We schedule appointments for tomorrow. We go to the valet to get the car (another advantage of St. Jude patients). It is nearly 6:00 when we are leaving. We are exhausted from hardly any physical activity all day. How does that happen?

Getting Annie back in the room, I go get the mail. She has tons of cards from her classmates at school and a couple of packages too. She is all smiles. That means I am all smiles too. I am cherishing when she is happy.

As she goes through the mail, I go get a nutritious dinner of pizza rolls for us from our half-shelf in the freezer…at the end of the hall…downstairs...and pop them in our shared microwave. Actually, I don't use the one assigned to us because someone has beat me to it. I use the next one over. From another family's shared kitchen. I am hoping I won't be written up at the clown house.

The hubs calls to say the washing machine is broken at home. He is going to Lowe's to buy another. Since we are planning on being broke for some time to come, I encourage him to get a good one.

Back in the room, Annie watches the CMAs while I work. Tim McGraw comes on to sing. Things just got better. I work a while longer. No IV to change tonight since the fluids will run all night. Annie puts in ear plugs to drown out the sound of the pump. I go to bed exhausted.

DAY 22 – Thursday, November 6, 2014

I wake up and call Red Bull at 5:30. I hate the 5:30 alarm, but love hearing her sweet voice. I go back to sleep until the sound of a beep wakes me up. It only beeped once or twice. It's 7:02. Another beeping. It's 7:16. It keeps going off intermittently. I finally get up. I think it is Annie's IV pump, but she is sleeping soundly, so I don't disturb her to check. At least it got me up and moving.

I get dressed and I go for coffee….at the end of the hall…downstairs. Surprisingly, there is coffee in the pot. A hallelujah moment! I get two cups and go back upstairs. Sitting down to work, I sip my first drink. It is bitter, bitter coffee. How do you mess up pre-measured coffee? Should have known something was up when there was coffee in the pot. My coffee addiction has me drinking it anyway.

Back at the room, the alarm on the pump starts going off like a loud siren. The battery is dead. That explains the earlier beeping. Annie is now up and remembers the nurse giving us a spare battery. She changes it and restarts the pump. I'm glad the nurse doesn't know I failed the battery changing test.

Annie's appointments at the hospital start at 11:30. I work until time to go. Something must be wrong because we are on time for a change. They take her blood and we go back to the clown house while we wait for test results. She lays down on the bed and starts to cry. She wants to go home. She wants this to be over. She doesn't want to carry this stupid bag or wear a mask in public anymore. I sit on the bed with her rubbing her back and saying I'm sorry. There is nothing more I can do and my heart breaks.

At 1:00 we meet with the doctor and he tells us her kidney function looks the same. At least it isn't worse. He will let her leave the hospital without the bag of fluids if she will take one more bag today at the hospital and agree to start drinking like a camel when we leave. She agrees and is much happier.

St. Jude has an accredited school with certified teachers. I have an appointment with her teacher. He tells me he will get with the homebound coordinator at her high school and he will help her finish the school year. I am thankful. Annie is bummed. She doesn't want to go to school. I tell her she needs normal. I want to do normal things like be unable to help with her homework. She wants to graduate with her class. She will start school next week. We miss normal.

We go back to the clown house and I work until bedtime while she watches TV and guzzles water. I am happy we are no longer messing with the IV at night. I go to bed exhausted, but looking forward to a good night's sleep.

DAY 23 – Friday, November 7, 2014

I wake up for my 5:30 call to Red Bull. I remind her I will see her tomorrow and fall back asleep until I get a text from a co-worker stuck in traffic. One advantage to my clown house office is my two-step commute. I can't manage to get out of bed until nearly 8:00, and I remember I promised Annie I would go to Kroger for her. She made a list yesterday. I get ready and head to Kroger.

I take work calls on the way and at Kroger. I have trouble doing two things at once on a normal day. I circle the unfamiliar store several times getting everything on the list except Rice Krispy treats. Annie's new favorite. After more wandering, I get off the phone and recruit the help of a sweet girl who looks about Annie's age. Seeing her makes me wish again for Annie to do normal things. I check out at Kroger and call back in to work before I get too weepy.

Back at the clown house, I just get everything organized when the clown house manager knocks. Time for room inspection. I am sure there is a reason for this, but I feel like a child who has been rebellious and must be watched and monitored. She comes in with the maintenance man, takes a quick look around, looks inside the mini-fridge, smiles and says "You're fine". Passed inspection. Get to stay at the clown house. Great.

I work until time to go to A Clinic for lab work and another lesson with the line nurse in changing the dressing and claves. We are on time for our 11:30 appointment. On time twice in one week. New record! While waiting for test results, we go see the line nurse. I commit the steps to memory and don't hurt Annie too badly as I change the dressing. She only yelps a couple of times when I accidentally tug the line or drip alcohol on her sensitive skin. The line nurse says I pass. She will work with the hubs next week. Maybe between the two of us, we won't harm her!

We wait for the doctor. Both typing on our laptops. The doctor walks in and asks why I work so much. I don't reply. What I want to say is that I should have been a doctor. Then I would have enough money to take off work and be present 100% while my child fights cancer. As it is, I need to keep my job. I am told by a nurse that usually one or both parents lose their jobs when their child comes to St. Jude. I hate cancer even more.

The doctor tells us Annie needs another platelet transfusion and her kidney function is no better than yesterday. She has also lost another pound. Not what I wanted to hear. He allows her to go through the weekend without IV fluids if she will promise to continue guzzling water. She agrees. We leave and Annie says she has the blahs. I give Annie more of her anti-nausea medication and take a Zofran myself.

Back at the clown house, I start changing sheets, doing laundry and cleaning the room. Again, missing my cleaning lady. The hubs and Red Bull come tomorrow. We are both excited. Annie gets more mail and another package. Opening mail has become her favorite part of the day. I make her a nutritious microwavable meal for dinner, work until 1:00 a.m. as I wait for the laundry to finish, and go to bed exhausted.

DAY 24 – Saturday, November 8, 2014

I don't wake up until the alarm goes off at 8:00 for Annie's meds. Nice. I get up, give her the pills and we both go back to sleep. At 8:45 my phone rings. Not immediate family. Not answering. Then the smell of bacon hits me. Ahhhhh. Saturdays at the clown house. Unlimited bacon. I give Annie a yogurt and go downstairs in my pajamas and bedhead. Looking like a true refugee, I get sympathy smiles from the church group. And they are cleaning the community kitchens. Bonus! With an extra-large cup of coffee (yes, there was some in the pot) and a plate of bacon, I go back to the room.

Annie is still keeping up with the Kardashians. I don't understand why anyone wants to keep up with this family. I'm certain my IQ is dropping the longer I keep up with them.

We leave for the hospital a little late. Shocker that. Annie needs a transfusion and we wait over an hour at the hospital for the platelets to get to the Medicine Room. No surprise. We Facebook, text and e-mail to pass the time. I have been waiting on doctors, nurses, medicine, test results, etc. for over three weeks. I should be happy to get a break going home. But I am already weepy about leaving her tomorrow.

Back at the clown house, we get a call from Red Bull that they are in the parking lot. Annie takes off for the lobby as fast as I have seen her move in weeks. The hubs and Red Bull have ridden with the boyfriend and his mom from Tulsa. When his dad couldn't fly the plane, the boyfriend's mom offered to drive. I like the boyfriend's family. Everyone visits a while and they offer to let the hubs and me go out to eat while they stay with Annie. Wow! Time alone. Free time. No agenda. We take off like prisoners on a jail-break.

We drive down the road I know that has Kroger and Target. We find an On The Border and go inside to begin our date. Neither of us have an appetite, but we order, pretending things are normal. Until I mention I can't believe this is our life. End of pretense. Then we both cry and eat and talk and cry. I have no idea what the waitress must be thinking.

Back at the clown house, the boyfriend and his mom leave for a hotel. I go to bed sad to be leaving tomorrow.

DAY 25 – Sunday, November 9, 2014

I wake up anxious about the day. I start packing my week's worth of clothes that I have worn for three weeks. I make sure the hubs has all the right medicines and times to give them on his phone app. I tell him he needs to take the classes with the line nurse so we can change her dressing. I remind him she has school. He tells me he has it all under control. I take a Zofran.

The boyfriend and his mom come back to visit with Annie while the hubs, Red Bull and I go for breakfast at our community kitchen…at the end of the hall...downstairs. I fix a bowl of Frosted Flakes, the hubs has instant oatmeal. Red Bull wants Ramen noodles. As I start to use the microwave, a woman brushes me aside and starts using the stovetop to make eggs and bacon. She doesn't look like she sees me. I tease her and thank her for making that nice breakfast for us. She looks at what we are eating and says, "I just got here. After I've been here a while, I'm sure I'll be making breakfast like you are." I have no idea if this is supposed to be funny or mean. I give her a pass. She is new to the clown house.

Red Bull and I get our things loaded in the SUV and I give Annie a hug goodbye. I am all teary, but she is looking past me at her boyfriend. He is the one she will miss the most. I hug the hubs goodbye and try not to be sick. The boyfriend's mom keeps pleasant conversation going all the way home. They drop us off in the evening. Dead plants on the front porch greet us. Evidence of the twenty-year-old's caretaking. But after three weeks away, there's no place like home.

We get a text from the hubs that Annie is running a fever. If her fever gets to 100.9 she has to go back to the hospital. It's 100.6. Red Bull is crying. She says it is her fault. She slept in the bed with Annie and she might have given her a cold. I tell her it's not her fault. This sickening disease and all the complications that go with it are nobody's fault. It's a disease from hell, straight from the devil. I don't think she is convinced it's not her fault. We get another text. The fever has broken. Relief.

A friend has brought dinner. Lasagna, salad and garlic bread. I play with my adorable grandson and eat a dinner that is far better than anything I would ever have made. I have a financial report to review for work in the morning and Red Bull has unfinished homework. We both work for a couple of hours, then go to bed exhausted.

DAY 26 – Monday, November 10, 2014

I wake up when Red Bull's 5:30 alarm goes off. Not wanting to get up, I call her instead of going to her room. At 6:00, it is time to get up. I can wear different clothes today. Not the same five-day rotation I have been wearing. I can shower in my own shower. I can have good lighting in a bathroom I don't have to share. And though it is nice to get ready without collecting anything Annie has carried off to her room, I miss her and can't quit thinking about her. What if something happens while I am here? What if she needs me? What kind of a mother leaves her sick daughter to come home and go to work?

I get to work and it's good to see all my friends again. People come in my office all day for updates on Annie. I don't get much done, but it's good to be back.

I text the hubs and ask if he remembered to give Annie her medication. Did he remember she has school today? Did he take her temperature? He texts back he could do all of the above, if I will quit texting him. I'm sure he needs my help, but choose to leave them alone.

I get the report from the hubs later in the day. Annie's kidney function is the same (still not too great), but she won't have to do IV fluids if she will keep drinking lots of water. Her blood counts are good. No transfusions needed. Our lives have become all about test results.

I work through lunch and make it home by 7:00. Red Bull and I eat leftovers for dinner, play with my adorable grandson and watch a few episodes of Days of our Lives. We haven't watched in months and it takes us a few minutes to get all caught up. I answer a few work e-mails and we go to bed exhausted.

DAY 27 – Tuesday, November 11, 2014

I wake up Red Bull at 5:30. I am taking her to school today and stopping by the car dealer to sign papers for the car Annie's daddy bought for her last week. We left my car in Memphis and the hubs' car is too unreliable for me to drive on my seventy-mile round-trip commute each day. Annie has seen pictures of her new (used) car. She loves it. Good motivation to get her back home and get that driver's license.

The person with the papers I need is not in this early. Mission not accomplished, and I am late for work. It's Veteran's Day and a celebration is going on in our lobby for my co-worker who is a veteran. Everyone sees me coming in late. No big deal until a co-worker tells me that someone has been complaining about our department only working from nine to four. Seriously? I'm not sure why God allows people in our lives who enjoys pushing our hot buttons. I need Him to push the Easy Button right now.

I hear from the hubs that they are having a boring day at the clown house. I think boring sounds good. Annie's school was cancelled because the teacher's daughter was sick. I wonder what it is like to have children of your own and work with children who are fighting cancer every day. Do they panic when their children get the sniffles? Do they want to put them in a sterile bubble? Do they want to get their blood tested every time they are tired and don't feel good? Will I want to rush Annie to the ER every time in the future that she says her stomach hurts? It's hard for me to imagine people choose to be surrounded by severely sick children and care for them every day. The people working at St. Jude did not choose the Easy Button. And I am very grateful that they didn't.

A few of us in the accounting group work until 8:15 getting ready for a mail-out for our board of directors. My new boss e-mails that she is sorry she cannot help us, but she is having dinner with the CEO and some bankers. Nice. I am hungry. Maybe I should ask her to bring me back some leftovers. I make it home by 9:00. I have missed seeing my adorable grandson who is already in bed. I am feeling guilty that I have not been there for Red Bull, so we stay up eating popcorn and watching more episodes of Days.

Annie will have a bone marrow biopsy tomorrow that will tell us how she responded to Round One. She will also get another injection in her spine to kill leukemia in the spinal fluid. I go to bed praying God will remove my anxiety and for good test results.

DAY 28 – Wednesday, November 12, 2014

I wake up and call Red Bull at 5:30. I think about getting on the treadmill. The new one I got for my birthday that has barely been used. I need to find out if the Target House has a fitness center. No sense getting sore if I can't work out in Memphis. I justify not getting out of bed and convince myself that just thinking about working out puts me in better shape. I drag out of bed and start the day.

Red Bull is off to school and I am off to work. The hubs texts to tell me Annie's hemoglobin and platelets are coming up. No transfusions needed. Her ANC is still 0. No ability to fight infection. Doctor says she is doing as expected. Her tests are completed and we are awaiting results.

The hubs gets the news that we get to move into Target House on Friday. We are all very excited. No more going for coffee....at the end of the hall...downstairs. The anticipation of popping popcorn in our very own microwave in our very own kitchen has us giddy. It's the little things!

Some of my co-workers had pink bracelets made that say "Strength for Annie." They are all wearing them at work. I am overwhelmed at this kindness. My previous boss, who I had not spoken to in a long time, sends a big bag to Annie and a tumbler, both with her name on them. My other co-workers fill it with all sorts of stationery and snacks. Other friends send cards and presents. It is like Christmas for Annie several days a week. My Texas friend sends presents for me! Friends at home bring meals during the week. We will be spoiled when this is all over!

I leave at 5:00 to go back to the car dealer. This time I get the papers signed and make it home by 6:00. My sister-in-law calls and says she has money to bring me that people have donated to help with expenses. This reminds me I need to pay bills. Ugh! Some things never go away!

My eighteen-year-old comes over with his girlfriend. They are hungry. He has a new job working for a tree-trimming service, but it's never enough money. I offer to make macaroni and cheese. He tells me he has eaten that for the last week. Red Bull is making us leftovers. I ask her to make him some too. He hasn't shaved in a while and has a scraggly looking beard started. I say I can tell he is broke since he can't afford a razor. He says "Mom, I'm a lumberjack now!" His sister hands him the plate she made for him and says, "Here you go, Paul Bunyan." At least we still have our sense of humor.

I spend the rest of the evening with Red Bull watching TV. We go to bed late.

DAY 29 – Thursday, November 13, 2014

I wake up Red Bull at 5:30 and she asks if she has time to wash her hair before school. What she really means is will she have time to dry it. Her hair, just like Annie's, is very thick. The blow dryer nearly overheats to get it all dry and most of the time they leave it damp. But today is very cold. She can't go out with wet hair. I tell her to be quick and save extra blow-drying time. I wonder again when Annie will start to lose her hair and how awful will that be? I remind myself to keep my focus on today.

I ride to work with a co-worker. We sometimes ride together and it's nice to just ride along this morning. He comments on the scenery. The leaves have their fall colors and it looks beautiful out across Keetonville Hill.

Yesterday marked four weeks since the nightmare began. In some ways it feels like four months. When we left for Memphis, the weather was warm. We took short-sleeved clothes. Now it's cold and the weathermen are calling for snow.

In other ways, it feels like one long day. The day that never ends. Like life for us has stopped while we hold our breath and wait for Annie to be home and well. But life goes on around us. Everyone is talking about football, getting ready for the holidays and living their normal lives. It feels like everything else is changing while we are stuck in time. And the leaves turned when I wasn't looking.

I text the hubs, but still no word on yesterday's bone marrow biopsy. Since they gave her a lumbar puncture with the chemo injection, the hubs says Annie has been sick and throwing up again. She has lost more weight and I am concerned that she is losing too much weight too early. We are anxious because we haven't heard anything from the doctor. He tells me Annie has an appointment at A Clinic so he will find out the test results. He also tells me that he passed the dressing change class with the line nurse. He says I am not signed off. What? I thought the line nurse and I had an agreement. I'll have to step up my game. I sit with my phone all day waiting for test results that don't come.

I leave work at 5:00 for a change. I pick up Red Bull and we run to Walmart for a few items before a couple of my friends bring over dinner. Everything we have to get is within one aisle in the store. No one is in one of the express lanes. We are in and out of Walmart in twenty minutes. This has never happened in our long history of Walmart visits. I hope it's an indication our luck is changing.

My friends bring a Mexican dinner, but make some lousy margaritas. I enjoy it anyway. I recount everything that has been happening. We laugh and we cry together. Good times! One of them has suggested some supplements that will be good for Annie to take that supposedly cure cancer. I tell her I haven't had time to look into it. She tells me I need to. One of the things that is hard is how everyone wants to help with alternative remedies. Apparently, places in Arizona have things she can drink that cure cancer. Just change her diet, give her supplements, pray the Word, watch this video, buy this book. How could we pump poison into our daughter's body without first taking the time to check out these alternatives? Why do we follow the lies propagated by the liberal doctors using traditional medicine? I look up some of these sites and do some quick research. One of the supplements recommended by a friend was actually tested twenty years ago and no evidence was found to support it cures anything. More often than not, the experts are not MDs. One guy with quite a following is a CPA. One website's info actually says "there are natural forms of chemotherapy, like medical marijuana..." Really? Please pass me what they are smoking!

The friends leave. My sister-in-law comes over. She has brought us money raised through donations from friends. I feel guilty living in a nice house, eating well, wearing nice clothes and accepting money. But at the same time I am a bit panicked over the medical bills I see, even with insurance. The round trips to Memphis are expensive. And the hubs no longer has his bus driving job. I take the money knowing we can use it. Again, I am overwhelmed at everyone's kindness.

My sister-in-law leaves at 11:00, and I go to bed thankful tomorrow is Friday.

DAY 30 – Friday, November 14, 2014

I wake up and call Red Bull at 5:30. She is crying. She doesn't feel good and doesn't want to go to school. Should I take her temperature? Should I take her to the doctor? No. She just wants to stay home. Permission granted. I text my twenty-year-old and tell him that he will not have to drive the fifty-minute round trip twice today. I am sure he is having a hallelujah moment.

My turn to drive to work. Running late as usual. Carpooling with me is risky. We get to work only five minutes past eight. Though no one should care, I have become a bit of a clock watcher. Making sure I get the job done leaving no room for complaints. Since I have already put in thirty-eight hours this week, I am hoping to cut the day short and go to happy hour. I haven't been since the night our nightmare began. I want to catch up with everyone else. TGIF!

For lunch, several of us go to a chili cook-off sponsored by the recruiter we use in accounting. I win a door prize. Dinner for two at a restaurant in Tulsa. I hope it doesn't expire since I won't be together with the hubs in Tulsa for at least five more months. I also hope this means our luck is changing.

We still don't have test results from Annie's tests on Wednesday. The hubs and I are anxious. Is this good news or bad news? The nurse in A Clinic says it simply means no news. Annie has been going to school this week at St. Jude. I ask how it is going. She says it is like doing all your work with a good friend. Her new teacher is my new BFF.

We have an accounting meeting at the bar across the street at 4:00. I love this group. It is fun to relax with them and I have been looking forward to this. They wear their pink bracelets for Annie. We pick on one of the single guys and tell him that he needs to propose to his girlfriend. The conversation turns to what makes a successful marriage. Being married for twenty-six years, I should know this answer. But who can say? Sometimes the perfect church-going couple doing everything right can't make it work. Sometimes the hillbilly couple from near Arkansas who began their relationship on a school bus are still together. I save my marriage-wisdom for another day with stronger drinks. I miss the hubs!

The hubs e-mails pictures of Target House. It is small, but it looks nice. We still will share one small bathroom. But in addition to our own kitchen, the hubs and I have our own bedroom. No more sharing with the teenagers. Nice.

I get home and get a call from the hubs. The test results are back. No trace of leukemia found in blood or spinal fluid. The leukemia is in remission after one round of chemo. Exactly what we longed to hear! Such relief! The tears are back. I sit and cry and cry. We both immediately begin texting and e-mailing the good news. The hubs puts a message of Praise to God on her Facebook page, Annie's Army, that she is cancer-free. Our luck has changed. God found the Easy Button. I pray He will keep pushing it. I go to bed relieved.

DAY 31 – Saturday, November 15, 2014

I wake up to texts and Facebook messages asking when Annie is coming home. People do not understand her daddy's Facebook message. They think a miracle has happened and she is cancer-free for good. Truth is a miracle *has* happened – delivered via the doctors and the chemo treatments. But this is just remission. She must endure several more rounds of chemo in order to protect against relapse. She will not be considered cancer-free for ten years.

I get upset with the hubs. He posts another message on Facebook trying to explain. She is not coming home. Please don't stop praying. Not nearly as many people read this message as the last. Friends tell me of people asking them "Is it true? Is there really no cancer? Is it over? Is Annie coming home now?" If only.

Time to pay bills. I haven't updated the checkbook since the nightmare began. The charges I haven't written down go all the way back to Annie's birthday night at Chili's. Back when life was normal. (At least when we thought it was normal.) I decide it is a good thing God doesn't let us see the future. It allows us to enjoy the "normal" days more.

I finally remove the dead plants from my front porch and sweep off the piles of leaves. A friend brings over some wooden pumpkin decorations for my porch. Time to get rid of the haunted house look. I go to the mailbox and collect the mail. A huge pile from a week's worth of uncollected mail and about two pieces of mail worth keeping. My nurse friend invites Red Bull and me over for dinner. Sweet.

The hub's sisters have gone to Memphis to visit. They are spoiling Annie with all her favorite things. I am glad someone is there to keep them from being so bored. Red Bull and I go to dinner at our friends. This is the nurse friend that helped us make the decision to go to Memphis. I haven't seen her since then. She breaks out dinner and a bottle of wine. I break out in big smiles. We visit until midnight when my twenty-year-old calls to ask if I'm okay. Yes...just laughing a lot with a good friend. I'm better than okay. He tells me I need to get home because nothing good happens after midnight. I hate when my own words come back to haunt me. At least he remembers something I have told him.

It is super cold outside. I miss summer already. I go to bed late and wishing I had an electric blanket.

DAY 32 – Sunday, November 16, 2014

I wake up and make coffee in my very own coffeepot...downstairs. I'm thinking houses should have coffee bars by the master bathrooms. And laundry rooms by the master closets. I should design houses. I could design multi-family houses. I talk to the hubs about Target House. I can't help thinking of the store when I mention it. We start calling it the store house. From the sorority house, to the clown house, to the store house. I think this will be our last move until we come home with Annie. The hubs tells me the store house has a cleaning lady that comes to clean the bathroom once a week. Sweet.

It is snowing outside and I spend the day in my pajamas. I also babysit my adorable grandson. I have forgotten how much energy babies take. He is eleven months old and needs constant attention. I video him in the bathtub and send it to his papa (aka the hubs) in Memphis. His papa tells me Annie is wiped out after visiting with her aunts, cousins and grandma. His family has gone back to Oklahoma and Annie is sleeping. She hasn't finished drinking all the water that she should and she will likely need blood tomorrow when they go to A Clinic. He is bored and irritable. I am getting more and more into a funk as the day goes on. Starting to get e-mails about the next morning's meetings. I am already dreading work.

I do all the laundry, watch a movie with Red Bull, snack on junk food all day, and go to bed depressed.

DAY 33 – Monday, November 17, 2014

I call Red Bull at 5:30 (yes, she is just across the hall, but I am lazy), and I start to feel sick about going in to work. I get ready and check to make sure one of the twenty-year-olds is up to take Red Bull to school. I hear my adorable grandson crying. His mom is in the bathroom, he is still in the crib. His dad is in the bed, oblivious to the crying. I can't resist picking up my adorable grandson, and I carry him to go get a bottle and change his diaper. I wish I had enough money to stay home and keep him all day. I could help his twenty-year-old parents out by letting them work the long hours instead of me. But I haven't won the lottery yet. And since I haven't bought a ticket, I go to work.

At work, we get ready for a board meeting next week with an audit committee meeting today. I am able to provide explanations and make sure the committee's questions are answered. Speaking of me, the committee chairman asks if we have other resources we use to answer all these accounting questions or "Is it all in her head?" Huge compliment for me. Some payback for the long hours.

The hubs said they spent most of the day at A Clinic. Annie's blood was tested and no transfusions were needed. They will even get a day off tomorrow. She is still randomly sick off and on, but overall has been feeling better. Good news. One less thing to worry about. On the other hand, her daddy is feeling anxious. He is calling his doctor to ask for something to calm his nerves and help him sleep. Not being used to being confined with nothing to do, he is getting stir crazy. He misses his teaching job. And in addition to losing his bus driving job, he can't work his second business. He jokingly asks me if he can set up his taxidermy shop in the store house. Fortunately, there isn't enough room in the freezer for deer heads. Maybe that's why they have room inspections.

I work until 7:30 and get home to Red Bull by 8:10. She is feeling neglected. I tell her I have a seminar Thursday and Friday so I should be home earlier. But in the meantime, there is a lot of work to do for our meetings. She tells me I always say that. Yes, I do. But I cannot lose this job.

We eat popcorn and watch *Days*. I text the boyfriend's mom to see about travel plans for the weekend. They have weekend plans. The boyfriend wants to see Annie, but his mom doesn't want him staying by himself when he gets to Memphis or driving home alone. Understandable. I text another friend who has offered a plane. She says the little plane can't fly in bad weather, and the forecast isn't looking good. Commercial tickets are very expensive and there are no direct flights. The time it takes to get there by commercial flight is nearly the same as driving. Red Bull gets tired of all my texting and planning instead of watching TV with her. She goes to bed. I go to bed looking forward to next weekend.

DAY 34 – Tuesday, November 18, 2014

I call Red Bull at 5:30 and stay in bed for thirty more minutes trying to pray and not to think about work. My prayer life has actually gotten worse. Reading my Bible used to be daily. Now I am reading it a couple days a week at best. What kind of Christian prays less when times are bad? Isn't suffering supposed to make me more Christ-like? I have so many issues, my mind is clouded. I cannot keep focused to pray. I have read hundreds of Facebook "praying for you" messages. I hope they are all true.

Red Bull and I get ready, and I go make sure my twenty-year-old son is up to take her to school. Of course not. My adorable grandson is crying in the crib again. I get his bottle, lay him in bed with his daddy, and remind the twenty-year-old that he needs to take Red Bull to school. His daddy seems agitated. Ugh!

I get to work and start responding to e-mails rapidly filling my inbox. Reviewing the quarterly financials, next year's budget and ever-changing fourth quarter forecasts, I have more than enough to keep busy. My department needs me to help with closing the current month's books too. Revenue needs me to review the distribution. Our property tax consultant calls with questions. The President asks me tax questions about a new deal they are working on. It's nice to have problems I can solve.

The nurse phones from Red Bull's school. She is sick. Stomach hurts. Can I come pick her up? No. But I will try to contact a twenty-year-old. My daughter-in-law is in class. My son will not pick up the phone. Normally, I would just go get her and work the rest of the day from home. But since this is my last week in Tulsa for a while, I am too afraid of the backlash at work. I text Red Bull to ask if she can just stay at the nurse's station. She says no, please come pick her up. I can't. After about fifteen minutes, the twenty-year-old calls back and I ask him to go pick up his sister. After long and loud sighs of agitation, he says he will. About thirty minutes later, he actually makes it to the school. Red Bull spent most of the day at the nurse's station. What kind of mom won't go pick up her sick daughter?

The hubs and Annie have had a day off. The doctor called and told him to stop all medications for twenty-four hours before they start chemo. The hubs will get a break. No late night meds for Annie. I am being a credit card watchdog because he cannot tell her no. I am seeing Amazon e-mails that thank me for my order. A soft-hearted daddy with a sick sixteen-year-old daughter is hard on the finances.

I leave work at 7:45 and go home to find a friend has had pizza delivered. The kids said the tip was already paid. Sweet! I scarf down two pieces of pepperoni and a bread stick. I contemplate a third, but my stomach has been so upset lately, I pass. My eighteen-year-old who lives in Tulsa scares me by walking in the door. It's late and I wasn't expecting him. He says he has been to the ER from a cramping stomach. They gave him some medicine. Lord, please don't let me get sick. I can't see Annie if I am sick.

I am carrying my adorable grandson to his crib and trip over something in the floor. The twenty-year-olds aren't much into housekeeping. As I fall trying to save the baby, I practically straddle their coffee table. Saved my adorable grandson. He cries because I have set him down. I cry because the corner of the coffee table connected with my leg. I'm going to have a nice bruise later. I get my adorable grandson to bed and go ask the eighteen-year-old if they gave him any pain medicine for the cramps. He says they did. I say he must share. He does. I go to bed crying...not due to physical pain.

DAY 35 – Wednesday, November 19, 2014

The alarm goes off at 5:30 and I think I have actually slept. Red Bull and I get ready. I go check on the twenty-year-olds and hold my adorable grandson for a few minutes before leaving for work.

Though I am registered for a seminar Thursday afternoon and Friday, I have a list of things to be finished first. One thing on my list is a power point presentation to the board. I gave my updates to a secretary yesterday, but have not had a chance to review them. I open the presentation the secretary sent back. For whatever reason, my slides have not been updated. Okay, looks like I will do them myself. I update and send for review. There is a problem with the font on the new slides. I call the secretary. She tells me to try enlarging the box within power point. It will make the print larger or smaller. I spend the morning trying to make my presentation look good on the page. No meaningful work accomplished for the morning.

I get a text from the hubs. He and Annie arrived at the hospital today to start her next round of chemo.

They have spent a lot of time sitting in waiting rooms. No surprise there. The test results of our family's blood tests come back. Red Bull's blood is a 100% match to Annie's. Tiger Lily and Red Bull – a perfect match! Though we don't think a bone marrow transplant will be needed, it is such a relief to know! It is a surprise that the one that looks the least like Annie, is the one that matches. We will have to quit telling Red Bull she was adopted. She may be disappointed for the confirmation that she is actually one of us. The other four of us, Annie's daddy, myself and her two brothers, all have blood that can be used to help if the NK cell therapy treatment is needed. I do not understand what it all means. I do understand we have all the blood we need for Annie's survival right here in our own family. I always hoped having four kids would be good for something (besides quadrupled challenges). It is a hallelujah moment!

I work until 8:30 getting everything finalized for the board meeting tomorrow. I eat a hodge-podge of leftovers when I get home. My adorable grandson is already in bed and Red Bull is playing video games with her twenty-year-old brother. Though I miss visiting with them, I enjoy reading a book. I am looking forward to only working a half-day in the office tomorrow until I leave for my CPE conference.

I read a little and go to bed feeling better.

DAY 36 – Thursday, November 20, 2014

I wake up Red Bull at 5:30. Looking forward to my day because board meetings will be all morning (thankfully, I am not allowed to attend) and I have my

CPE conference in the afternoon. I get ready and head to the office. Red Bull texts and says her twenty-year-old brother won't get out of bed to take her to school. I wish I could take her. But it's the opposite direction from my work, she would get there way too early, and it would make my commute an hour and a half. She texts again. He got up and she made it just before the tardy bell. Crisis averted.

I get to work and quickly send out an e-mail explaining an adjustment we made to yesterday's financials. I answer questions about my slides for the presentation. Fortunately, it is a short inquisition, because the meeting is starting.

With a little reprieve, I quickly make sure all the items on my list are being taken care of. I have a downtown lunch meeting with our tax consultant and then I will go to my conference. I pack up my computer and other things from the office that I will need for my two weeks away and tell everyone at the office goodbye.

The hubs says Annie is feeling good. She is getting randomly sick, but still has not lost her hair. They have bought paint supplies, a remote control helicopter (which he nearly flew into the doctor's head), and new sound equipment for their phones' playlists. She is also in good spirits. Relief!

I get a text from Annie. "Only awkward thing about having dad here and not u. Bath time at the hospital. I don't have my mother to wash me. I have a nurse. I said nope! I can take care of it myself lol." I text back "Ah. I'm so sorry. I'll be there Saturday. Just stay smelly tomorrow!" She texts, "Oh no. They've made it mandatory now that the patient has to take a bath every day. I'm not letting some random lady look at my goods. I told her wait by the door I think I got this one but if u hear something strange feel free to rescue me." I text back "Lol! You crack me up. I'm sure she's seen the goods before!" She texts, "No no [_____] (that really is her name) will not be washing me. I'm waiting till my mama is here. Until then I'll do it myself." I miss being her mama every day.

At the conference, Captain Awesome receives a text to call the office. We are past break time, so we both leave the conference and go to the lobby. We both answer questions, confirm we have taken care of everything on our lists and promise to look at anything else needed that evening after the conference. We get back in the conference and my sick stomach is returning. After the conference, they have happy hour in the lobby. Not feeling well and wanting to get home to Red Bull, I pass on happy hour. I don't remember ever passing on free drinks before. Things are definitely changing. Depressing!

I get home and start working on a number that needs filled in on our investor update. I thought one of our accountants had handled it, but she is new and hasn't figured out how to dig for all the info. I get another request for some information that isn't crucial and send it back asking the accountant to dig on this one. Knowing I will be out tomorrow, I finish up the numbers for the investor update along with the supporting spreadsheets and e-mail them off. Thinking I have taken care of everything that will be needed for tomorrow, I quit working at midnight and go to bed exhausted.

DAY 37 – Friday, November 21, 2014

I wake up Red Bull at 5:30. I start to get ready a little after 6:00 and check my e-mail. I have a list of issues to address that must be completed by noon. After a long phone call that goes south, I realize I will be going into the office after all. No conference for me.

I vent to a co-worker who tells me the company has made a lot of concessions for me to work remotely from Memphis, and I should not complain over missing a conference. With the amount of work that I have been doing, I have a hard time seeing "concessions." But I don't argue. I actually start crying. At work. Embarrassing. I think I must have lost all perspective. I take a breath. I need this job and insurance. I loved it once, I can love it again. I can do self-study for CPE in my spare time. Not the end of the world. I can do this.

I go to a meeting where we talk over an hour about what to update in the narrative of a report. Endless meetings (particularly those where the scheduler shows up late) have become the bane of my existence. I work all day on changing and re-wording reports. I review and actually work on several other items that I had put off until later. No question there is plenty of work. Just questioning if it required my physical presence. No longer questioning out loud.

I text Red Bull to tell her some friends are supposed to come over and bring dinner. They will be there before I am. Will she pick up the house? She calls me crying. The house is a mess. I ask her to do her best. I am sorry I am not there. She asks when I am coming home. It is 6:00. I tell her soon. At 7:45, we are finished with re-wording, reprinting, changing the order of the paragraphs, etc. We get some information from the rest of the departments that is supposed to be included. We get an e-mail that more information from other departments will be completed over the weekend. Huh? I thought we were behind because we didn't put this in by noon. Oh well, at least I am finished.

I get an update on Annie from the hubs. Everyone loves Annie at the hospital. She knows all the nurses by name and tries to find out all about them, their lives, their children, their pets. She is Chatty Cathy. Meantime, her daddy is very bored. I am looking forward to seeing them tomorrow.

I go home and visit with my friends. They have brought over a delicious dinner and make me a creamsicle adult beverage to calm my nerves. Ordinarily, I would suck down a couple. But I don't think my stomach can handle it. My friends cheer me up. They are all working moms too. They understand. They pray for me. They are lifesavers. They leave too soon, but I am exhausted. Driving back to Memphis tomorrow. I go to bed crying.

Closer to Graceland

DAY 38 – Saturday, November 22, 2014

I wake up at 4:13 when I get a text from my twenty-year-old telling me he needs gas money before I leave for Memphis. Of course he does. After all, he has been gracious enough to drive his sister to school. I should pay him for that. What was I thinking? I can't fall back asleep. I am nauseous. I need to quit thinking about work. I toss and turn until 7:00 when I get up and take a Zofran. Captain Awesome texts. I have his token to log-in to the bank website. When can he come get it? He knows I am driving to Memphis today and didn't want to miss me. I text him. 9:00? I am trying to forget about work and not get sick so I can drive. I ask him to pray for me. He assures me he is. He gives me good advice. Go read the Psalms until you feel better. I take the advice. I feel better. God is good.

I start to reflect that out of everything going on in my life, my work is causing me the most stress. I resolve to do better, take the high road, and try to smile no matter what. No push back. Play nice. I send an e-mail to three people at work who have had to listen to my complaining. I apologize for bringing them into my drama. It is out there now. I am committed. I will do better. The Zofran has settled my stomach. Red Bull and I pack and leave for Memphis.

Annie and her daddy are calling from the hospital. They tell us to turn on our location services on our phones so they can watch our progress. The only thing I think would be more boring than actually driving for hours is watching a green dot move on a map while we drive.

Red Bull and I make it to Memphis and go straight to St. Jude. Annie and her daddy are in a good mood. They are playing music on the new Bluetooth speaker he bought her. We watch funny videos and Annie is a Chatty Cathy. More chatty than normal. Is it the medicine? Or is this normal and we have been so long away from normal that we have forgotten? Her counts are all still good enough for no transfusions and her ANC is approaching normal, even half-way through the chemo. My mood is lightening. I get a little tickle in my throat. I cough a little. Everyone stares at me. No coughing allowed. I can't get sick.

We leave for the store house. It is beautiful. It is a small two-bedroom, one-bathroom apartment. A cleaning lady comes to clean the bathroom once a week, and the trash only has to be taken to the end of the hall and dropped in a trash chute. Nice. The laundry room is next door and we are allowed our very own ironing board and iron. We also have our very own coffee pot and microwave. No more going down the stairs….to the end of the hall…to an empty pot. There are random room inspections, but who cares? It will keep everyone from being a slob. Maybe they start you with the clown house so you will think the store house is paradise. Mission accomplished.

We cook some pizza in our very own oven, pop some corn in our very own microwave, and watch a Tim Hawkins video until we are laughing so hard we are crying. The hubs and I sleep together in a bedroom of our very own for the first time since we came to Memphis. He is a very happy man! I take a Benadryl to take care of the tickle in my throat and go to bed feeling good for the first time in a very long time.

Target House

DAY 39 – Sunday, November 23, 2014

I wake up to stomach cramps. I have medicine to ease the cramping. I am a physical mess. God, please help me not get sick! I get up to take my medicine. I try not to think about work. It will only bring the cramps back. I sit at my computer and start to write. Writing it down is keeping me sane.

The hubs gets up, makes coffee and starts cooking bacon. Two of my favorite things in the world. Oh my goodness, I love that man! Then he starts playing George Strait and Tim McGraw from his new

Bluetooth speaker (another Amazon purchase). Can this time just stand still?

Annie is calling. She wants us to come to the hospital. Wants us to bring food. Her daddy tells her to order from the hospital. She doesn't want hospital food. She tells him the sandwich she wants him to make. He can't tell her no.

He starts making the sandwich and tells her we will be there soon. The hubs and I take some of the drops of different concoctions my Texas friend sent. We have no idea what is in it and the hubs says it tastes like horse butt. Not sure when he has tasted that. One says it will build our immune system. Another will relieve stress. Relieve stress? I want to guzzle the bottle, but make sure to follow the recommended dose.

At the hospital, Annie's first bag of chemo for the day is just finishing. The nurse says she is doing so well that it would be a good day to get up and walk around the hospital. She will still be connected to her IV fluids and antibiotics, but no more chemo until 8:00. She doesn't want to walk around the hospital. She doesn't like the hospital smells. She wants a shower. She showers, we listen to music and watch TV. The hubs flies the remote control helicopter around the room all afternoon. Boring. Boring is good.

At dinnertime, we tell Annie to order from the hospital while we go out to eat. We argue over where to eat. First world problems. Red Bull's first choice is always McDonald's. Always. But burgers don't sound good to me. She suggests Taco Bell. Crunchy tacos sound yummy, but her daddy isn't sold on that idea. We see IHOP. We all agree. Who doesn't like bacon? I eat today's second breakfast. It does not disappoint.

When we get back to the hospital, Annie hasn't eaten. She says she is not hungry. We say she has to eat. She is taking a medicine to increase her appetite. It doesn't appear to be working. We get her a Gogurt from her supply. She eats it to make us leave her alone. I am hoping the Gogurt doesn't reappear. Her nurse starts her last bag of chemo for the day. Though she doesn't feel good, Annie is still in good spirits. Her daddy leaves to go watch TV in The Kennel because he cannot stand to keep up with the Kardashians. Instead, he would rather watch Swamp People. My IQ drops in either room. I stay with Annie and write.

When the chemo finishes, Annie says she doesn't need us to stay with her. We say goodbye to Annie for the night and go back to the store house. The hubs only spent one night at the hospital with her during this round of chemo. I am so happy she feels comfortable and safe at St. Jude. Once again, I am so tired that I cannot wait to get into bed. I am amazed how tiring sitting in a room all day has made me. Tomorrow I am supposed to be on vacation, but I have told the President that I will look at a few things for him. He is my friend and trying to make things better for me at work. I want to keep him happy. I go to bed dreading the work week, hoping I won't hear from the office and can take a day off.

DAY 40 – Monday, November 24, 2014

I wake at 5:30 when the alarm goes off. The alarm that I forgot to cancel. Ugh! I doze for a while and decide to check my e-mail. Why do I do this? Sure enough, I have two e-mails before 7:05, asking me questions and to send files. So much for a day off. I get up and start working.

At 11:00 the hubs and Red Bull leave for the hospital. I stay behind to work. On my day off. I work until 1:30 when my parents call to say they are in Memphis on their way to Nashville to see my sister. They want to stop by to see Annie. They are stuck in traffic, so I take a quick shower and get ready to go with them. At 2:00, they arrive and we go to the hospital together.

Annie is doing her normal chattering, but she is more irritable today. I make a mental note to talk to the doctor about changes in her personality. Seems like taking eighteen different types of medications could have some effect. Trying to smile and be nice when you feel like crap probably has an effect too. Her counts are all good. She hasn't had a transfusion in several days. She is on her last bag of the harsh chemo. Tomorrow and the next day she will only need chemo twice a day – at 8:00 a.m. and 8:00 p.m. – and it should only take about thirty minutes each time. The doctor says she can be checked out of the hospital tonight and be outpatient for these last two days of chemo. She is happy. When Annie is happy, we are all happy.

The hubs, Red Bull and I eat lunch with my parents in the St. Jude cafeteria. It is similar to the food court at the mall. At lunchtime, it is hard to find a place to sit and the food choices are plentiful. By 3:00, most places have closed up. The grill is always open and the Bacon Cheddar Burger has become my favorite. Of course it has. It starts with bacon.

After lunch, my parents leave and I go back to work at the store house. I am still sitting at my computer when everyone, including Annie, comes home from the hospital at 9:00. The girls are in a good mood. The hubs reminds Annie they have to be back at the hospital by 8:00 a.m. "So get to bed and stop texting by 10:00," he says. He even uses his serious daddy speaking voice. The girls reply "Sure, dad." Meaning they are sure to text and Facebook half the night. I am glad for some normal.

I take calls from work until 10:00. Finally, the investor packet is finished. I work until after midnight on the project I promised for the President. I am hoping to catch a break tomorrow. I go to bed exhausted.

DAY 41 – Tuesday, November 25, 2014

I wake up to the stupid 5:30 alarm that I forgot to turn off. I feel anxious and sick. I try to pray. I cry instead. I am tired of trying so hard to be a good mom and good wife and good friend and good employee and good Christian. I think I am failing at all of them. I try to keep the crying quiet and not wake the hubs. I get up and start working when I get an e-mail from one of the accounting staff that he is sick and will not be in today. He was scheduled for a meeting today. The meeting schedulers will not be happy.

Annie gets sick just as she and her daddy are leaving for the hospital. They will be late. He hates to be late. They return after the chemo and she tells me she has been throwing up. She feels better now and is talking too much for us to get a word in edgewise. She is very hyper. Her hands are shaky. This is becoming her new normal. What is this medicine doing to her?

She watches TV with Red Bull, and they even go to the fitness room together. Annie walks one-tenth of a mile on the treadmill. When they return, she complains she isn't able to do as much as Red Bull. I am happy she even feels like walking to the fitness room. She feels better than me.

I get several e-mails of things needed today and things needed first thing Monday morning. So much for scheduling vacation. I sit at my computer and work until 5:30, which was when I told the office I would be unavailable. The only way I could think to keep from getting calls until 10:00.

We plan what to eat before Annie goes back for her second chemo treatment at 8:00. Finally a kitchen. Nothing to cook. The hubs says he will grocery shop tomorrow. Meantime, Annie has a corndog and the hubs goes to Sonic for the rest of us.

The eighteen-year-old calls and needs new tires on his car. Of course he does. The twenty-year-old calls and says someone ran over one of our cats. He saw it in the road. He has collected the cat in a bag and plans to bury it in our pet cemetery out back. I am impressed by his effort, and I make a mental note to buy mouse traps. Annie is saddened by the news. Red Bull distracts her with putting another selfie on Instagram. Cat forgotten.

The eighteen-year-old calls again. He has gone over to our house to help the twenty-year-old bury the cat. As he is in the garage getting the shovel, he notices both cats playing. Both cats? He calls the twenty-year-old to the garage. "If we had two cats, and I see two cats, whose cat do you have in the bag?" Huh? I appreciate the twenty-year-old trying to take care of things. Now we have a cat in our pet cemetery that we never knew. The grave of the unknown cat. I feel sorry for the family that lost their cat. They will never know because the twenty-year-old will not go door-to-door with the cat in the bag to find the owner. But, I haven't laughed like that in a while. I laugh until I cry.

Annie and her daddy get home late after chemo. We try to find something entertaining on TV without much success. Red Bull and I watch some weird chick who calls herself Lorde on The Tonight Show. Her hair resembles a bird's nest and she wears black lipstick. She dances like Elaine on Seinfeld. Enough TV. I go to bed pondering the unfairness of life.

DAY 42 – Wednesday, November 26, 2014

I wake up when the hub's alarm goes off at 7:00. Yes, I remembered to turn the 5:30 alarm off. He knocks something off the dresser trying to turn the alarm off. Finally, he finds the alarm. What a fiasco. I check my e-mail. Surprisingly, nothing yet. I cherish another few moments of sleep.

The hubs gets Annie up and they take off for her first chemo treatment of the day. I sit down and read my Bible. I have been out of the habit when I have needed it the most. I love to read it out loud. I shout out and repeat the good parts. I wonder if Red Bull will come to see what is going on. She must be sleeping soundly. I read for about an hour. I ask God if he still has my back. Not feeling it. But trusting it. I get up and go to work at my computer.

The hubs and Annie return and once again she is very chatty. I have never seen her so animated or wanting to talk to me so much. I talk to her for a while, but need to get back to work. I really want to get everything done and have a few days off.

In the afternoon, some friends from Oklahoma come through Memphis on their way to their family holiday in Alabama. They stay at the store house with us for a couple of hours. It is a nice break from work. We go over to the other Target House and visit the Amy Grant room, the Shaun White room and the DreamWorks room (with lots of movies to watch). We come back to our house and show them the crafts room, the fitness room and the Brad Paisley room. The common rooms here are very nice. They all have comfortable chairs and couches. They all have TVs and game consoles. The Brad Paisley room has a pool table. The hubs plays pool with my friend's hubs and the rest of us visit. If you have to be a cancer refugee, this is place to be. I make a mental note to quit working so much and enjoy the family.

The friends leave and I go back to work. The hubs has moved my "office" to the bedroom because they are tired of having to be quiet. He brings me snacks while I work. Later, I begin to smell something burning. Then, the smell of fish and burning. Red Bull comes into my bedroom to inform me that her daddy set the pan on fire while he was making salmon cakes. Ugh! The only thing worse than the smell of fish is the smell of burning fish. Salmon cakes are my favorite, but maybe not such a good choice in small living quarters. I wonder if the manager will come. I don't want to get kicked out of the store house. Red Bull sprays enough air freshener to freshen the planet. It helps for about ten minutes.

I can still smell fish at 8:00 when I quit working. I leave the room and go look for everyone. Red Bull tells me they left for Annie's last chemo treatment. I spray more air freshener. I sit down and read my Kindle until they come home. I have read very little since the nightmare began. Working from home is worse than working at the office. When the office is in your home, you never really leave the office. I have a hard time separating. Harder still when I get nearly round the clock e-mails. But tonight the e-mails have stopped and I try to relax. The hubs and Annie come home from the hospital. She has finished the last of the chemo for Round Two. She is tired and goes to bed. The other three of us watch a little TV. The Tulsa office is closed for Thanksgiving and Annie has no appointments tomorrow. I go to bed looking forward to a day off.

DAY 43 – Thursday, November 27, 2014 – Thanksgiving Day

I wake up when the hub's alarm goes off to take Annie's eclipse out of the fridge. Thankfully, he is on top of the meds. He comes back to bed and I wake up a second time when the alarm goes off at 8:00 to give the medication. Again, I lay near comatose while he gets up and takes care of Annie. He stays up and I get up a little later and read my Bible. I resolve to get back in this routine of spending time praying and reading my Bible and thinking about God in the morning. My soul needs it. I read the Psalms where David expresses a lot of what I feel. I recite Psalm 143 – one of my favorites. Most people recite Psalm 23 or all the loving verses. I like the ones that ask God to destroy my foes. How about some Psalm 35. Contend with those who contend with me. Or even Psalm 40. May all who desire my ruin be turned back in disgrace. That's praying for my enemies, right? I continue to trust God has my back and knows what he is doing. I can do this.

We receive lots of Happy Thanksgiving texts. I am overwhelmed at the prayers and gifts we continue to receive. A friend on Red Bull's soccer team knows Barry Switzer. Barry Switzer donated Bedlam tickets to be raffled and her soccer teammates sold raffle tickets and worked a concession stand to benefit Annie. A 5K run is being planned by our church. A guy from church organized Chili's to give a percentage of sales on certain nights to Annie. My parent's church, in the hometown where the hubs and I grew up, has organized an "Event" with a dinner where lots of items will be auctioned and Annie will receive the proceeds. A cousin I lost touch with sends us money. A teacher from elementary school sends us money. Old friends and new friends and people we don't even know are sending gifts and money. The hubs and I are overwhelmed at the outpouring of love and gifts. He says we need to pay more attention when our nightmare ends and we see others in need. Agreed! We have always given to the church, but this makes me want to be more aware of specific things we could do to help others. We have much to be thankful for!

We go downstairs at noon to collect our Thanksgiving dinner from the store house. Turkey, dressing, mashed potatoes, green bean casserole, rolls and pumpkin pie. All cooked and ready to go. Annie doesn't join us. She is too sick to eat. Red Bull, her daddy and I eat until we are stuffed. Clean up is over by 1:00. The hubs sits down to football. Red Bull is complaining because she is bored. Annie is still in bed. I decide bed sounds like a good idea and take a long nap. After I wake up, Red Bull and I go watch *A Series of Unfortunate Events* in the DreamWorks room. It's a fitting title.

No one is in the room except us. We lay on the big couches a while and then switch to the giant bean bag pillows on the floor. Fun room and fun time. We return to our room and Annie is up and eating. The hubs is finishing up football. Annie talks to the boyfriend who is coming tomorrow. Red Bull and I play word games. I don't get a single e-mail from work all day. It's a Christmas miracle at Thanksgiving. I go to bed thankful for a good day.

DAY 44 – Friday, November 28, 2014

I wake up when the hubs alarm goes off. I get the eclipse out of the fridge and go back to bed. I wake up again when it's time to give Annie her meds. I get up and give her the medicine. The hubs gets up and makes coffee. The boyfriend comes today. Annie is awake earlier than usual. We all try to get in the bathroom at once. We finish just in time. The boyfriend and his dad have flown in and they come to visit us in the store house.

Annie has appointments at A Clinic at 11:30, and I take Red Bull shopping for some Black Friday specials. We go to JC Penney and Target. Our old standbys. We get lots of discounts and I get to eat Target popcorn for lunch. Life is good. We return to the store house and the hubs is watching movies. Annie has gotten a good report. Counts are low, but no transfusions needed. No more appointments until Sunday. I take a nap. When I wake up, I tell him it would be a good night for us to have a date night. He doesn't want to leave Annie. I tell him I am sure she will be fine – even with the boyfriend. Red Bull is chaperoning. And the boyfriend knows he cannot even kiss Annie – too many germs. With much persuading, the hubs agrees to take me out.

We go to Buffalo Wild Wings and have a beer and some appetizers. He is in a funk. He has gone stir-crazy and is having some anger issues over our whole situation. I understand. We are just beginning the whole leukemia thing and it seems like a lifetime already. I tell him of the dream I had last night where I was flying. I flew to a place where no one knew me. I had no responsibilities and just started over. Even in the dream I knew something was missing. Without our family, nothing else matters. We can get through this. We can do this.

The hubs and I return to the store house from our date. While we are still in the parking lot, Red Bull calls. Do we know it is time to give Annie her 8:00 meds? Yes, we will be right up. Everyone's life revolves around Annie taking her medicine. We can't mess this up. We only get one chance. We give Annie her meds and she finishes watching a movie with the boyfriend. Red Bull and I play some computer games and the boyfriend's dad shows up to take him back to the hotel. Check-out time at the store house is 10:00. They say their goodbyes. We will see them again tomorrow. I am happy the boyfriend makes Annie happy and gives her something to look forward to. I am happy he still wants to be with her.

I come back to my computer to write in my journal and see Captain Awesome has been e-mailed a list of things to have ready for Monday morning. Thank goodness he is playing nice. He is one who has made concessions. I go to sleep hating that I have to work for a living.

DAY 45 – Saturday, November 29, 2014

I wake up when the alarm goes off to take Annie's eclipse out of the fridge. I offer to get up and do it. The hubs mutters some kind of reply. I stumble to the kitchen, take it out and lay it on the table and crawl back into bed. I wake up again when I get a text from my parents saying they are on their way back from Nashville. They have spent the holidays with my sister and will stop back through on their way back to Oklahoma. I wake up again when the alarm goes off at 8:00 to give Annie all her meds. Why am I so tired? I get up and give Annie her meds. Knowing the boyfriend will want to come back over soon, I go ahead and shower and the hubs gets up and makes coffee. Love that man!

I get ready for the day. The hubs starts doing laundry. He and Red Bull will go home today. I am already sad. The boyfriend comes over with his dad. There is unexpected cloud cover outside. The boyfriend's dad says they will have to leave as soon as the clouds break up. He tells us they will also have to fly into the wind. Though I can tell he is not happy they made this flight, I am glad they came. Annie is happy that the boyfriend came to see her. When Annie is happy, I am happy.

The "Event" is today. I know lots of people have worked hard for this day in order to support Annie. I am once again overwhelmed at everyone's kindness. And I am trying not to get in a funk as I know Annie and I have a long, lonely week ahead.

The boyfriend and his dad come over to the store house. My parents arrive at the store house. Too soon, it is time for them all to leave. The boyfriend and his dad are the first to leave. I pray they will have a safe trip. I cannot take more bad news. The hubs and Red Bull leave. Then finally, my parents leave. Once again Annie says, "And then there were two." It is all I can do to hold it together.

The boyfriend's mom sent wine with her hubs. After everyone leaves, I complete a self-study CPE course (no conferences for me), pass the test and get my certificate. Then I sit down to take a little break. I end up drinking all the wine she sent. It helps me through my evening. The boyfriend's mom is my new BFF.

The hubs calls to tell me the organizers of the "Event" told him over $13,000 was raised today. I cannot believe the news. People we have not seen in years and some we do not even know have given generously and sacrificially to help us. And not just money. The time it took to organize the Event is incredible. All of the auctioned items were donated - most were handmade. I am shocked. I cry and cry. My usual response these days. The income lost from the bus driving and the taxidermy has been replaced before it even became an issue. Transportation costs are covered. God is good. I go to bed grateful.

DAY 46 – Sunday, November 30, 2014

I wake up with a pounding headache. I go to make coffee and get my Bible out. After all, it's Sunday. A good time to talk to God. I ask God for strength, and I ask him again to relieve my stress from work. I decide I will not work today. I decide the non-emergency e-mails can wait until tomorrow. And they are all non-emergencies.

Annie has to be at A Clinic by 11:30 to test her blood. We are late. Shocker that. She goes in to give blood and we await the results until 2:00. I work on another CPE self-study course. At 2:00, they tell us her hemoglobin counts are low. She needs a blood transfusion. They order the blood. We wait. I finish the CPE course. At 4:00, the blood arrives. It will take a couple of hours. Annie asks me if I will go back to the store house and get her laptop. Of course I will. I cannot tell her no. While I am at the store house, I get another CPE self-study course.

At 6:00, we leave the hospital. Annie wants to go to Target and get a Christmas tree for the store house. So, of course, we go to Target and shop for a Christmas tree. At home, we have a multi-colored tree with a hodge-podge of decorations. Annie decides she just wants two colors. We get a tree with white lights and pick silver and red as the colors.

Our neighbors back at the store house have decorated their door with Frosty the Snowman. Complete with the top hat. It is the cutest door on the floor. Of course, we have to compete. We get red and white wrapping paper with ribbon and prepare to gift wrap our apartment door.

When we get back, we play Christmas music and set up what Annie calls our Charlie Brown Christmas Tree. We put the topper on top. A star. I plug in the light. It is a strobe light all over the ceiling. I feel like I am in a disco. We both get a good laugh but decide we cannot live with the strobe-star light. We also didn't make it home with our ribbon for the door. We search the car and apartment. We find we also don't have the tape and some face cleaner that we bought. Looks like we will be going back to Target…tomorrow.

The hubs calls. He has e-mailed a spreadsheet to me detailing the donors from the day before at the Event. He is proud of his spreadsheet. I am proud he tries to please me and grateful for all the people who gave – most of whom I don't even know. Unexpected blessings.

Annie and I watch *The Cat in the Hat* movie and eat chicken nuggets and fries for dinner. Annie makes a dessert of brownies with melted marshmallows and chocolate chips on top. Ooey, gooey goodness. It is so rich, we can't even finish two pieces. I put the rest of the pan in the freezer. It smells nice in the apartment. I go to bed feeling grateful that Annie and I had a special little Christmas celebration.

A Charlie Brown Christmas

DAY 47 – Monday, December 1, 2014

I wake up when the alarm goes off to call Red Bull. I hear her sweet voice tell me she is already up – it is a hair washing morning. I get ready and walk my two-step commute to start work at 8:00. I have e-mails from work. One from Friday, one from Saturday, two from Sunday and two already this morning. It has been a slow weekend.

I already feel the stress coming on. I don't know how much longer I can continue to do this job. I get really sick as soon as I sit at the computer. I have three prescription medications. One for indigestion, one for nausea, and one for lower abdominal cramps. All three major digestive issues are covered. This morning I am more in pain than I am nauseous. I take two pills – the ones for indigestion and cramps. I can do this.

I work until 12:30 when I take Annie to St. Jude to go to school. Her teacher has scheduled her for three days this week. It is super cold when we go outside. I forgot my coat at home. All I have is a jean jacket. Thank goodness for valet parking at the hospital. Annie goes to her class and I work while she does her schoolwork. She finishes and we go back to the store house. I tell her I will work until 5:30 then we will go back to Target. She plays on Instagram and orders on Amazon. She makes a scrambled egg. She scorches the egg on the pan. The apartment now smells like burned eggs. I keep my comments to myself since I wasn't helping. I work until 6:30 and we leave for Target.

We pick up the few items we never made it home with yesterday. We exchange the strobe-star light for an angel. The angel is huge on our Charlie Brown Christmas Tree, but at least we got rid of the disco. Annie gets upset at Target. She says she hates wearing the mask. She thinks everyone is staring at her. She says "They will stare at me worse when I am bald." I really have not noticed anyone staring and try to convince her. But she is in a funk. When we get back, Annie says she feels "blah" and doesn't feel like decorating the door. I tell her to go lie down before she starts puking. When she feels blah, I feel blah.

I eat several non-nutritious microwavable items for dinner while watching *Holiday Commercials* on TV. I miss watching *Days* with Red Bull. I give Annie's meds to her and change her dressing. I am terrible at changing the dressing. I make Annie nervous. The tape is super sticky. I get it all tangled up and have to start over. I redo and recut a couple of times before Annie tells me to quit with the OCD – it is good enough. I go back to the kitchen, scrub the scorched pan, sweep and mop our floor and take the trash to the trash chute. Tomorrow is room inspection day. I don't want to get kicked out of the store house.

I go to bed feeling blah.

DAY 48 – Tuesday, December 2, 2014

I wake up and cannot go back to sleep. I look at the clock. 2:38. Ugh! I toss and turn until 4:30. Might as well get up. I read my Bible and try to pray. I pray for Annie to heal. I pray for her to keep her hair. I pray for me to not be so anxious about my job. I pray for direction. I pray for peace in my soul. I pray for God to increase my faith so that I will keep praying.

I get ready for work and sit down at the computer. There is a call with our investors at 9:00. I read through the transcript for about the tenth time and help with last minute questions.

After the call, I get back to work until 11:00 when it's time to wake Annie to get ready for school. As I am going to wake her, I remember that I didn't give her the meds she is supposed to take at 8:00. She has taken medicine at 8:00 a.m. and 8:00 p.m. for weeks. How could I have forgotten? I give her the medicine and she gets ready for school.

As we are walking out the door, she says she doesn't feel good. I tell her it is probably because I got her off of her schedule. She will be fine. We get in the car. We are on the way and she pulls out the barf bag that she always carries with her and begins to throw up. I turn the car around and we go back to the store house. I feel like a big loser for not giving her the meds on time. I think I have caused her to be sick. I think my job is making me crazy. I am not remembering to do the very things that I am here to do. I get sick and take some medicine for myself. Thank God for Zofran. Then I sit back down, get over feeling sorry for myself and get back to work.

I quit working at 6:00. Annie is feeling much better and wants to decorate the door. I am not much of a decorator. I have no creative bone in my body. But I make Annie think I have this under control. I've got this. We can do this.

We wrap the outside of the door in wrapping paper and go through two rolls of two-sided sticky tape. We put ribbon going across and down. The ribbon was much more sparkly and bright in the store. Oh well. We put a big red bow on it. Mission accomplished. It actually looks pretty good. We take some quick pictures just in case it all falls down in the night.

We go to the other Target House (there are two – we are in #2) and check out *We Bought a Zoo*. Annie doesn't want to stay in the DreamWorks room to watch it. We bring it back to our room to watch. I love the movie. Lots of laughs. But the parts where he is grieving over his wife who died? Too much for me. Too close to home.

I talk to Captain Awesome about Plan B. The backup plan when I have had enough. I tell him about missing Annie's meds. He says maybe it's time to seriously consider Plan B. I begin to seriously consider a plan that just focuses on Annie. It makes me more peaceful just to consider it. I go to bed thinking of new opportunities, and I finally get a good night's sleep.

DAY 49 – Wednesday, December 3, 2014

I wake up when Red Bull's alarm goes off. I hear her sleepy voice tell me she loves me. How I love the sound of her voice. I get up, make the coffee and start getting ready. Annie has to be at A Clinic for blood tests at 7:30. I wake her and tell her she should eat something. She says she isn't hungry. We get ready to go. Along with my laptop, I pack breakfast. A Twinkie for me and a granola bar and fruit snacks for her. Water packed. List of meds needed. Out the door by 7:25. We are going to be late.

I drop off Annie and quickly find a parking spot because it is still early. She is still checking in when I catch up with her at Registration. The lady at Registration is an elderly black lady that we love. As she puts the armband on Annie, she always prays for healing for her. "In the name of Jesus, may you be healed for now and forever." Amen! She always makes me tear up. I have had my make-up on less than an hour. I don't want to wash it all off with crying. Love that lady, but she needs to stop making me cry!

We get Annie's blood test results. She is low on platelets. Also, the doctor says none of us have the right type of blood (the certain mismatch) for NK cell therapy for Annie. They just got the results today. We had previously misunderstood. Red Bull is a perfect match for the bone marrow transplant (if needed), but we won't be able to use any of our blood to do the NK cell therapy. And even though Annie is standard risk (not low risk like we thought), the NK cell therapy does not have enough proven benefit to look outside the family for the right type of mismatch in the blood.

Again, we are just trying to understand all the info being given to us on a daily basis. The doc says each round of chemo means her white blood cell counts and ANC go to zero. When they build back up again, she will have a bone marrow test. If the bone marrow test shows she is still in remission, she will have only two more rounds of chemo. But it could take longer in between to recover with each round. It's a waiting game. Waiting and hoping.

Annie's hair starts to fall out. It is everywhere. Strands are on her coat, in the bathroom, on her pillow in the morning, on the floor…everywhere. She is in a funk. We start talking about wigs. The doctor says she has kept her hair the longest of anyone he has seen. She is ready to shave it all off because it is driving her crazy. I tell her to wait for her daddy to bring the clippers on Saturday. Truth is, I don't want to see her hair go. It has me in a funk.

Annie gets her platelets and we come back to the store house. I work until 5:30 when she begs me to go to Kroger. I tell her to make a list. She brings a list full of junk food. More junk food. I cannot tell her no. I go to Kroger. I have found a newer Kroger. It is much nicer than the ones I have gone to before. Like the others, it has several security guards, both outside and inside the store. I can't decide if this makes me feel safer or more scared. Like always, I'm packing just in case. I get the junk food and get back to the store house just in time to take Annie's meds out of the fridge. I will not miss her meds again.

I make a skillet-dinner out of a bag that has a ten-minute prep time. My kind of meal. It is delicious. I drink a V8 Fusion spiked with a mini-bottle of vodka which my new BFF sent. (The same friend who sent the wine.) Yum! Annie gets on Facetime with her Tennessee cousins and her aunt (my sister). I visit too. We have fun seeing them all and they are making us laugh. Good times. At a time like this, I thank God for Facetime, Skype, Instagram and texting. Thank God for people who cheer us up. And thank God we can still laugh.

I receive less than ten "I need this right away" e-mails from the office all day and the last one was at 5:35. I wonder if there has been an accident at work. I write a little and go to bed hoping for better days.

DAY 50 – Thursday, December 4, 2014

I wake up at 5:30 and call Red Bull. She hangs up on me. I call back and she says, "Why did you hang up on me?" We joke about who hung up. I love her sweet voice. I go back to sleep until 7:00 when the alarm goes off again. I take the meds out of the fridge, make the coffee and get dressed. At 8:00, I give Annie her meds then make the two-step commute to work.

Annie's hair continues to fall out. She is upset. I tell her to go ahead and wrap her head in a scarf so it won't fall out while she is at school. She wraps a blue scarf around her head and puts on her mask. For the first time, I think she looks like a cancer patient. We are both in a funk again.

At noon, I take Annie to school at St. Jude. The entire campus is overflowing with people. We are running late as usual, so I drop her off in front of the hospital. Big mistake. Now I can't valet park and there is nowhere to park. The garage is full. People are in cars sitting in lanes in the parking lots waiting for someone to leave. I end up driving over to the sorority house where we used to live and get the last spot. I call her and tell her to call me when she is finished. I will work from the car. Then I discover I have no wireless. I work off my phone. Not too bad because I get several work calls anyway.

After school, we go back to the store house. They are giving tours to groups inside the store house. We hear them tell the groups how everyone is just like family to them. They are very kind to us here and I don't disagree. Annie gets on the elevator and quickly pushes the button to close the door. She is upset. She says, "I am a patient – not a tourist attraction." I explain that the store house operates from donations. People are seeing how their money is spent. They didn't come to look at her. They came to help us. She doesn't seem convinced. She is tired of being here. I don't disagree with that either.

I go back to work. Annie looks at wigs online. She picks out a couple of cheap ones. I tell her to go ahead and get them. If they don't look good, we will get others. Annie says she is going to get the mail. I finish working and offer to go with her. The mailroom is in the other Target House – a short walk away. She says she needs to be alone. She doesn't want me to go with her. I'm shunned.

When she gets back, I cook another skillet meal out of a bag. This one takes twelve minutes and is not quite as yummy as the last. But I am proud of myself for cooking a meal. Annie checked out movies when she went to get the mail. We watch *How the Grinch Stole Christmas*. It cheers us up. I go to bed trying to not let cancer be the Grinch that steals my Christmas.

DAY 51 – Friday, December 5, 2014

I wake at 5:30 and give Red Bull her morning call. TGIF! I get ready, give Annie her meds and get to work. I get an e-mail from a secretary. The "State of the Union meeting" for accounting won't take place today. Sorry for the inconvenience. Inconvenience? That's answered prayer. Though it is rescheduled for two weeks away (another day when I won't be in the office), I don't even care. A reprieve from this meeting means my Friday is off to a good start.

Annie has to be at the hospital at 10:30. We are late. Of course we are. We check in, they take her blood for testing and we are in the A Clinic waiting for results by 11:00. Lots of groups are touring the hospital today. Annie is in a funk. The waiting room is packed. Not a good sign. I pull out my laptop and start to work. It is frustrating not having my second monitor or my ten-key. I get frustrated at the slow pace I am working. I get frustrated from waiting. I get irritated with Captain Awesome. I go to the cafeteria and get Annie some pop tarts and Gatorade (her requests). I come back and work in the waiting room with screaming children and weary parents.

After two hours, Annie goes to make sure we are still on the list. They assure her we are. We have never waited this long before. Finally, at 1:45 my phone rings. It's a nurse in A Clinic. She says they have been looking for us. I tell her we have been sitting here for hours – even went to check on things. She says the nurse couldn't find us. I'm thinking she was always the loser at hide and seek.

Annie's counts were low, but not low enough to need transfusions. The nurse says it is too bad they couldn't find us because we could have left hours ago. I'm thinking she really shouldn't have said that.

We get back to the store house and I get back to work. Annie makes us Chili's chicken nuggets and Arby's curly fries. Since she can't go to restaurants, she loves that we can buy them at Kroger. She says she is serving us linner (instead of brunch). I work until 6:00, when she starts playing Christmas music and asks me to walk with her to get the mail. Things are looking up. We get a text from the hubs that his flight from DFW is delayed. No surprise. He won't arrive in Memphis until 10:30. I'm not too keen on driving at night to the airport, but Annie and I are both excited to have his company. I cook a DiGiorno pizza while we wait.

We drive to the airport hoping not to have to stop at too many red lights. Memphis at night is scary. I reassure Annie that I'm always packing. It gives riding shotgun a whole new meaning to her.

Annie is excited to see her daddy walking out of the airport. She chatters all the way back to the store house. She tells her daddy that she wants her head shaved – now! He cannot tell her no. I am sadder than she is to see her hair go. He shaves her head and she is actually beautiful. I am trying not to cry. She is smiling and I take her picture. We all go to bed. I fall asleep exhausted.

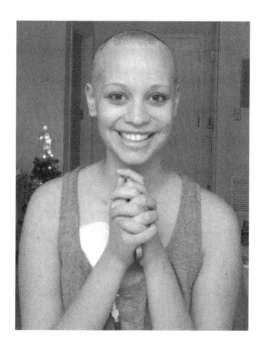

DAY 52 – Saturday, December 6, 2014

I wake up at 7:00. No alarm went off, I just woke up. Time to take Annie's meds out of the fridge. I go back to bed and wake up at 8:00. Right on time again. I get up and give Annie her meds. The hubs gets up, makes coffee and starts cooking bacon. Ah, life is good.

At 9:00, I decide to get ready and go watch the runners in the St. Jude Marathon. They are supposed to be running down the street that goes right in front of the Target Houses. It is very cold outside, and I still only have my jean jacket. The hubs and I walk to the front of Target House #1. (Annie didn't want to get out of bed.) We see the runners. Hundreds and hundreds of people running. There is a DJ playing music and a group of cheerleaders on the street. Very fun. I call Annie and tell her to get ready and join us. She texts back. We forgot to unhook her from the IV before we left. Ugh!! Her daddy quickly goes back to our apartment and takes out the IV meds. Then they join me to watch.

Annie is wearing her mask and waving at the runners. A photographer from St. Jude is there and asks us if he can take her picture down on the street with some runners. He tells us every runner wearing a red vest has donated at least $500 to St. Jude. It is very humbling. We go out into the street and someone hands Annie a "Thank You for supporting St. Jude" sign. She holds the sign along with another girl on the street and they take their picture with runners. He tells us they are looking for marathon pictures to put on the big screen in Times Square. Maybe they will use hers. She is very happy. This makes her daddy and me very happy. After about an hour, I am turning into a popsicle. Annie and her daddy stay another hour and have a lot of fun talking with some runners. The photographer comes back to the store house to have us sign consents, but tells us Annie's picture wasn't selected for Times Square. Too much red tape for a current patient. They want to make sure all goes well for us at St. Jude first. He saves the pictures for their files anyway. She will have to be a star another day. Doesn't matter. It was great fun.

When we get back to the room, her friends who are supporting Annie's Run back home call her on Skype. For the entire run, they Skype with her. She gets to wave from the computer as runners cross the finish line. Our U.S. Congressman, Markwayne Mullin, gets on Skype and wishes her well. She has a great day! Better still, we find out Annie's Run made $4,000 in donations.

This is one of the best days since the nightmare began. We all watch a little TV afterward and go to bed. I go to bed early since my flight leaves at 6:00 a.m. I fall asleep dreading leaving in the morning.

DAY 53 – Sunday, December 7, 2014

I wake up – sort of – when the alarm goes off at 4:00 a.m. Is it morning already? I get up, get dressed, pack up and we are on the road by 4:50. We drive back through the scary streets – not so scary with the hubs. I get to the airport at 5:10. I kiss the hubs goodbye and walk inside. There is a line going out the door. The man behind me is Mr. Talkative. Talks about how he left his debit card on the dresser and other such nonsense. I don't turn around to look at him. I don't want to be nice or make conversation. We stand in line so long without moving that finally they say at the counter all passengers going to Chicago can come to the front of the line. Yes. That's me. I'm going to Tulsa via Chicago. (The consequence of no direct flights from Memphis to Tulsa.) Under two minutes and I'm all checked in.

I find my seat on the Eagle and notice though it is a full flight, no one is next to me. Finally, the passenger we have all been waiting for arrives. He comes down the aisle and heads for my row. So much for sitting alone. He goes to sit down and spills the contents of all his pockets all over the floor. He apologizes to everyone for making us wait. He explains that he had to dig for cash and take everything out of his pockets because he forgot his debit card on the dresser. Huh? I'm next to Mr. Talkative?

I try to avoid conversation. Mr. Talkative falls asleep. I work on another CPE course. When we are close to Chicago, Mr. Talkative wakes up and starts talking. He is actually a nice guy. I find out he has been to Memphis for a funeral. Sad. He finds out I have been to Memphis because of my sick daughter. He says he will look up Annie's Army on Facebook. I have made another new friend.

I get back home. Red Bull brings my adorable grandson out to greet me in the garage. I have really missed them. They are both smiling. I love them so much! I go in the house, have some pizza rolls and try to stay awake, but have to go lie down for a long nap. After my nap, Red Bull and I go to Walmart. She tells me on the way that she knows how her friends feel whose parents are divorced. I ask her to explain. She says, "I'm one week with mom and the next with dad, wondering will I be in Memphis for the weekend or at home." Cancer has lots of baggage. I make a mental note to pay more attention to the one left behind.

The hubs calls and says they have spent the entire day at the hospital. Annie needed blood and no one moves fast on a Sunday. But they are back at the store house now and she is feeling better. She calls me to complain that Justin Timberlake was supposed to come to St. Jude later today and her daddy wouldn't wait with her to see if he showed. I reassure her that I would have waited. I would have liked to judge if he really did bring sexy back.

Red Bull and I get home and unpack the week's worth of groceries and supplies. I get in bed and plug in the electric blanket I brought from the store house. Red Bull says, "I can't believe you took that." I say I thought her daddy bought it for me. She tells me the store house provided it for Annie. I've been misled. I will have to talk to the hubs about his so-called gift of the electric blanket. But since I have stolen it anyway, I plug it in and go to bed feeling very warm.

DAY 54, Monday – December 8, 2014

I wake up at 5:30 and call Red Bull. Trying to keep my stomach settled, I make a point not to think about work. I get to work and actually make it until after 1:00 before rapid fire e-mails begin demanding all my attention. Some kind of record.

The twenty-year-olds' mini-van we have given them is in the shop, and my son has a new job that he can't miss. Red Bull is riding to school with a teacher. The teacher lives on my way to work, and like so many other people who have helped us get through this crazy time, her teacher volunteered to chauffeur Red Bull to and from school. Red Bull doesn't like having to ask for favors, and it means she has to get to school early and stay late, but it's the best I can do. Arriving early and staying late is her contribution to curing cancer.

Annie had school today. Just like when I took her the last time, the hubs cannot find a parking spot. He waits for her in the parking lot and picks her up in front of the Chili's Care Center. He is already sounding bored. I pray he will make it through the week without going stir-crazy.

I work until 6:30. On my way home, I find out that one of my friends had pizza delivered. Awesome! Some of my other friends want to redecorate Annie and Red Bull's bedrooms. Their contribution. I find out they want to come over the next night to measure and look at their rooms. Their rooms are a pit. We all pitch in and spend the evening cleaning the bedrooms. We load up four lawn and leaf bags full of clothes for goodwill. I feel better to have accomplished something today, but I go to bed exhausted.

DAY 55 – Tuesday, December 9, 2014

I wake up at 5:30 and call Red Bull. I ask her if she has a ride to school. She tells me she has taken care of it. But after school her teacher has a teacher's meeting. Can I pick her up at a friend's house when I get off work? I cannot tell her no. I tell her I will leave work on time today for a change.

Captain Awesome is at a seminar today (one I didn't dare to ask to go to) getting his CPE. I try to spend the day answering all the requests of my department and helping solve the normal issues of the day. I am peppered with e-mails all day as well. It's a struggle juggling the requests without Captain Awesome. I manage to get through the day without getting sick. A huge accomplishment.

The hubs and Annie have a day off from going for appointments at the hospital. She sleeps all day. The hubs is stir-crazy again. There is an Elf Workshop at the store house today. Her daddy tells her they should go. She says she doesn't feel good and cries to try to convince him to let her stay in the room. He tells her she has ten minutes to get ready. They are going. They get to the dining room and Annie decorates cookies. Since she is on the low-bacteria diet, she will not even be able to eat the cookies when she is done. The hubs tells her to keep decorating. (After all, he can eat them). Annie also gets a free red apron. Bonus! The hubs sends pictures of Annie in her red apron and elf hat decorating the cookies. He says that she actually had a good time. The pictures aren't convincing, but she is the cutest little frowning elf I have ever seen.

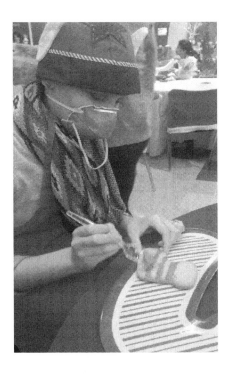

I leave work at 5:30 and drive for an hour to pick up Red Bull at her friend's house. I had no idea how far away this friend lived. After picking her up, I get a call from one of the friends who wants to re-decorate the girl's rooms. She pulls up behind me in the driveway as I get home. Having worked through lunch, I am starved. She has brought a bottle of wine. I decide to drink my dinner.

She comes inside and measures, talks and visits. I play with my adorable grandson. She stays until 9:30. I enjoy her company – and the wine – but am exhausted. Another friend wants to come by. No, I text back. I am going to bed.

Before bed, Red Bull and I have a late leftover pizza snack. The hubs calls. He was worried. I forgot to give him my nightly call. I try to explain about everything that was going on today. He doesn't sound appeased. I finish my pizza and go to bed exhausted.

DAY 56 – Wednesday, December 10, 2014

I wake up and call Red Bull at 5:30. I get up and try not to get sick about going in to work. I take my medicine for indigestion. I pick up the house as today is the day my cleaning lady comes. The one I have not paid in weeks. I wonder how long she will keep this up. She is a sweetheart for not charging me. I think she is much nicer than I am.

As I am backing out of the garage, the twenty-year-old calls to tell me to be careful driving down our county road. The county sheriff is catching speeders on their way to work. I ask how he knows this. I don't really want to know. He says he is one of the speeders the sheriff ticketed. Dang! I tell him to please let his daddy help take care of it so it won't show up on his driving record and increase our insurance.

I make it to work by 8:00. I start my normal day of putting out fires. I get a text from Red Bull. "It's trash day. Did you take the trash out?" No I did not. Not looking forward to the heap that will accumulate over the next week, I call my twenty-year-old daughter in-law and ask her to take the trash out. The last time we forgot, we had a mini-landfill by Week 2. The twenty-year-old tells me she has already taken out the trash. The day is looking up.

Annie has an early appointment at A Clinic. Her daddy texts that her platelet count has a slight improvement today (from 24 to 27) and her hemoglobin is high enough for no transfusions. It is a good day. They decide to go see The Nutcracker which is showing at the St. Jude ASLAC pavilion. I text the hubs that I am jealous. He texts later that Annie got sick before the show even started and they had to leave. Maybe next year. She did get a free T-shirt, though.

The eighteen-year-old texts. He needs money (of course he does) to pay a ticket. What is it about tickets today? He was driving the girlfriend's dad's pickup and the tags were expired. He took the verification that he paid the tags to the courthouse, but he owes $110 for the courthouse fees. Our county has a new courthouse. Apparently, I will help pay for it.

I get my nails done over my lunch break. No matter how bad things get, this is a luxury I don't want to give up. Tom, the alias of the Vietnamese man who does my nails, asks if I am ready for Christmas. Christmas? Is that coming soon? I haven't bought a single present and haven't written my annual Christmas letter. I have a reputation with the Christmas letter. Next week just got busier.

I make it home by 6:30 and pick up Red Bull to take her to Walmart. She is going to two birthday parties over the weekend and needs gifts. The twenty-year-olds need diapers for the baby too. Of course they do. I make a wrong turn on the way to Walmart. We have lived here eleven years and I suddenly make a wrong turn. Is that a new stop light? No. Red Bull tells me I am losing it. I agree. We get the few items we need, wait in one of the few open lanes for what seems like an eternity, and go home to put a fresh diaper on my adorable grandson. I eat some chicken my daughter-in-law has made, play with my adorable grandson for a while, and go to bed exhausted.

DAY 57 – Thursday, December 11, 2014

I call Red Bull at 5:30 and lay in bed until 6:00. Two more days until I can return to Memphis. Bittersweet. I will miss seeing Red Bull. But I also miss Annie and know the hubs needs a break. He is calling more often. He has prescription medication to help him sleep and also saw a dermatologist this week because his skin broke out in a horrible rash. We are falling apart. But we cannot get sick. We have to be strong for Annie. We can do this.

Annie had a day off today. She and her daddy hung out at the store house together all day. He wants her up early. She is becoming nocturnal. He is frustrated and bored. He needs a break. He calls and says he cooked her pork chops, but she didn't want applesauce. I always serve pork chops and applesauce together. A longstanding joke based on a Brady Bunch episode. But she wanted corn with the pork chops. That's just crazy. I need to get there fast.

I leave work at 5:50. Just enough time to make it home before my friends arrive. One of them texts. Let's meet for coffee instead. Even better. On the way I call Red Bull. She tells me to get home soon because this will be our last night together for a while. I remind her that I will be here one more night. But she wants to go to a slumber party at a friend's tomorrow night. I tell her I will make it quick with my friends so we can have some time together. I am feeling guilty already. On the interstate, all the cars come to a dead stop. We are sitting….and sitting….and sitting. Must be a wreck, but I cannot see anything up ahead. I call my friends and cancel our coffee night together. It will be too late and I cannot miss seeing Red Bull. One week at home is rapidly flying by.

I get home, watch *Days* with Red Bull and play with my adorable grandson until bedtime. I go to bed already dreading the next week when we will be apart.

DAY 58 – Friday, December 12, 2014

I wake up and call Red Bull at 5:30. The last time I will see her for a week. She is packing for her slumber party tonight. I am glad she is able to have some normal. I get ready for work and give her goodbye hugs. Each day seems harder just to keep it together.

I get to work when someone comes to my office and talks solidly for over 38 minutes. I speak 25 words in this time. Keeping these insignificant stats is my new hobby. It helps pass the unproductive time. At 10:00, another meeting, quickly followed by another meeting at 10:30. The scheduler shows up 15 minutes late, and I think I will lose my mind. This meeting lasts over an hour and could have been a five-minute phone call. I have never spent time more inefficiently.

Annie has blood tests at A Clinic. The hubs texts and says her counts were very low. She needs two pints. By the time the blood comes and she receives two pints, they have spent the day at the hospital. Tired and weary, they come back to the store house and he makes chicken fingers and fries. Finally, he is not making me look bad with all his yummy home-cooked meals. They eat and go to bed exhausted.

I leave work at 6:00 and head to my nurse friend's house for dinner. She has made pork roast, mashed potatoes, green beans and dinner rolls. Yum!

She opens a bottle of wine. Love her! We visit until 9:00 when I know I have to leave because my flight leaves Tulsa at 6:00 a.m. in the morning. Ugh! I go home and go to bed hoping I will not be sick from having to get up in the middle of the night to leave.

DAY 59 – Saturday, December 13, 2014

My alarm goes off at 4:00 a.m. I plan on getting ready in thirty minutes. I get up, finish my last minute packing, rush around getting dressed and am backing out of the garage at 4:43. I can make it. I drive like a bat out of hell and arrive at the airport at 5:03. I can make it. I park and struggle to get my new humongous suitcase (compliments of the hubs) out of the trunk. I take a few pictures for the hubs of where I parked the car. I walk into the airport, but I am a long walk from the American counter. I finally make it to the ticketing counter and see the line. It's 5:21. I get in the non-moving line. I'm not going to make it.

I am nearly in tears when the lady at the counter says they start giving away stand-by thirty minutes before check-in. It's 5:40. My flight is missed. She puts me on the next one in an hour. Not bad, except now the delay in DFW is 3 ½ hours instead of 45 minutes. I won't be in Memphis until 1:00 in the afternoon. I have no one to blame but myself. I make a mental note to start being on time. I think this one may require more effort than just a mental note.

I get through security in record time (of course I do now that my flight is missed). I walk slowly to the gate. It's 5:50 and my original flight hasn't even left yet. I look longingly outside as it backs away from the gate.

Oh well. I will make good use of the time. I pull out another self-study CPE course and dive in.

We begin to board forty minutes later and I continue to work on CPE through the short flight to DFW. At DFW, I find my gate for my next flight is at the farthest terminal. But I have three hours. Who cares? I feel like a little train ride. I go upstairs and catch the tram. I still don't fly enough for this to get boring. I like being at a big airport with all the hustle and bustle. I like people-watching. I get off at Terminal A making a mental note to watch for a gate change. The hubs ended up going back and forth all over the airport on his last flight when they changed his gate. He wasn't so fond of the hustle and bustle when he was the one doing it. Off the tram at Terminal A, I see a Dunkin Donuts. Yum! Three donuts and a large coffee later, I am looking for a place to sit. A martini bar has no one in it. I ask the gal at the counter if I can sit at a table to eat my donuts. She says sure.

I sit in the bar, eat my donuts and people-watch. People see me in the bar as they go by. They start to come in and order drinks. I think I am good for business. I talk to the bartender. She looks really young. She tells me she loves her job and once bartended at the Super Bowl. She says she is very good at what she does. I'm convinced. I ask what sort of drink is good to follow-up donuts for breakfast. She makes something with Violet liqueur and violet sugar around the top of the glass. Yum! She brings the bill. That small yummy drink was $15. Yikes! I make a mental note not to order drinks at an airport bar. I work on some CPE and go to find my gate.

It's a bumpy flight to Memphis but we make it on time. I have finished two CPE courses on the trip. I am smarter. Time well spent. Just as I get to baggage claim, the hubs is walking in. A sight for sore eyes. I run up to him, drop my bag and squeeze him hard enough to smother a smaller man. But he is a big man. He lifts me a little and we kiss. It's too bad we look like old and weary travelers. That would have made a great movie scene. He wrestles my humongous bag from the carousel and we walk to the car. Before we drive off, I see a little brown bag next to my seat. He has brought whipped cream vodka. I say it's too bad we don't have any shot glasses. He pulls me out a plastic one. I love this man! Two shots later, I am ready to ride to the store house.

Annie is on her phone when we arrive (of course she is). I give her a big hug and go to unpack. I am really tired, but don't want to miss anything by taking a nap. I unpack all my stuff and give Annie everything people have sent from home. Every time someone arrives, it is like Christmas for her all over again. She will be so spoiled when this is over. For now, I don't care. My two sister-in-laws and their girls come by to visit Annie. They are on their way to the Gulf to go on a Christmas cruise. They are a loud bunch and have us all laughing. Too soon, it is time for them to go. Hugs all around and I try to hold together and not cry.

The Optimist Club is serving pizza in the dining room and giving gifts to the kids. The hubs and I go down for pizza. Annie doesn't want to come. When we see all the gifts they are giving away, including some really cute knitted hats and scarves, we call Annie and tell her to come down. She comes down all masked up and not looking happy. I take her around to the tables to collect her gifts. She doesn't want to stay and eat with us. We let her go back to the room. I look around the dining room. You can definitely tell the Optimists from the rest of us. They are cheerful and smiling. We are weary and trying to show grateful-ness. It is truly better to give than to receive.

Back in the room, we all watch *Home Alone* together. One of our must-see Christmas movies. Annie got a new nerf gun as one of her presents. She keeps shooting her daddy. He is not amused. He actually tells her to stop in his mean daddy voice. It doesn't work, but I am impressed he still has the voice.

At 7:00, I cannot hold my eyes open and go to bed. I doze and keep waking up at every noise in the store house. I also have a hard time sleeping since the outside is lit up like daylight coming in through the window. At 8:30, I remember I left an update running on a computer at work and wonder if I should have let our IT guy know. I text him. He tells me I should probably check on it tomorrow to make sure everything is okay before Monday morning. Now I am awake. The hubs comes to bed. He is all warm and snuggly. I go to sleep pretending we are back at home and life is normal.

DAY 60 – Sunday, December 14, 2014

I wake up early and the hubs suggests we go out to breakfast after Annie gets her 8:00 a.m. meds. I agree and get ready. We find a little restaurant called the Blue Plate Grill. Biscuits and gravy, eggs and bacon, and three pancakes later, I am stuffed. We gas up the car and go through the touchless car wash. It should be called a touchless car rinse. The grime is still there, but the dust is knocked off at least.

Since Plan B is on my mind more and more, I decide I need to get everything personal off my work computer. We go to Best Buy. A salesman greets us to help us. We tell him we need a laptop. He starts to "help" and I think "oh brother." But it turns out he is the General Manager of the store. He is very helpful (of course he is). We end up buying a new laptop and several other things we "need" to go with it. We go back to the store house and we play some Tim McGraw music (much to Annie's dismay) while the hubs sets up our new computer. Too soon, it is time for him to pack his bags and return to the airport.

I take him to the airport and this time it is not one of those good "hello" hugs. It is the "goodbye" hug. Much different. I am so tired of this! We are only halfway finished. It seems like the last two months have been a lifetime. I am not sure I remember normal. I watch the hubs walk in the airport and cry.

Back at the store house, I remember to check on my computer at work. My IT guy from works helps me. Good thing we checked. There is an error message. I get the update off and running again and keep tabs on it until it finishes. All should be good for the computers at work tomorrow. I see I have several e-mails, but I have resolved not to answer them until normal business hours.

I remember today is my younger sister's birthday. I am not good with acknowledging birthdays, but send her a text so she will know I am thinking of her. I am going to miss my adorable grandson's birthday. They are having the party next weekend. The hubs is staying to celebrate with them. I miss home. I make Annie a microwavable meal for dinner and I make popcorn for myself. I write while she keeps up with those darn Kardashians. A couple of them are having a hard time in the Hamptons now. Apparently, it is really hard to be super-rich. I go to bed wishing I didn't have to work for a living.

DAY 61 – Monday, December 15, 2014

I wake up at 1:30 to Annie crying. She doesn't feel good and can't sleep. I tell her to take a warm bath and try to relax. I go back to bed and pray I will be able to fall back asleep. Prayer answered. The alarm goes off too soon at 5:30. I call Red Bull. She says she has been up for a while. It is a hair washing day, plus her daddy has a teacher's meeting at 7:15. They have to leave very early. I can tell her mood is better since she is getting to ride with her daddy to school. The alarm goes off again at 7:00 and I get up to take Annie's meds from the refrigerator and get ready for work.

I work until it is time to take Annie for her noon appointments. Blood tests first. Then she has a day of school. A day for her only means about one hour in the classroom. I work from a desk at her school while she works, then we are off to see the doctor. The nurse meets us right away and tells us Annie's counts are going back up so they will test her bone marrow again on Wednesday. If the leukemia is still in remission, she will start her third round of chemo on Thursday. If all goes well, she will be outpatient for Christmas. I am excited. Annie looks disappointed.

After we leave, I find out that she is disappointed because the boyfriend is coming this weekend and now she will be inpatient and likely very sick. I remind her this just means she will be going home that much sooner in the spring. Round Four is the end. She doesn't look appeased. She has trouble seeing past this weekend. She is sick of cancer interfering with her plans. That makes two of us.

We come back to the room and Annie says she wants to take a nap. She is in a funk. She comes in later to show me the "funniest YouTube video" of a dog going to get ice cream from an ice cream truck. Funk ended. Thanks YouTube! Annie says she wants ice cream. I tell her to make a list and we will go to Kroger. I work until after 6:00 when Annie reminds me I promised to take her to get ice cream. Annie masks up and we go back to the nice Kroger we found where the police are out in full force. We buy all of our favorite quick and easy meals, snacks, and of course, ice cream. Back at the store house, it is taquitos, chips and monterey jack queso for dinner. We fill up, but leave room for ice cream – which Annie informs me is actually gelato. It's delicious and it's Italian. I enjoy being an ice cream snob.

We search for something on TV and find one of the *Home Alone* movies. I remember when my twenty-year-old was little and he looked a bit like Macaulay Culkin. I look up Macaulay online. Yikes! I am hoping that's where the similarities ended.

Captain Awesome texts that we are getting rapid-fire e-mails. But I have resolved I will no longer answer non-emergency e-mails after hours. I clean up the kitchen and go to bed hoping I can sleep all night.

DAY 62 – Tuesday, December 16, 2014

I wake up at 5:00, before the alarm goes off to call Red Bull. I stay there thinking about things until it's time to call Red Bull. She sounds very tired. I talk to her until I am sure she won't fall back asleep. I get up and start writing. Writing it down always makes me feel better.

Annie is up by 7:00. She can't sleep either. We go ahead and run the Heparin through her lines since her IV antibiotics have stopped until after the next round of chemo. She needs a dressing change. I forgot yesterday. The line nurse would be so disappointed in me. Annie asks if we can do the dressing change later. She wants to go back to bed. As long as she will keep her silence from the line nurse, I will wait until noon. We have an agreement. She goes back to bed. I start getting ready for work.

At 8:00, I give Annie her meds and go to work. Knowing how busy the next two days should be with Annie, I ask for a couple days off. In our morning staff meeting, it is approved. I am looking forward to it already. As penance, I am tied up all through the lunch hour and until the evening. I am on the phone with work for over two hours. Annie wants me to go downstairs with her for the Santa shopping that is going on in the dining room, but I cannot break away from my work phone calls. She goes by herself and comes back with gifts. She tells me they let them select three people to "buy" gifts for. Then they gave them tickets to "buy" the gifts. A very nice thing for the kids here. She shows me the gifts she bought for her dad and two brothers. Huh? That's the three people she chose? I ask, "What about me?" But I think she has already gotten me something. She says, "Mom, you're easy. You're always cold." Not sure what that means, but hoping it's a trip to Hawaii. Finally, I e-mail off some schedules and announce I will not be available after 8:00 p.m.

Annie and I watch Tim Hawkins videos and I go to bed looking forward to a day off.

DAY 63 – Wednesday, December 17, 2014

The alarm goes off at 5:30 and I call Red Bull to wake her. I am barely awake myself. Annie and I have to be at A Clinic at 7:00, so I need to get up. I am having a hard time moving. Finally at 6:00, I drag myself to the bathroom and start getting ready. A little later, I wake Annie. We leave at 6:55. We are going to be late.

Annie gets her blood tested and we go to wait for the results in A Clinic. We meet a girl and her aunt from Missouri in the waiting room. They are asking Annie questions. She is, of course, Chatty Cathy. They become fast friends and tell us all about their experience too. Her niece had lymphoma. They were previously in Memphis for seven months. They are back for a monthly check-up. It's nice to talk to someone getting a happy ending.

We also meet the nurse who helped us to get here in the first place. Her husband was the doctor we talked to over the phone when we were still in Tulsa. She comes to find us in the waiting room. She gives me a hug when she meets us. I try to thank her, but I break down and start bawling like a baby. She probably thinks I need medication. She would be right. It is not my best moment. I think I appear to just be sad and weary. I hope she knows how truly grateful I am. I want to encourage everyone to come to St. Jude. Even healthy people. It is full of more kind souls than I have ever seen in one place.

Back at A Clinic, we are told Annie's blood counts did not come up as expected. They do not want to start chemo until at least Friday. Annie is now disappointed. She goes for her procedures. Another bone marrow test and lumbar puncture with a chemo injection. As she is waiting for the anesthesiologist, the doctor comes in and asks if she wants to wait until Monday for the next round. A few days ago that is exactly what she wanted. Now that she has gotten used to the idea of being inpatient when the boyfriend is here and outpatient for Christmas, this news from the doctor has her all shaken up again. They are teasing her in the procedures room about her boyfriend and I can tell she is close to tears. Little changes in schedules are a big deal to her. Her emotions are very fragile. She is wound up tight. I feel her pain. I tell the doctor she really wants to be outpatient for Christmas. She really wants to get going with Round Three and get home that much sooner in the spring. He understands and says they will test again Friday. If the counts are up well enough, they will admit her and begin the chemo Friday. I put that out on the Annie's Army facebook page and ask for prayers.

After the procedures, she is loopy. We walk to the car and unbeknownst to me, she begins texting friends. Later, I find out that she texts some pretty confusing things. I make a mental note to take away the phone after the next procedure. She asks me to go get the mail, but is asleep when I return. I go to the pharmacy and pick up the medicine that she has to take tomorrow to neutralize the chemo. Thinking I might forget a medication is probably the worst part of the whole process. The burden of constantly thinking, "Am I forgetting something?" is sometimes overwhelming. And then when I actually do forget something, I feel like a complete failure. What kind of mom would forget to give their child their medicine, or forget that it is dressing change day, or forget to change the claves, or forget to flush the Hickman line? I am not very good at this new job. I think again about letting the old job go.

The doctor calls in the evening. Test results in. Great news! No leukemia found in blood or spinal fluid. Annie is still in remission. I text the hubs and the rest of the family. I find out later the hubs was very emotional over the news and purposely waited a while to call me to talk about it. We don't realize how tight we are wound.

Annie and I eat an eleven-minute PF Chang skillet meal. Not bad. We have more of our gelato for dessert. Yum! I post test results on Facebook and we watch a little TV. I text the hubs and find out he and Red Bull are having a busy night.

Some friends had called and asked if they could paint Annie's room at home. I find out this is a result of her posting some things she likes on Pinterest. I tell Annie to be careful what she tells anyone she likes or wants. We are in unchartered territory. Everyone wants to help in some way. They are eager to give her everything. It is nice, but it is overwhelming and makes me feel guilty. There are lots of less fortunate children. I'm not sure redecorating Annie's room should be a priority. The hubs calls and tells me the room painters are there. They are putting the primer on Annie and Red Bull's walls. I am glad they also remembered the child left behind. They are still there when I text and tell him goodnight.

I remember today is the day to change Annie's dressing. I get out all the supplies. I can do this. Annie coaches me through the steps when I get them out of order. Mission accomplished. She actually compliments the finished product. I start to write, but am too tired. Annie and I go to bed exhausted.

DAY 64 – Thursday, December 18, 2014

I wake up at 5:30 and call Red Bull. She sounds tired. I remind her just a couple more days and she is out for two weeks. This perks her up. I miss her. I start checking e-mail from work – mistake. Even though I am supposed to be on vacation, there are questions that need answered for a meeting later in the day. Shocker that. Knowing Annie will be checking into the hospital tomorrow, I start working on the answers and e-mail along with a note that I will be available until noon today, but then I will start my Christmas vacation. It seems to work. Only a few more e-mails for the day. Maybe my luck will hold out.

In the afternoon, we have plans to go look at wigs. We find the shop that has been recommended and Annie tries on several types. She looks good no matter what wig she puts on. She looks good bald. She finally decides on a reddish-blonde wig and a long, wavy brunette wig. She decides to test them out and see if blondes really do have more fun. She wears it out of the store and wants to go to Target to buy some last minute Christmas presents. Last minute for her, since she will be checking into the hospital tomorrow. I have not even started shopping. Christmas Eve is traditionally the day that I get it all done.

We pick up the items and I realize that she forgot to wear her mask. She cannot get sick. I tell her she can't touch anything and to hold her breath as much as possible. This gets an eye roll. Back in the car, she starts saying she is sick. I panic and ask what she needs me to do. She laughs and tells me to lighten up. At least she still has her sense of humor.

We get to the store house and I tell her I need to work for just about thirty minutes. A couple hours later, she tells me dinner is ready. I finish working and we eat taquitos and mozzarella sticks. We try to watch a movie on Netflix, but everything we want to watch does not come in streaming video. We do the same with Amazon Prime. We have fifty channels, two movie services and a DreamWorks room to rent movies, and we can't decide on one thing to watch. Finally, we both agree on the second *Hunger Games* movie. The first *Hunger Games* was so depressing, I am hoping this one will redeem the series. No. It does not. Is there one funny scene in these movies? I make myself finish it and go to bed depressed.

You're a Mean One, Mr. Grinch

DAY 65 – Friday, December 19, 2014

I wake up and call Red Bull. TGIF. I cannot fall back asleep. I have put my autoreply on my e-mail that I am unavailable, but I have a few things to do before actually taking vacation. I get up and finish up a few things at work. A little later, I get out my Bible. I have gotten way behind in my Bible Study class and read the passage for the next lesson. It's a Psalm where David is asking God to have mercy on him and be his help and deliverer. It is the one that says "May all who desire my ruin be turned back in shame and disgrace." Thanks for writing that down, David. I like it. I pray it over and over hoping God hears.

I get ready to take Annie to the hospital and wake Annie earlier than she wanted so we can be on time. We are only five minutes late. I drop her off and get the last parking spot in a far-off lot. I trek back with my laptop and we begin the wait. First, blood tests. Next, an EKG/ECHO of the heart to get a baseline since her next round of chemo can be hard on the heart. After that, back to A Clinic to wait on test results. Lots of people in the hospital today. Lots of screaming kids. The healthy ones get bored waiting with the sick ones. Some days they literally will make Annie sick, but today she doesn't mind. She is in a good mood and actually enjoying watching the little kids.

We finally get admitted to a room. Annie is wound up and Chatty Cathy. I am exhausted. I still don't know how I can be so tired from sitting and waiting all day. She gets in an isolation room. Not because she needs the isolation, but because it is the only room left. It has two sets of double doors to enter and exit. You have to wait while one set closes completely before the other will open. It's a big ordeal just to come and go. Think I'll be doing more sitting.

We arrive just in time for the hot chocolate cart. One of the best things about St. Jude is the hot chocolate and coffee cart that comes around every day. It's like waiting for the ice cream truck as a kid. We get our hot chocolate and settle in. We hear that celebrities sometimes come visit for Christmas. We are on the lookout for celebrities.

Annie wants her bag, so I tell her I am going to move the car closer and will bring the bag. On the way, I talk to people from work. I move the car and sit and talk over the day's problems for a while. It is cold and starting to rain. I get off the phone and walk back to the hospital. I am walking in the hospital's front revolving door when I remember I was supposed to bring Annie's bag to her. Ugh! Back across the parking lot to the car to get the bag. Then back to the room. My hands feel frozen when I get back. I have Raynaud's and my fingers are solid white. Annie enjoys pointing this out to the nurses. She jokingly tells me that I am a freak of nature. Nice.

I sit and visit with Annie until they get her chemo going. She tells me she is fine and I don't have to stay. A hallelujah moment! I am bone tired. I kiss her goodnight and go back to the store house. Being alone should be relaxing. Instead, it just feels lonely. I eat some cheese crackers and find *A Christmas Vacation* is on TV. My Christmas favorite. We have watched it every year with the extended family for years. I text my sisters. My older sister asks how my job is going. I tell her Plan B isn't looking so bad. I remind her that Cousin Eddie was out of work for seven years. She texts back, "Uh have you seen his home?" Yeah, if I didn't like the clown house, I probably really wouldn't like RV living.

The movie goes off. I go to bed lonely.

DAY 66 – Saturday, December 20, 2014

I wake up at 5:30 without an alarm. Ugh! I want to sleep in. I lay there and think about work. I can't sleep. I decide I might as well get up and clean the store house. The boyfriend comes today. He will get Annie's room in the store house since she is inpatient. I spend the morning cleaning and doing the laundry. At 10:00, everything looks great. I pick up a few items from Annie's list of things she wants. I head to St. Jude.

The weekends are so different at the hospital. For one thing, plenty of parking. I go up to Annie's room, through the two sets of double doors and walk in smiling big. I am greeted with a very sick looking girl. The worst I have seen her look in a long time. She already scolds me for being too loud and asks me to bring her the green bag (the barf bag). It's going to be a long week.

I turn out all the lights for her and sit down to write. I get really sleepy. I try to lay down in the recliner but it won't recline all the way. I pull out the chair and look for another lever or button. I jerk and wrestle around until Annie looks at me and says, "Mom, please?" Okay, how about the too-small couch. I curl up on the blue vinyl and think I'll never be able to rest. The sound of my own snoring wakes me. It's an hour later and I'm freezing. A nurse comes in and offers me a pillow and warm blanket. Ah! My new BFF. Annie hasn't moved. I go back to sleep until the boyfriend arrives at 3:00.

The boyfriend and Annie start watching TV. She is feeling better, so I use it as an opportunity to go run errands. I have typed my annual Christmas letter, but forgot to buy Christmas stationery when we were at Target. I go to Target, get the stationery and call to see if Annie wants anything. Roarin' Water Capri Suns and Smuckers crustless peanut butter sandwiches are her requests. Done! I go back to the store house, print off my letters and print my labels. I am ready to stuff Christmas cards. I forgot the return address labels at home. I text the hubs to bring them. He and Red Bull can help me tomorrow when they get here. Most people would let it go and not send the letter, but I have a Christmas letter reputation to uphold.

I think I will do a little reading before going back to the hospital and remember I left my Kindle charging at the hospital. I end up playing Solitaire on the computer and get addicted. At 9:00, I pack up the snacks and go back to the hospital. Annie and the boyfriend are watching the first *Harry Potter*. I feel old looking at how young Harry is in this first movie. The nurse starts Annie's nightly chemo, the movie goes off and we begin watching the last episode of *Harry Potter*. I can't hold my eyes open and wake up when Harry is old and sending his own kids off to school. How the time has flown.

After the movie and after the chemo finishes, the boyfriend and I head back to the store house. I am too wound up to go to sleep, so I make myself a yummy drink, grab a Twinkie and play Solitaire until I can't hold my eyes open. I wake up in the middle of the night freezing, so I get the electric blanket out and put it on the bed. I put it up when I knew the hubs was coming, but I got the days mixed up and put it up a night too soon. I get too cold without the hubs, my human electric blanket, next to me. He will be here tomorrow. I go back to sleep.

DAY 67 – Sunday, December 21, 2014

I wake up at a few minutes after 8:00. The latest I have slept in weeks. I get up and dressed. The boyfriend and I eat some instant oatmeal and head to the hospital.

As we are walking in to St. Jude, we hear honking. We keep talking and head into the revolving door. The honking continues. I look up and it is my two sister-in-laws and their girls. They are on their way back from vacation and have stopped by to see Annie once more. They go up to the room with us. Annie is still not feeling well, but she sits up and visits for hours. They are loud and lots of fun. They have lots of funny stories of the vacation and they have brought us all presents. It makes Annie perk up for a while and brings her out of her funk. Too soon it is time for them to go.

After they leave, we watch *Alice in Wonderland* and eat junk food. The hot chocolate cart comes by. I receive my daily portion. Yum! I lay down on the little blue vinyl couch again and next thing I know I am waking up to the sound of the boyfriend's voice talking about the movie, but I am dreaming he is telling me it is time to get up and go to the hospital. I think it is morning and I am all confused. I realize where I am and see the credits rolling up on the movie. I text the hubs and find out he is twenty minutes away. I tell him I will meet him at the store house and I leave the boyfriend to have some time alone with Annie. I feel sorry for the boyfriend. He acts like he really cares for Annie, but if he doesn't, he is stuck. What kind of a boyfriend would break up with his girlfriend when she has leukemia?

I get back to the store house just as the hubs and Red Bull arrive. Hugs, hugs, hugs! It's so good to see them. We visit a while and he wants to go to the hospital to see Annie. I opt to stay behind. Red Bull goes with him. She wanted to spend the night, but Annie didn't want her to stay. Annie gets really crabby when she is on chemo. The boyfriend is the only one she likes. The rest of us decide you get a pass when you are on chemo and fighting for your life. Red Bull comes back disappointed. We all go to bed exhausted.

DAY 68 – Monday, December 22, 2014

I wake up when my alarm goes off at 5:30. The alarm I forgot to turn off since Red Bull is here with me on Christmas break. I go back to sleep until 7:45. I am on vacation at work this week. I keep thinking it is the weekend, so it is easy for me to keep from working. I go into the other room and begin assembling Christmas cards, letters, mailing labels and stamps. The Christmas cards came in a care package compliments of my sister's mother-in-law's church, which I lovingly refer to as The Pentecostals. How people I don't even know care enough to think up such great random gifts still amazes me. The hubs gets up and gets in the assembly line. We spend a couple of hours getting them ready to mail.

The boyfriend gets up and the hubs takes him to the hospital. Red Bull and I stay behind and relax. I play Solitaire and she does some target practice using Annie's nerf gun with Chapstick tubes lined up across the store house as targets. She is a very good shot and is enjoying killing the Chapstick. A bit unnerving. The hubs comes back to take Red Bull and me to the hospital to stay with Annie while he drives the boyfriend to the airport. Annie is sad to see the boyfriend leaving. I am sad when Annie is sad. We are all getting a little crabby. After the hubs gets back, he and Red bull go to the cafeteria and bring me back a Bacon Cheddar Burger. Ah, bacon! Love that man! But he and Red Bull are restless and irritating Annie. They decide to go back to the store house. I spend the afternoon with Annie while she sleeps.

I take a few e-mails and calls from work. I write in my journal. It is a boring day. Boring is good. The doctor comes in and talks to Annie about moving up the chemo by a few hours. If they do that a couple of times, she could be discharged tomorrow evening instead of Wednesday, assuming she doesn't get too sick or run a fever. We are going to give it a try. Outpatient is easier since we aren't running back and forth to the hospital, but it is harder to keep up with everything. When and what did she last eat? Is she going to the bathroom regularly? Is she running a fever? Is she in pain? Is it time for her medicine? Is time to change the dressing, or the claves? Have both lines been flushed today? Does she need refills on any medication? Are the dressing/cleaning supplies stocked? Does she need her mask? Mentally, inpatient is easier.

I stay at the hospital with Annie until her chemo finishes at 10:00. I call the hubs. He and Red Bull have been playing pool in the Brad Paisley room. He finally got a nice pool table in his house. Sort of. At home, he has a pool table in the garage. It is usually piled high with rejected junk from the house. Makes a nice drop-off location. My treadmill in the guest room is currently serving the same purpose. I tell the hubs it is time to come pick me up. Annie is down for the night. No more chemo until 6:00 a.m.

Annie talks to her daddy on the phone and wants him to come spend the night with her. She doesn't want me. I am relieved. He begs her to be able to sleep at the store house. I convince her she will be sleeping anyway and her daddy will be in a much better mood tomorrow when she comes "home" if he gets a good night's sleep. She is persuaded and gives us a night off. A hallelujah moment!

The hubs picks me up in front of the hospital and we go back to the store house. The store house is beautiful at Christmas. We stop on Poplar Avenue to take pictures, but the pictures do not come close to showing how pretty it looks. Remembering Memphis has lots of places to look at Christmas lights, we make plans to look at lights Saturday night when the eighteen-year-old and the twenty-year-olds will be here with my adorable grandson. I see a Facebook message from the twenty-year-olds that my adorable grandson is sick. Annie is looking forward to seeing him. No one can get sick. Doesn't fit in the plans.

Back at the store house, we enjoy some yummy drinks and watch a little TV. We don't last thirty minutes. Neither of us can hold our eyes open. We go to bed exhausted. (My younger sister, who has been reading my journal comments that "exhausted" is not descriptive enough. As I explain to her, whenever I say I am "exhausted," this translates "wanting to curl up in the fetal position and sleep for four months.")

DAY 69 – Tuesday, December 23, 2014

I wake up at 7:45. No alarms went off. Yes! I check e-mail. Why did I do that? It only puts me in a bad mood to see all the e-mails. Nothing urgent. I resolve not to respond. I am on vacation. They are not important. I get up and make the coffee. Coffee always makes everything better.

The hubs gets up and we read our Bible together. Well...I read aloud and give a mini-sermon. He nods and says Amen. We pray together. Then I begin to talk about my job with him. My praise quickly turns sour. Need to quit thinking about work. I go to the hospital to sit with Annie. Red Bull and her daddy leave to do some Christmas shopping. They call from the Apple store asking about iPhone upgrades. This isn't going to be a cheap Christmas.

The nurse says discharge is planned for 6:00 tonight. The hubs plans to come back to help pack up all the stuff we have accumulated in her room over the last week. We have barely used The Kennel this time.

Only for "timeouts" when Annie makes us go away. Annie is crabby, so I tell her daddy to wait until time for discharge to come. No problem with that for him. I play Solitaire and write. I feel bad that Captain Awesome is having to deal with work alone. Next week will be my turn while he is out of the office. I feel even worse about that.

The hubs and Red Bull arrive, and true to form, they drive Annie crazy with their shenanigans. I get a call from work and go to The Kennel to avoid her wrath. Annie's chemo finishes and the nurse comes in to go over all the meds and her schedule. Here we go. I listen to the instructions as if studying for an exam. We can't mess this up. The meds are the same. Nothing new. But figuring out when to start each one after leaving the hospital and then trying to get them all back on the same twelve-hour schedule is challenging.

Annie is discharged but too weak to walk to the Chili's Care Center pick-up lane. We wheel her over, carrying all the stuff we accumulated in the five-day stay. Back at the store house, everyone is tired and irritable. The hubs has cooked beans in the crockpot all day and made cornbread to go with it. Much better than the pizza rolls I had in mind. The hubs and I load up on beans. Probably going to regret that later. Red Bull raids the freezer for the pizza rolls. Annie isn't hungry. We load her up on her medication for the night. The girls end up going to their room. The hubs and I find ourselves watching a movie they picked out. When this dawns on us, I agree to watch a war movie he has rented. I last about thirty minutes before I get up to clean the kitchen. I go to bed exhausted.

DAY 70 – Wednesday, December 24, 2014 –
Christmas Eve

I wake up when the hubs gets up. He tells me it's 7:00. I stay in bed for 45 more minutes. I check e-mail and Facebook. The last picture I posted of Annie on her Annie's Army Facebook page has reached 7,900 people. Unlike many of the other pictures where she is smiling and doing "normal" things, it is a picture of what things are like most of the time. She's sleeping. All bundled up. Pale and bald. Still beautiful.

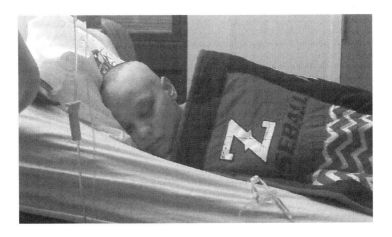

I get up and look at myself in the mirror. Yikes! I don't understand how people look good when they get up. My hair is a lumpy, jumbled mess. (But I also could never pull off the bald look like Annie can.) The overwhelming feeling that I could burst into tears at any time has my sinuses all messed up. I have big bags under my eyes. New wrinkles have emerged on my face, and my hair is turning gray. I look like the one who is sick. It is going to take a lot of time getting ready. The hubs agrees to take Annie to her 9:30

appointment at A Clinic. I start trying to make myself look presentable.

At 8:21 the hubs asks what time Annie gets her medicine. Crap! Supposed to be at 8:00! So much for keeping on schedule. We both set alarms for next time. He gives her the medicine and tells her to get ready to go. Annie moves as slow as molasses. Her daddy is antsy. She has misplaced her journal. He tells her to look for it later; it is time to go! She starts crying. They finally leave for the 9:30 appointment at 9:35.

Now that they are gone, I adjust the thermostat. They are freezing me out. Just like at home, the Thermostat Wars have begun in the store house. I always lose. I am getting dressed in the bathroom and someone knocks. Red Bull goes to the door. A Target House Elf is at the door with a big bag of presents. When we first arrived at St. Jude, Annie filled out a questionnaire about what she likes. They read it. All her favorites are in the bag. Annie and her daddy bring back fried chicken with them. I have heard about Pirtles, but not yet tried any. Yum! Colonel Sanders has nothing on Jack Pirtle. Annie goes through the new gifts and divides up the clothes, purses and cosmetics. We all get something. Nice!

We spend the rest of the afternoon playing board games and watching TV. A lazy day. In the evening, we decide to go check the mail and get more movies from the DreamWorks room – both things are in Target House 1. Annie doesn't feel like going. The other three of us walk over to the other store house and check the mail. Two letters...both in the wrong mailbox. Rats! We are picking out movies in the DreamWorks room when *Over the Hedge* starts playing on the big screen. We decide to stay and watch. Red Bull and I each lay on the giant beanbag pillows. The hubs takes the couch. No one else is in the room. I try not to fall asleep watching the movie. I only doze a little. It was a short movie.

After the movie, we go back to our apartment just in time to give Annie her evening meds. We all watch *The Help* together. I have seen it before, but this time it seems especially sad. When the maid tells of how her son died, we are all crying. I can think of nothing worse than the death of your child. The movie finishes and I go to bed feeling blue.

DAY 71 – Thursday, December 25, 2014 –
Christmas Day

I wake up at 7:00 when the hub's alarm goes off. He gets up and takes Annie's eclipse out of the fridge. I wake up again at 8:00 for the second alarm. Time for the meds. The hubs isn't stirring. Guess it is my turn. I start getting the medicine. Annie comes out of the girl's bedroom all cheery and wishing me a Merry Christmas. I tell her I am surprised she is up. I thought she was nocturnal. She reminds me it's Christmas. We don't sleep late on Christmas. What was I thinking? No one should sleep late on Christmas. She is ready to open gifts. I am enjoying her lightened mood. The Grinch of leukemia will not rob us of having Christmas morning together.

Annie plays Santa and we open gifts. Red Bull and I start playing a new game she got for Christmas. It is called Words with Friends. It has tiles where you take turns building words in crossword fashion. I tell her it's a Scrabble knock-off. She says, "No, mom. It's from a phone app." Maybe I haven't played Scrabble enough to know the difference, but I wonder how much money someone made off this clever "new" game idea. After the game, the girls go back to their bedroom to Facebook, Instagram and Skype their friends all day.

Feeling sure the store house would offer a free meal, I hadn't even thought about Christmas dinner. The hubs makes chili from a mix he got for Christmas. Not exactly our traditional Christmas dinner, but good enough. We lay around listening to Tim McGraw and George Strait. I play Solitaire and I teach Red Bull to play. Every kid should know how to play some card games, right? Annie stays in her room all day. But she is feeling good and laughing with her sister. It's a nice day. I decide (once again) to quit working so much. I go to bed looking forward to tomorrow's visitors.

DAY 72 – Friday, December 26, 2014

The alarm at 7:00 puts us in our normal routine. After I give Annie her 8:00 meds, I go back to bed.

Annie's brothers come today. They will bring the wife and girlfriend and my adorable grandson. Even though they sometimes drive me crazy, I love my boys and feel as if I have barely seen them since coming to Memphis. I can't wait for us all to be together again. I am so grateful they can all come. (Bribery with a weekend at the Embassy Suites helped!)

The hubs and I go to Kroger and get supplies. He makes sure he has cash for the weekend. We keep checking to see when they will arrive. We tell them to be sure and let us know when they are close so we can go with them to check in at the hotel and pay for their room. After not hearing from them for quite a while I call. They have just crossed the Mississippi River Bridge and are in Memphis. What part of "let us know when you are close" did they not understand?

We leave to meet them at the hotel to get them checked in. They call while we are still on the way. "Where are you? We are ready to check in." I take a breath remembering the blood tests confirmed they are really sharing my DNA. I love them. And yes, they are the ones I raised.

We arrive and get them checked in. Then we take my adorable grandson with us back to the store house and play with him until they have all recovered from the trip. Then they come over to join us. They make Annie smile. When she smiles, we all smile. We ask what they want for dinner. The daughter-in-law wants steak. Of course she does. We order online takeout from Outback Steakhouse and eat a late dinner together. Yum! Annie cannot eat takeout so we make her one of her microwavable meals. She doesn't mind. She is in a good mood and feeling good. The eighteen-year-old brought me a jigsaw puzzle for a present. We work on the 1,000 tiny pieces that all look the same until our eyes cross and it's time for them to check out at 10:00. I go to bed looking forward to seeing them again tomorrow.

DAY 73 – Saturday, December 27, 2014

Up at 7:00. Normal routine of meds. We all get up early and get dressed in anticipation of our

155

company coming back to visit. While we are waiting, I work on the jigsaw puzzle. The hubs and Annie are watching car crashes on YouTube. I tell the hubs that reminds me that we need to be sure and get our adorable grandson's car seat in the limousine. As soon as I say the word limousine, I realize I have let the cat out of the bag. We had a surprise planned all week. My friend from Texas sent us some extra Christmas cash. She wanted us to spend it on something fun. As soon as we saw a stretch Hummer painted with zebra stripes driving down the streets of Memphis, we knew we had to rent it for Annie (zebras are her high school mascot). The friend thought it was a great idea. We rented it for tonight and scheduled a Christmas light tour. Knowing I cannot keep a secret, the hubs and Red Bull took bets on how long I could go without spilling the beans. Time for someone to pay up.

Annie looks at me and says "Limousine? What Limo?" I look at the hubs. I am mortified. I begin apologizing. Then he says, "It's ok. I already told her." What? When I had tried so hard to not say anything? He tells me she has known since last night. Apparently, she knew we were planning something for tonight and had been badgering her daddy for more information. Unable to tell her no, he caved. I try to remember if my children have ever really been surprised with a gift.

The eighteen-year-old and the girlfriend come over and we spend the afternoon together working the jigsaw puzzle and watching one of *The Lord of the Rings* movies. It's the one with never-ending battles that is way too long to hold my attention. (Or does that describe them all?) The twenty-year-old and the wife are too busy enjoying themselves at the hotel, sans my adorable grandson. Since the limo will arrive at 6:00, the eighteen-year-olds decide to go back to the hotel in time to get ready. First, everyone is hungry. Of course they are. We order take-out from Huey's. A burger place with delicious burgers. Everyone is fed and ready. We wait for the limo to arrive. Ready for a night on the town.

Right on time, the limo pulls up in front of the store house at 6:00. The driver rolls out the red carpet (literally) when we come out of the building. We haven't seen any celebrities, so we decide to be celebrities ourselves. Fun!

Inside the limo, the floor, ceiling and seat cushions are also zebra striped. A multi-colored flashing light is going. I must find the "off" switch. We have three TVs, a PlayStation and of course an ear-splitting speaker system to connect to our iTunes playlists. We go to the hotel and pick up the hotel-stayers and take off for the Shelby Farms lights. We sing and dance and the hubs breaks open a bottle of cheap champagne. We serve to everyone over eighteen (I wonder if can I go to prison for this?) and I enjoy myself despite all my music selections being rejected.

After Shelby Farms, we travel to see Southern Lights. Someone sees a "Welcome to Mississippi" sign out the window. Mississippi? I was never good at geography. Didn't realize we were so close. (I think going to prison in Mississippi sounds even worse.)

Before driving through Southern Lights, we need a potty break. To impress all our peer-group, the driver stops at a Walmart. Nothing classier than a Zebra-striped hummer limo at a Walmart in Mississippi. I can't go in without spending some money. We use the potty, buy snacks for my adorable grandson and climb back in the limo. The Southern Lights do not disappoint.

After the lights, we travel back to Tennessee. We take our second potty break at the Peabody Hotel. It is swarming with people. I want pictures of the children in front of the giant, beautiful Christmas tree. Annie looks at me and says "Mom, I don't have my mask!" Crap! I tell her not to breathe. We quickly get the picture and get back to the limo. We drive in front of Graceland and get out again to take pictures with the mansion in the background. Our time is up. Four hours passed in a flash. We drop off the hotel-stayers and take the last limo ride back to the store house. Everyone agrees it was a blast. I go to bed smiling.

DAY 74 – Sunday, December 28, 2014

I wake at 7:00 to the hubs alarm. I wake again at 8:00. My turn. I didn't hear the hubs get up and take the meds from the fridge, but there is the eclipse on the table. I give Annie the meds, start the IV and crawl back in bed. Though we were back by 10:00 last night, I feel like we were out all night. We talked about going to Graceland today, and it sounded fun last night. Now I know there is no way that is happening. We hear it has been snowing in Oklahoma. We see the pretty pictures. We hear from the hotel-stayers that they are on their way over to say goodbye. They are anxious to get started on the road-trip home.

They come by and we give hugs all around. They pack up the room full of my adorable grandson's toys. How does one child have so much stuff? Annie asks them to drive through the circle drive in front of the store house as they leave. We wave from our second floor apartment window as they drive away. I miss them already.

I work Sudoku puzzles for a while. Then Red Bull and I work on the jigsaw all afternoon. Complaining about the light, the hubs feels sorry for us and goes to the store to get a brighter light bulb above the table. He is proud of his purchase. The brighter light makes a glare. Red Bull and I try to decide if the glare, making the colors of the pieces harder to see, is worth being able to see the jigsaw shapes better. I try not to spoil the day by thinking about work. We work on the puzzle until time for bed. I go to bed exhausted and dreading the work week ahead.

DAY 75 – Monday, December 29, 2014

I wake to the 7:00 alarm and get up. It's a work day. Since Captain Awesome is on vacation, I cannot take the day off. New rule. It means I will lose some vacation days. But I am told it is a very generous policy anyway and I am not the only one who couldn't take all their vacation. Translation = too bad...move on.

I take meds out of the fridge and see Annie is on the couch. I get ready for work (even though I am actually only going back to my desk in the bedroom). At 8:00, I wake Annie for her medicine. She says she couldn't sleep. Her back and stomach hurts so bad, she has thrown up. Though she has an appointment at noon, I am afraid to put her off. I call and they say to get her in through isolation as soon as we can. At least since it is early there should be better parking. I feel guilty for even thinking about the parking situation.

The hubs takes her. He has the sniffles and wears a mask around Annie. We cannot get sick! At the hospital, they get right in. Blood tests confirm her counts are low. They settle in as blood and platelets are ordered. He mentions the upside was they got a good parking spot. I feel a little better knowing I am not the only one thinking about parking. I settle in to work. I have to work on Plan B. Dealing with this job every day is making me lose my mind. I feel like no one really understands what I am dealing with every day. Every. Single. Day.

I put in a full day at the computer and finally stop when the hubs calls to ask me to get together some of Annie's things. Red Bull and I go to gather her things. Their room is a wreck. Just like home. I start making beds and picking up clothes, jewelry, electronics, fingernail polish, etc. I decide to do the laundry. Our room in the store house is next door to the laundry room for our floor. Closer than my laundry room at home. At home my laundry room is next to the garage – the furthest room from any of the closets. I should design houses. The downside to being so close is hearing the thumping sound of the washers at almost all hours. But it has a nice rhythm that I have grown accustomed to hearing. The store house has three washers and dryers. Easy to get lots of laundry washed at one time. I don't want to hog all three washers, so I do two loads at a time. Saving a washer for another homeless cancer refugee. It's my contribution to the store house.

Annie has had an allergic reaction to the platelets. The hubs says her stomach pain was so bad, they are giving her morphine. They are running more tests and going to admit her into the hospital for observation overnight. This is fine with me. When too much starts happening, I feel safer if she is admitted and the professionals are taking care of her. I am also thankful she was well enough to enjoy the holidays and the time with her brothers and nephew before she started feeling bad again.

The hubs says her non-stop talking has started again. He comes back to the store house to get the things she wants. Though we went grocery shopping and stocked up on food, he stops at McDonald's and brings dollar menu chicken sandwiches and fries. Just like home. We eat the junk and watch a little football. He goes back to the hospital to sit with Annie. Red Bull and I play Text Twist until time to go to bed. I go to bed feeling anxious. The hubs comes home sometime in the night, but I am too tired to ask him any questions.

DAY 76 – Tuesday, December 30, 2014

I wake up at 5:10 thinking the sun is up. It is so brightly lit outside the store house that it never feels like night. I have tried sleeping with sleep masks to cover my eyes. They help with falling asleep, but I end up pulling them off in the middle of the night. The windows have blinds, but not curtains. I need a dark sheet to somehow hang up at night. I fall back asleep thinking about this and wake back up later knowing it is daylight. Annie is in the hospital. The hubs has turned off his morning alarms. I have overslept. It's 7:26. I go to make coffee. We are out! I forgot to put coffee on the grocery list. It's going to be a long morning. I get ready and do my two-step commute. It's 8:15.

I start to work and the hubs gets up. He leaves the store house for a bit and comes back with McDonald's coffee along with a bacon, egg and cheese biscuit and a hashbrown. Love that man! As my work day is already going with calls and e-mails, Red Bull is still sleeping and her daddy takes off for the hospital to check on Annie. I sit at my computer doing very little of the work I enjoy. My job has changed so much I have been unable to be the accounting nerd I want to be. Today I am a diplomat trying to keep the peace. Not what I signed up for.

The hubs calls and says Annie is doing better. They will be releasing her to come "home" soon. The room inspectors come by. They use the excuse that they are making sure everything works. It's incredible that they can get this information by opening the oven door and looking in the bathroom. I don't mind. The store house is so much nicer than the clown house, they can open my underwear drawer if they want. The cleaning lady comes today too. She only cleans the bathroom, but it is still nice to have one less thing to do. When Annie and her daddy arrive, the apartment is clean and ready to be messed up again. She is very tired and sleeps on the couch all afternoon while her daddy watches TV and I work a few more hours.

Everyone has snacked all afternoon, so the hubs cooks a frozen pizza for dinner. Annie is upset to find out the boyfriend cannot come for the weekend. The weather is supposed to be too bad for his dad to fly the plane, and his mom doesn't want to make the drive. The boyfriend's mom is going to help with the project on Saturday to finish painting Annie and Red Bull's bedrooms at home. Annie doesn't care. She wants to see the boyfriend and somehow it has become my fault he is not coming. She goes to her room to sulk.

Red Bull and I play Text Twist. But she gets upset to learn from home that her episodes of *Supernatural* have not been recording. Apparently, the twenty-year-olds have messed up her DVR schedule. Now she is in a funk too. The hubs and I watch TV and try to ignore the teenage girl drama filling the small apartment.

I go to bed trying not to think about all the drama in my life – including work tomorrow.

DAY 77 – Wednesday, December 31, 2014

I wake up at 7:00, take out the meds and go take a shower. My last day of work until the new year – two days away. At least I will get a day off tomorrow. I can do this.

I wake up Annie at 8:00 to give her the meds and remind her she has an appointment at 9:30. I remind her that her daddy doesn't like to be late, so please get up soon. I go to make coffee. There is no coffee. Ugh!! I wake up the hubs and ask him if he will get coffee before he takes Annie to her appointments. He asks if I want him to buy coffee to make a pot or just want a cup of coffee. I tell him a cup is fine if it is a LARGE cup. He heads off to McDonalds and promises to go to Kroger later. In a short while, I have a large cup of coffee and a sausage biscuit to go with it. Nice.

Annie is slow getting ready. At 9:33, they have not yet left for the hospital. Her daddy has his jacket on and is standing by the door telling her to hurry up. Not helpful. He is also lamenting that he will never find a parking spot. She is making an attempt to hurry. She starts crying. She can't find her shoes. There are four small rooms in this apartment including the bathroom. It is amazing we can lose anything. They finally leave for the hospital taking Red Bull with them. I'm ready to start my work day.

It is a slow day at work with fewer e-mails and calls than usual. With three on vacation, I call and talk to two of the three remaining. They are feeling lonesome. I know the feeling. While it is slow, I take a load of laundry to the laundry room next door and pick up a little. I get several texts from Annie that her daddy and Red Bull are driving her crazy. They are kidding around in the waiting room and taking selfies. I text them to please try to control their horseplay while they are waiting. Annie texts that she never wants to come with the two of them again. They send a picture of themselves taking pictures. Oh brother. Apparently, they did not heed my text to stop with the shenanigans. At least they are able to have a good time.

They return with a good report. Annie doesn't need blood or platelets and she is feeling better. They have also been to Kroger and have coffee. But they forgot the sparkling apple cider Red Bull wants for tonight. Back to the store. Just like home, we never get it all in one trip.

Early in the afternoon, I get an e-mail from an accountant that my department has been told they can leave for the day. Was I told? Of course not. I may be called the Controller, but clearly I am no longer in control. At least this means I can quit working too. Only one more work day until I can be back in the office and discuss plans for the future. I can do this.

All evening we watch TV, work the jigsaw puzzles and relax. After our limo celebration, this is good enough for us. The girls drink the sparkling cider and the hubs fixes me a couple of yummy adult drinks. We ring in 2015 as the ball drops in New York and we ring it in again at midnight in Memphis. We are watching the downtown Memphis fireworks on TV at the same time as we are hearing them outside. We can't see them because of the buildings, but they are loud and make our little celebration fun. I can imagine the sound of rapid-fire gunshots that we usually hear back home. We stay up to put a few more pieces in the jigsaw and I go to bed looking forward to a day off.

Happy New Year!

DAY 78 – Thursday, January 1, 2015

I wake up when the alarm goes off at 7:00 and my stomach is cramping bad. Happy New Year! I get up to take out Annie's meds from the fridge and lay on the couch for an hour. Before the alarm goes off at 8:00, I start looking for the medicine in my purse. I take all three of my medicines for digestion, but the cramping doesn't stop. I give Annie her meds and go running to the bathroom doubled over with cramping. To save the gross details, I am having a rough morning. My stomach hurts so bad, it is making me sick. I take an Oxycodone when I think I am going to die. I have one more "episode" and my pajamas are soaked with sweat. I take a shower, put on more jammies and lie down on the couch. Annie tells me later that it sounds I have exactly what she had. Now I understand the morphine they gave her. I sleep on the couch all day. I start feeling a little better, finish reading the book I had started and order two more books on my Kindle. The hubs and Red Bull finish the jigsaw puzzle and we all watch football together the rest of the day. Boring. Boring is good.

For dinner, the hubs makes black-eyed peas. I love them but we rarely eat them. Supposedly, you will have good luck for the year if you eat black-eyed peas on New Year's Day. I ask the hubs if we ate them last year. Neither of us remember. Maybe that's where we went wrong. If black-eyed peas have anything to do with it, this year should be better. I eat plenty.

One more work day, then the weekend. The hubs' sister comes this weekend. She will stay the week with Annie. Her daddy and I are taking a break together and going home. We feel we both need to be on the job for the first week of the year. He wants to get his new classes going and get lesson plans set up. I want to have some serious discussions about my future with the company – but in person, not over the phone. It's the first time neither of us will be with Annie since the nightmare began. I am nervous to leave her, but know that her aunt will probably give her better attention than I do. We give Annie the evening meds, finish watching Alabama beat Ohio State and I go to bed dreading work the next day.

DAY 79 – Friday, January 2, 2015

The alarm goes off at 7:00. I am still exhausted. I lay there so long that the hubs gets up to take Annie's meds from the fridge. He comes back to bed and I stay snuggling for a few more minutes. Last work day this week. I can do this. I get up and start getting ready. At 8:00, I give Annie her meds and make the coffee. Yes, coffee! When the hubs went to the grocery store the last time, I told him not to bother coming back if he didn't have coffee. A little harsh, but desperate times call for desperate measures. He came back with coffee.

I start filling the pot with water, forgetting that I had already filled it days ago before I realized we were out of coffee. Water starts pouring out the back of the coffee pot onto the counter. Ugh! A half-roll of paper towels later, I have a sparkling counter and, finally, a delicious cup of coffee. I'm ready to start my work day.

I put out some morning fires. Only two in the accounting department are in the office today. The e-mails are so slow, I call one of them to make sure things are okay. I don't want to jinx things, but I have not gotten my usual e-mails. One of the two tells me he will check to see who is downstairs (the accounting department is upstairs). I tell him not to check – just enjoy the quiet.

Annie and her daddy come back to the store house. Since St. Jude was packed today, they didn't wait at the hospital for test results. He gets the last cup of coffee. I ask if that is his first one. "Yes, why?" Because that explains my shaking hands. A little later, we get a call from A Clinic that Annie needs platelets. Her daddy fixes some Arby's fries for them for lunch before they head back to St. Jude. They come back several hours later and Annie says she wants to make mini-pies. She makes a list for Kroger, and when I quit working at 5:00, the hubs and I go shopping again.

We return to the store house with all her supplies. She bakes us yummy blueberry and apple mini-pies. I eat so much, I am almost sick. *The Fugitive* is on TV for the 2,000th time and we watch it for about the 20th time – until another football game comes on that the hubs wants to watch. Sharing the TV with the hubs has almost made me a football fan. I even know what teams are playing in the different bowls. I enjoy it slightly more than keeping up with the Kardashians, but still miss watching *Days* with Red Bull.

While the hubs watches football, I read Bill O'Reilly's *Killing Patton* until I can't keep my eyes open. In the last week, I have stopped in the middle of reading Condoleezza Rice's *No Higher Honor*. I like reading about what happened behind the scenes at the White House, but her book is very long and slow reading. Instead, I decide to start reading various books recommended by friends. I finished *Wild* by Cheryl Strayed. She was too wild for me, but I enjoyed reading about her hiking trek. Steve Harvey's *Act Like a Lady, Think Like a Man* was hilarious and on point from my marriage's perspective. Now I am reading about World War II. Makes me wish I had paid more attention in history class. I was the one who would raise her hand in class and ask how knowing about this was going to help me later. I wanted to learn about something that would help me make money in the future – like accounting – not learn about history. But this is interesting stuff. I never knew Stalin was just as cruel as Hitler. It depresses me to realize just how mean and cruel people can be to one another. All to have more power. To try to be God. I go to bed feeling very philosophical.

DAY 80 – Saturday, January 3, 2015

I wake up at 7:00 when the hubs alarm goes off. I am paralyzed with exhaustion. His snooze alarm goes off and he gets up to take the meds out of the fridge. Repeat at 8:00. He gets up to give Annie her meds, and then closes the door to the bedroom to let me sleep. But now, I am awake. I reach over to my Kindle and finish reading *Killing Patton*. Finishing it makes me wish I had the actual book, because I would like to look up all the footnotes at the end. Instead, I come out of the bedroom and read Patton's speech in the appendix to the hubs. I am sure he gets tired of my reading things to him, but he never complains. I have to tone down the language because the girls are within earshot. Patton's speech, while saying a lot of nothing, is a great motivating (and entertaining) speech.

The hubs fixes a breakfast of eggs, sausage, toast and coffee. We are out of bacon, but sausage is the next best thing. There is no part of the pig that isn't yummy. Very glad my religion doesn't require a kosher diet.

Annie gets up and she is in pain. She has had back pain and pain from hemorrhoids for days. We have tried everything. Even though the cancer is in remission, the side effects of the chemo are brutal. Red Bull is getting a migraine. She has started having these recently. She can tell when she is getting one because her vision blurs. I take Annie an oxycodone and give Red Bull an Excedrin. I mix strong drinks for the hubs and myself.

The hub's sister is on her way from Oklahoma. She will stay with Annie for the week. The hubs calls St. Jude to make sure they are aware of our plans, and he orders supplies that may be needed for the week. Both of us are a bit apprehensive to leave her for a week without one of us with her in Memphis. I also feel guilty for looking forward to a "normal" week in Oklahoma.

While the hubs watches football, the rest of us lie down for naps. The store house is a hard place to take a nap because everything can be heard through the walls. But today is either especially quiet or I am especially tired, because I fall instantly asleep and don't wake up until two hours later.

I get up and start doing laundry so we won't have to pack dirty clothes. The hubs teases me because

I can barely open the laundry room door. It is so heavy, when I am wearing my slippers, I slide backwards as I try to push it open. He tells me I need to start working out and muscle-up a bit. When I return to get the girl's clothes, Annie says she would help with the laundry, but she can't even open the laundry room door. Aha! Validation! But the hubs laughs and tells me it doesn't help my case to compare my strength to that of a cancer patient. I don't manage to get out of doing laundry.

Annie's aunt and cousin arrive from Oklahoma. They come over to get the week's instructions for appointments and lessons in giving the meds, hooking up the IV and changing the dressing. We give them maps of the area and the floorplan of the hospital. Fortunately, Annie is old enough to help.

I am so glad they are here. I would be so intimidated with all the things required, but they handle it well. My brother-in-law (the hubs' sister's husband) just passed away last summer. Annie's aunt had been caring for him for a long time. I am surprised she would volunteer to step back in and do it again for a week. But she is a very caregiving person and is eager to help. I make a mental note to be nicer to the hubs' family.

They stay and eat a dinner of frozen pizzas with us. The hubs takes them to a hotel for the night. I go to bed apprehensive about the week ahead.

DAY 81 – Sunday, January 4, 2015

We wake up to the usual 7:00 alarm. Meds out of fridge and back to bed. At 8:00, I am dragging, but get out of bed, give Annie her meds and take a shower.

Annie's aunt is supposed to be here at 9:00 and we want to be ready to go. By 10:00, we are packed up and waiting, but her aunt has not yet arrived. Hating to wait, the hubs asks me to call. About twenty minutes later I call and they have just arrived at the store house. The hubs begins getting the things ready for a dressing change for Annie. He wants to give her aunt one last lesson before we go. I can tell he is as apprehensive as I am about leaving her. I tell him Annie will probably get more attention from the aunt than she would with me.

Finally, we are ready and take off for Oklahoma. The drive is long and boring. Red Bull has her ear buds in place, so no chance of any meaningful conversation there. I read aloud to the hubs for a while. Our usual routine is several chapters of James Herriot's classics. Today it is *All Things Bright and Beautiful*. Each chapter is like its own short story and always good for a laugh. After my voice starts wearing out, I switch and start reading my newest Kindle purchase, *Gone Girl*. I get really sleepy, but feel it is my duty to stay awake since I don't drive. We take a couple of potty breaks, but the hubs (unlike me) is all about the destination, not about the trip. Few stops. Make it quick. Gotta get back.

We find out that our eighteen-year-old has borrowed the hubs' Honda Passport. We call to say we are coming to get it. One detail that the eighteen-year-old failed to mention in our earlier discussion is that the Passport isn't actually running. We arrive at the eighteen-year-old's apartment complex at 5:00 in the evening. It is 28 degrees. The hubs and the eighteen-year-old work on the Passport a while. The hubs thinks maybe it is just the battery. We go to Walmart, get a new battery and return to the apartment complex. It is now dark. The hubs is not happy. They work on the Passport a while longer. It is not just the battery. The Passport is still not running. The hubs gives up and gets back in the car with Red Bull and me (where it is warm and toasty and I have been reading my book). He says he will call a tow truck tomorrow to tow it to our mechanic. The eighteen-year-old will have to borrow the mini-van from the twenty-year-old. I call the twenty-year-old to ask if there is gas in the mini-van. Clearly, my exhaustion has taken over, because this is a ridiculously dumb question. Of course there is no gas in the van. How would it have gas? We have not been home to fill it.

When we get home at 7:00, the hubs gives money to the twenty-year-old son to go fill up the mini-van with gas. The twenty-year-old tells his dad he will do it as soon as he finishes the video game he is playing. He is in the middle of a battle, but he will get it taken care of before morning. The hubs and I eye each other warily and drag our bags upstairs to get unpacked.

The hubs checks on things in his garage. This is the first time I have been home in three weeks and the hubs in two. I walk around the house looking for things that have not lasted through two weeks of the twenty-year-old's caregiving. At least there are no Christmas decorations to put away. It was a very Bah Humbug kind of home over Christmas. No tree, no lights, no decorations. It must have been depressing to have stayed here. One look at the mail that has stacked up feels me with dread. I'll tackle that later. But one look at my adorable grandson and I am hooked for the night. I hold him and hug him. He looks a little under the weather, but he is in a good mood tonight and we play until bedtime.

The hubs and I go to bed together in our own bed, in our own house for the first time in nearly three months. He is a very happy man! Red Bull announces she does not need me to wake her. She can sleep a little later since she is riding with her dad. I go to sleep dreading the work week ahead.

DAY 82 – Monday, January 5, 2015

The alarm goes off at 5:30. I am sick to my stomach not wanting to go into work. I have early meetings and can't be late. I drag myself out of bed and start getting ready. I have decided to go in early and resign. Life is too short. I get a text from Captain Awesome that he will not be in today. Still driving in from Denver after a white-out stranded him there an extra day. My biggest supporter won't be there. Ugh!

I have asked to meet with our President. He has been a friend to me the past three years and understands my situation. We meet and it runs long. He is very understanding, but tells me he cannot accept my resignation. I need to meet with the CEO. The CEO is out until Wednesday. Ugh!

I go back to my office and greet all the people I have not seen in three weeks. Everyone wants to know about Annie and how things are going and it is after 9:00 before I sit at my desk. I haven't even plugged my computer in. When I do, it doesn't cooperate. I can't get to my normal desktop. I do all the high-tech things I know to do with a computer…which means I restart my computer and hope it fixes everything. It does. I should work in IT. It is now nearly 9:30 and about twenty e-mails pop up. As I am sorting through, I notice I have missed a 9:00 meeting. I have also forgotten to mention that Captain Awesome is out today. I shoot a quick e-mail of explanation, knowing my oversights will not be well received. It's a Monday.

I work on putting fires out all day. I should be planning for the upcoming busy season, but it is hard to care. When I am actually doing my job and working with the accounting staff, I love what I do. I try to stay focused on this and get through the day. I get a meeting request for a rescheduling of this morning's meeting. Apparently, I did not dodge that bullet after all. At least Captain Awesome will be back to join us.

The hubs has spoken to his sister. After today's blood tests, Annie needed two pints of blood. They spent the day at the hospital, and afterward Annie still felt like shopping at Target. Of course she did. Her aunt is there to buy her things. A new victim who cannot tell Annie no. Her aunt also cooked them a yummy spaghetti dinner and they watched movies together. Annie is enjoying the time with them. Relief!

I leave work and arrive home at 6:00 to a strange car in the driveway. As I am pulling into the garage, I notice a good friend of mine playing pool with the hubs. She has also brought pizza for dinner. Nice. Another family from church brought over a yummy soup which will keep until tomorrow night. Not having to think about dinner for two nights straight? Priceless. I think my friend must just be humoring the hubs to play him a game of pool. But, she says she enjoys it and was really good in her college days. How did I not know this about my friend? Game on. I have not seen too many people beat the hubs, but she does. I try to console him by telling him I must have distracted him. He agrees. He hates to lose. I can see a re-match in their future.

We eat dinner. My friend has brought Christmas gifts. I apologize for having nothing. Not that I didn't think of her, but that I didn't buy a single gift. She understands my Grinchy mood. As we talk, I watch her completely clean my kitchen. She is washing my adorable grandson's highchair and scrubbing down my cooktop. Another day I might have been offended or insisted I will get it later. Instead, I just sit there and talk while she works like an indentured servant. We catch up until 9:00 when the kitchen is sparkling and I start yawning. Afraid of overstaying her welcome, she gives me hugs and takes off for home. Love that girl! I go to bed feeling anxious about the week ahead.

DAY 83 – Tuesday, January 6, 2015

I get a text from Red Bull at 3:30 asking me to come in the bathroom. She is lying on the floor sick. She has been throwing up. Not good. I give her some Benadryl and wait until she feels good enough to go back to bed. I wake up again at 5:30. I feel like I took the Benadryl. I am dreading the day. I get ready for work slowly, run by the cleaners on the way and make it into the office by 8:20. I can do this.

The morning meeting has the same long agenda I see each week. Oh boy. It drags on for an hour. Finally, some relief and I head back to my office. I get a text from Red Bull. She has stayed home and says she feels like eating, but there is nothing to eat. Also, the twenty-year-old is getting ready to leave and Red Bull does not want to be by herself. I call and talk her into going back to sleep and convince her that before she knows it her daddy will be home from school. Not a good time for me to be missing work. I feel like a failure as a parent.

I work all day trying to get caught up on things I had put off while I was in Memphis and on wrapping things up so they won't be left hanging since I don't plan on staying after next Friday. Not feeling hungry, I eat a lunch of macaroni and cheese and mashed potatoes. Later, I start feeling sick to my stomach. I figure the stress and nerves are taking their toll. I take a Zofran and keep working. I get a call from the hubs when he gets home from school. Red Bull is running a fever. I tell him I will leave right on time and we will all get some much needed rest tonight.

The hubs gets the day's report from his sister. Annie is doing okay and has a day off. No tests or getting blood today. They stock up on groceries at Kroger and her aunt cooks a yummy beef stroganoff for dinner. She is making me look bad. And setting the bar too high. Annie will never be happy with the formerly delicious and satisfying microwavable meals I routinely serve. Clearly, I left out an important part of the instructions for my sister-in-law. No cooking anything that takes longer than ten minutes in the kitchen.

I am driving home from work and notice my gas tank is nearly empty. Since I despise having to pump my own gas, I call the hubs. I ask if he will come with me to put gas in my car. He knows it is a rhetorical question. I pick him up and we go to QuikTrip. We visit about our day. This is one of my favorite small things to do. Just the two of us. No distractions. Catching up. He fills the car with gas and we go back home to face the troops.

My adorable grandson still hasn't made it back with his mom. They are spending the week with her family. Probably just as well since Red Bull and I aren't feeling well anyway. I visit with my twenty-year-old son a little. I sit at my computer and type a resignation letter along with a list of reasons I am leaving. No one feels like eating and we all go to bed with the blahs.

DAY 84 – Wednesday, January 7, 2015

Red Bull and I are up in the night again at about 1:30. We are taking turns in the bathroom. She is throwing up. I am wishing I could. After about an hour, we each take Benadryl and try to go back to sleep. It works. The next thing I know, the 5:30 alarm is going off. I have to make it to work today. This is the day I meet with the CEO. I cannot be sick. I take all three of my digestive medicines including the Zofran. Red Bull says she feels better now and wants to go to school. If she can do this, I can do this.

I get to work and get a text from the President asking if I am meeting with the CEO today. Yes, at 9:00. I tell him I am so sick I am trying to keep from throwing up. He texts back. "Don't throw up on the CEO." Good advice. I have been praying about the meeting all morning. I pray I will feel well enough to be able to speak intelligently. Finally it's 9:00. God, please don't let me throw up on the CEO. I pray I will be clear in explaining the problems in the department and save the next Controller from the same.

I go down to the CEO's office. I hand him the resignation letter and start talking with him about all the issues I am having at work. We talk for nearly an hour and he is very receptive to my concerns. This is the first time I have ever spoken to him one-on-one about anything serious. I expected him to help me find boxes to pack. I am pleasantly surprised to learn that he does not want me to resign. He wants a day to think about this. Ugh! Another day of waiting. As I am walking back to my office, I realize God answered my prayer. I did not feel sick as I was talking to the CEO. And most importantly, I did not throw up on him. Thank you, God!

The hubs calls and Annie is having a bad day. She has gotten really sick. They figure out that she hasn't pooped in nine days. I didn't realize it had been that long and feel bad that we weren't monitoring it closer. We had started giving her Mirolax before we left and knew there had been no results. But, nine days? Yikes! The doctors want to admit her back into the hospital. His sister wants to know if it is okay with us if she is admitted. Actually, we feel fine knowing she is being closely watched by the nurses.

After they get Annie settled into her hospital room, we get a call from her aunt that the laxatives have taken effect and now Annie is screaming with pain as she attempts to empty out nine days of backup. The aunt says it is a big scene and they haven't give her pain meds because that is what was so constipating in the first place. The hubs asks if he needs to take the next flight back. But his sister tells him he might as well stay put. It is horrible to watch and would be even harder for a parent. We both feel totally helpless.

I work for only a couple hours after my meeting when I start to feel so sick I need to lie down. Thinking it was just nerves and the sickness would go away, I had kept going. But now, I can't. I send out an e-mail that I am going home. That won't be well received. When I get home, my sweet cleaning lady is still there. I can't lie down in my own bed because she is in the middle of cleaning. I take a Benadryl and lie down in the twenty-year-olds' room. I am freezing and cannot get warm. I get back up and find an old thermometer. My temperature is 102.6. No wonder I don't feel good. I lie back down. I get a few texts over the next few hours but mostly I sleep. I take my temperature again. Now it is 101. Feeling better, I go get into my own bed. I wake a few hours later when I start getting some calls from work. I take my temperature again. 98.9. Nice. I go downstairs to find the hubs. He welcomes me back to the land of the living.

I am a little hungry and think of the diet that settles a stomach. The BRAT diet. I remember this from when the kids were little. And I love a memorable acronym. Bananas, rice, applesauce, toast. All easy on the stomach. I find some applesauce and have it for dinner. The hubs asks how I like the new thermometer. What new thermometer? I only found an old one. He texts the twenty-year-old daughter-in-law. She says she must have left it on the kitchen counter when she was using it on my adorable grandson earlier in the week. He had been sick. He was running a fever. Red Bull and I had kissed and loved all over that child as soon as we got back from Memphis. That info about his fever might have been nice to know. Oh well. We all go to bed feeling better.

DAY 85 – Thursday, January 8, 2015

I wake up to the 5:30 alarm. I would think after all the sleep I got yesterday, I would feel rested. But I am still bone tired. I get up and start getting ready. I am feeling better.

I get to work and find out that the CEO wants to meet with me at 4:15 to go over my options. I agree to meet with him again. It's going to be a long day.

The hubs gets a call from his sister for the daily Annie update. Annie is still having a hard time with digestive issues. Another day of trying to get the plumbing moving again. Another long day for them.

I meet with the CEO at the end of the day. He has had some conversations with others in the office and tried to resolve some of the issues. He really wants me to try to work things out. I tell him I will have to sleep on it. I cannot decide if I care enough anymore to want to work things out or if I just want to leave.

I work for a couple more hours and am on my way home when the hubs calls to say my friends are looking for me. Crap! I was supposed to meet them for dinner at 6:30. I call them and tell them I am on my way and I make it there by 7:00. We eat dinner and visit and laugh and get caught up. I haven't seen them since the holidays and they give me Christmas presents. Once again, I have to explain that Christmas wasn't part of my plans this year. They understand. I had planned on leaving in time to be home by 9:00. But I was having too much fun. I leave for home at 9:00.

I get home to a quiet house. Everyone is in bed. I creep upstairs and go to bed wondering what to do. I don't sleep well, but pray off and on all night.

DAY 86 – Friday, January 9, 2015

I wake up at 5:30 and don't want to get out of bed. I have tossed and turned all night. I get to work and have an e-mail from the CEO saying he hopes I will at least give it the college try. I think he has no idea how much I have tried with this job, but I agree to try to work things out.

After another meeting to talk over issues in the department and I leave the meeting thinking there is a possibility I could actually enjoy my job again. I let the CEO know. He is pleased. Nothing better for job security than pleasing the CEO.

The report on Annie is good today. She is feeling better. Less pain. They are letting her go back to the store house. I am so glad her aunt has been there for her this week. Though I am sure it will be a long time before they are brave enough to volunteer again. They all get settled back in to the store house and have a yummy pot roast with scalloped potatoes for dinner. Of course they do.

I spend the rest of the day trying to focus. It has been a hard week. I leave on time for a change so I can spend some time with the hubs, but I find out on the way home that he and Red Bull have gone to a basketball game.

I come home to a quiet house. My adorable grandson is still with his mom and her family. I go to bed and read *Gone Girl*. The hubs comes home sans Red Bull. She has decided to spend the night with a friend. The hubs and I go to bed without a house full of children. Strange. I go to sleep dreading seeing the hubs leaving tomorrow.

DAY 87 – Saturday, January 10, 2015

I wake up when the hubs alarm goes off at 6:00. He is riding with the boyfriend's mom and boyfriend to Memphis today. I am in a funk to be back on our schedule of only seeing each other briefly on weekends. Unlike me, he is ready to go early. Of course he is. I get up and visit with him while he waits. We talk over everything going on. Who would have thought on Annie's birthday, October 10, that this would be our life? If someone had told me what was coming, I would have been sure I could not do this. And yet, here we are. We are doing what we have to do. We will be different than we would have been. We try really hard to see the silver lining.

The hubs' ride arrives and I kiss him goodbye. As soon as he drives away, I remember a present he was supposed to take for Annie. I call him to come back. He leaves for the second time at 7:30. And we are both single parents once again.

I make coffee. A friend gave me some pumpkin latte coffee that I mix with the Maxwell House. It is a great cup of coffee. I drink the whole pot. I gather all the unopened mail and bills that have accumulated. The hubs has not opened anything when he was here and we didn't go through it this week. It's overwhelming. How can the post office not be having a good year when one family receives this much mail? I go to pick up Red Bull at her friend's house. Then I spend the entire day going through bills and getting everything organized. I feel better.

The hubs calls to say they have arrived. The first part of their day goes well. Annie watches TV with the boyfriend while her daddy runs errands. But then she has to go to the bathroom and the pain begins. The hubs has no tolerance for her in pain. He cannot deal with it. He takes her back to the hospital and they admit her. They are not exactly sure what is causing the pain and sickness. They think she might have an infection, but until her blood counts show ANC, they cannot thoroughly check her out. They start her on several different antibiotics, but other than managing the pain, there is nothing they can do for her. They start her on morphine. We get ready for her morphine personality to kick in. It doesn't turn out to be a very good visit for the boyfriend.

Red Bull and I have been invited again to my nurse friend's house for dinner. My friend fixes a pot pie that is yummy! And of course, she has saved a bottle of wine for me. Love this friend! We eat and talk and laugh until after midnight when the twenty-year-old texts to say it's time to come home. He reminds me nothing good happens after midnight. I promise to drive carefully. Red Bull and I make it home safely by 12:30 and see that our house has several extra twenty-year-olds in it. They want to cook something to eat. I tell them to make sure they clean up their mess and don't wake me. Clearly, the wine has affected my logic.

I am still a little wound up so I read *Gone Girl* until I get sleepy. I go to sleep feeling relaxed.

DAY 88 – Sunday, January 11, 2015

I don't wake up until 11:00. I can't remember the last time I slept this late. It feels good. I go downstairs to make another pot of the pumpkin latte coffee. I look around at my kitchen. The kitchen that was supposed to be cleaned after the late night cooking. I clean the sink enough to be able to get the coffee pot under the faucet. Must. Have. Coffee! I ignore the mess and sit down to write when I remember I need to go to Walmart. I also need some new pants that fit, so I go to a couple of department stores first. Why is it when I don't have money, I can always find plenty of things I want, and when I am ready to buy, I can't find anything? I give up and go to Walmart. I actually find some jeans that fit. I spend over an hour in the store and spend way too much money. As soon as I get home, Red Bull tells me about a few items not on the list. Figures.

The twenty-year-old fixes pizza rolls. I do laundry. It's a boring day. Boring is good. Red Bull and I watch *Facing the Giants* for about the fourth time. We do our usual job of criticizing the acting, but crying in the end. I go to bed dreading the work week ahead.

DAY 89 – Monday, January 12, 2015

I wake up at 5:30 and start looking at Facebook on my phone. I don't understand why I can't keep my newsfeed in chronological order. I keep seeing posts that I have missed. At 6:11, I decide enough time has been wasted. This could take up my entire day. I have to get ready for work.

The twenty-year-old daughter-in-law is taking Red Bull to school this week. I am hoping she is keeping track of how much gas is in the mini-van since the gas gauge is broken. After having to bring them gas on the turnpike in 100 degree weather last summer, one would think they had learned a lesson. But when I ask if there is gas in the van, I hear, "Hmm...there should be." I am praying they do not run out of gas now that it is 15 degrees outside.

I go to work and have a quick meeting with the accounting department. I am doing so many things I had decided I wasn't going to have to do since I was leaving. Now they are stressing me out. We get all caught up and plan the next happy hour. Priorities. I really like this group and hope we will be able to continue working together for a long time.

I stay in meetings most of the day and don't hear a report about Annie until I am on the way home. She is still having problems with pain and is on morphine. Her daddy puts her on the phone and she talks to me all the way home. She is upset that the boyfriend lost his part-time pizza-making job because he was missing weekends to come and see her. She is also upset thinking she ruined his visit. She is in a funk. I am sad that she is not doing better.

I get home and find a friend has delivered pizza. Thin crust Pizza Hut pepperoni. Yum! I find an unfinished bag of my favorite chips to go with it. Though I know I will have severe heartburn later, I cannot resist. I think the seasoning on Cheese Doritos must be crack. I cannot stop until I have finished off the rest of the bag.

I sit down to watch the NCAA Championship football game. I'm still not a football fan. But the hubs got me interested this season from all the games we watched in the store house.

As I settle in to watch Oregon and Ohio State (and realize I am not the football fan I thought I was – I thought Alabama beat Ohio State…hmm), my adorable grandson is brought downstairs. His cheeks are pink and he feels warm. Of course, I can't find the new thermometer. I only manage to hold the old thermometer under his arm for a short time and it reads 100.3. The eighteen-year-old shows up to get his insurance card. He is on his way to Urgent Care because he is wheezing from his asthma. The hubs calls and says Annie is running a fever. Good grief! We are all falling apart!

Both the eighteen-year-old and my adorable grandson go to Urgent Care. The eighteen-year-old has inflamed lungs. My adorable grandson has an upper respiratory infection. The hubs calls again. They don't know what is causing the fever for Annie. But at least she is in the hospital and they are taking care of her. He is exhausted and goes back to the store house. I wait for my adorable grandson to come home from the hospital. So much for a quiet night watching football.

I watch until Oregon has clearly lost and I cannot hold my eyes open. I go to bed thinking the hubs would be proud of me for watching a football game without him.

DAY 90 – Tuesday, January 13, 2015

I wake to a text from Red Bull asking me to come in the bathroom. Her stomach hurts. She is crying and thinks she needs to go to the doctor. She comes to lie down in my bed. I give her ibuprofen and tell her she will be fine. She says "That's what you said when Annie told you she was sick." Nice. I tell her I will take her to the ER. She says she is feeling a little better. I tell her she can stay home from school and to call me if she feels worse. She goes back to sleep. I get ready and go to work feeling like a crappy parent.

I work all day and do not hear from Red Bull. I assume no news is good news. I hear from the hubs that Annie is still running a fever, but they think it may be due to the morphine. Lots of doctors have been in to see her, but since they can't do any invasive procedures, they still do not know what exactly is causing the pain. The hubs has bought our plane tickets for the weekend. He made sure not to get mine too early. I am dreading spending another weekend traveling. I am ready for this to be over.

After work, the whole accounting department goes to happy hour. I really enjoy this time and am hopeful that my decision to stay with this job was a good one. I go home and find Red Bull playing with my adorable grandson. They are both smiling when I walk in the door. They make me smile. Red Bull says she started feeling better about lunchtime. I wonder how much is nerves or anxiety with this whole situation, but I don't say anything. I am just glad she feels better.

I play with my adorable grandson and clean up the kitchen. Red Bull wants to watch TV. We cook a frozen pizza and watch *Big Fish* together. Much to her dismay, I cannot hold my eyes open for the whole movie. I disappoint her by going to bed before the movie is over.

DAY 91 – Wednesday, January 14, 2015

I wake to the 5:30 alarm. I am sooo sleepy. Red Bull feels better and wants to go to school, but the twenty-year-old who takes her is sick. I get ready for work, update the Annie's Army Facebook page that I have neglected and we leave at 7:20. After taking Red Bull to school, I make the commute to work. I have been in the car for 1 ½ hours. I use the drive time to pray. Good health is at the top of the list. I could feel sorry for myself, but when I think of all my friends and what is going on in their lives, I realize everybody has to deal with something difficult. Everybody's "something" is different, but no one is immune to problems. Everybody has something. I pray for everybody's "something" that I can think of. The song where the guy sings "I can only imagine…" comes on the radio. I try to imagine life in heaven without problems. I don't have that big of an imagination.

I get to work and start putting out fires. I haven't received the usual dozens of e-mails and calls. Nice. I get a lot done, but have a lot more to do. Job security. I work until time to go to dinner at a friend's house. I will be only a few minutes late.

The hubs calls to give a report about Annie. Though lots of doctors have seen her, there is nothing they can do for her. Her white blood cells have not built back up. Her ANC is zero. No immunity. They still have her on several antibiotics and she is feeling better. Of course, she is also still on morphine. That helps. She hasn't had a fever in 24 hours. If she continues to be fever-free, she will be able to go back to the store house tomorrow.

The hubs is frustrated. He is trying to do laundry at the store house and someone is hogging the dryer. I tell him when it happens to me, I take their clothes out and fold them, then set them on the table.

He says he will take their clothes out, but he will not fold them. What if someone walks in while he is holding their underwear? Good point. We don't want a scene in the laundry room. I pray that Annie will get well and her daddy will not go too stir-crazy at the store house in the meantime.

I eat dinner at my friend's house and visit until Red Bull calls at 8:30 to tell me it's time to come home. (Red Bull and her twenty-year-old brother have become the Curfew Police.) I obey and make it home by 9:00. We are supposed to watch the rest of *Big Fish*, but she starts watching *Maleficent*. I have trouble sitting through "regular" movies. Animated movies are worse. I beg for a reprieve until tomorrow night. Reprieve granted. I stay up and play with my adorable grandson for a while and go to bed happy that everyone is feeling good for a change.

DAY 92 – Thursday, January 15, 2015

The alarm wakes me at 5:30, but I am frozen in place. At 6:00, I finally drag out of bed. The twenty-year-old is taking Red Bull to school (a hallelujah moment!), but she announces that she won't be able to take Red Bull tomorrow because she is babysitting for someone else. I hope they are paying her. With no morning catastrophes, I get to work a little early.

The CEO has decided he needs to be more accessible to the rest of us. He has planned a breakfast with the accounting department. Bacon, egg and cheese wraps await. Yum! The day is off to a good start. He fields the hard questions such as, "How long can the company survive oil prices being so low?" with optimism. "No layoffs." "More efficient operations." "Good things on the horizon." I am hoping he is right.

I get a report from the hubs that Annie is feeling better, but had a slight fever again overnight. They are not ready to release her yet. She is on the morphine and getting into conversations with her daddy that they shouldn't be having. They start talking about her boyfriend. Boyfriends are not a good subject for a sixteen-year-old girl to discuss with her daddy. He reminds her what all seventeen-year-old boys have on their minds and not to let her guard down. But she is ultra-sensitive and irritable while she is on all the medication. He is stir-crazy and irritable. Not a good combination. She texts me that her daddy is being mean to her and talking bad about her boyfriend. I am hoping she doesn't post that on Facebook.

I come home and find the boyfriend's mom is working on Red Bull's bedroom. She is hanging pictures and has bought Red Bull new curtains and bedding. The boyfriend's mom works and has four kids of her own. I appreciate the gifts, but she is also setting the bar too high. I have no idea where she gets this much energy. We visit, and Annie's boyfriend comes over with a new desk for Annie's room. Apparently, Annie is tired of her old desk. Of course she is. They make Annie's room look beautiful.

After they leave, Red Bull tells me she has a ride from a teacher in the morning. The catch is that we have to be at the teacher's house at 6:45. Then she tells me she is sleeping over at a friend's house tomorrow night. This will be our last night together for over a week. She starts to pack for her sleepover. I start to get in a funk. We go to bed exhausted.

DAY 93 – Friday, January 16, 2015

The alarm goes off at 5:30 and I know I need to get up. We need to leave by 6:30. I need to get up. I need to get up. Okay, I'm up. I stagger to the bathroom and start getting ready. Surprisingly, we arrive at the teacher's house only three minutes late at 6:48. Red Bull gives me a hug, I give her my mantra ("I love you, baby. Have a wonderful day!"), and we do our usual routine of blowing kisses while she gets in the car to go to school. I drive to work feeling sad.

I drive into the parking garage before 7:30. It is deserted except for one car I do not recognize and there is someone inside. I park and grab my purse and phone. As I get out of the car, so does the person in the car. It is dimly lit in the garage, but as the person gets out, I can see it is a man. I reach into my purse and have my hand on my gun when I see it is one of my co-workers. Relaxing, I ask him what he is doing. He got to work early too and was just listening to something on the radio. When he saw I had arrived, he thought he would walk in with me. He has no idea.

I get a text from Annie that some country music singers are supposed to be at St. Jude today. This has her excited. She has texted her daddy to bring her make-up and clothes (something other than the pajamas she has worn for the last few days). They are hoping to see Brad Paisley. I tell them to be sure and get pictures and autographs. I am super jealous. They call later. They saw The Band Perry. Actually walked right past them before they realized it was them. And, Annie got autographs from Craig Campbell and Jackie Lee. I do not know either of these singers, but I am happy for her. She got out of the hospital room even though her daddy had to wheel her around along with the pole holding her bags of fluids and antibiotics. She is exhausted and sleeping when the hubs calls at night. It has been a good day. We are still looking for Brad.

My work day goes by quickly. I have lunch at Pei Wei with a friend I haven't seen in a while and my fortune cookie says my charming personality will bring me rewards. Okay…time to start being charming. At 5:00, along with my laptop, I pack up everything I can think of that I might need to work on next week in Memphis. I say bye to everyone and walk to the parking garage feeling like a pack mule.

The twenty-year-old calls and asks me if I will stop and get dog food on the way home. In a word, No! He says he doesn't mind going to get it himself, he just doesn't have any money. Of course he doesn't. And, by the way, if I will give him a little extra money, he will buy dinner for the two of us. So thoughtful. I come home to a quiet house and give him money for the errands. I start organizing everything I will need to pack for the week. But I am too tired. I will just have to get up early. I make myself a yummy drink and go to bed looking forward to seeing the hubs and Annie.

It's Just Another Day

DAY 94 – Saturday, January 17, 2015

I wake up at 7:00 and go to make the coffee. The twenty-year-old is up and returns my debit card from the night before when I asked him to fill my gas tank. He tells me he will pick Red Bull up at 11:00 and has the address. I am impressed that he is caring so well for his sister. Then I remember she is babysitting for him tonight. He wants to make sure she gets home.

I pack up and make it to the airport on time. I check-in with no problems and read some memos from work while I wait for the plane to take off.

After landing at DFW, I have a two-hour layover. I eat at TGIFridays and read a Time magazine. I finish reading *Gone Girl* on the flight to Memphis. Disturbing book. More disturbing is that I think I actually know some people that crazy who can also appear to be nice and innocent. Makes me want to watch the movie.

Smooth flight to Memphis. I sit by a college student headed back to Ole Miss. She is from California and wanted to go to a school in a different part of the country. I imagine Mississippi is quite a bit different from California. Mission accomplished.

The hubs comes to pick me up and we do another movie-like hug in the baggage claim. He has a new drink for me to try in the car. Something called Apple Moonshine. He is turning into a Tennessee Redneck. The Apple Moonshine is a disappointment, but spending time with the hubs is not. We go back to the store house to unpack my things and begin to pack the hubs things for his return trip.

Walking in to our apartment again makes me very emotional. I can barely hold it together. Then we go to the hospital to check on Annie. She looks like the poster child for St. Jude. She looks like a cancer patient. She is still in pain and cranky. How am I going to do three more months of this? Her daddy has brought her a snack and we make her eat a little, though she says she is not hungry. We talk about her getting released, but she is not happy about that. We drop the subject. I help her take a bath and we get her settled in for the night about 10:00. We head back to the store house to spend our one night together for the next week. I fall asleep dreading the week ahead.

DAY 95 – Sunday, January 18, 2015

The hubs wakes up early. I hear him get up, but I lay in bed unable to move. A while later, the smell of coffee has me looking to see what time it is. I brought the yummy pumpkin latte my friend back home gave me for Christmas. It's 8:00. I get up and get a cup of coffee, sit on the couch and start to watch some hunting show that the hubs is watching, when I get a text from Annie. It says, "Get here soon." They are talking about releasing her and she does not want to go back to the store house yet. We are getting concerned that she doesn't want to leave the hospital. We get ready quickly and head to the hospital.

The doctor comes in and we talk about her getting released today. He says the saying in the hospital is "The longer you stay, the longer you stay."

In other words, if you keep looking for excuses to stay, you will never feel like leaving. Annie is upset. I go tell the nurses to quit being so darn nice to her. I am pleased that they love her, but they have set the bar so high, I can never compete. Finally, we convince her that getting out of there will make her get well faster. I mention she needs to get up and moving. She panics – thinking I am going to try to get her on the treadmill at the store house. I assure her that I didn't even bring my jogging shoes. I haven't been on the treadmill since October when this nightmare began.

Her counts are low and she needs blood and platelets before we can check out. While she is getting the transfusions, I take the hubs to the airport. After I hug and kiss him and watch him walk into the airport, I think I am going to be sick. I turn off the radio for the drive back to the hospital and try to talk to God. I want to pray for strength and a good attitude. But I cannot even pray. I am too depressed. I am hoping all my Facebook friends that keep commenting "praying" are following through.

I get back to the hospital and the nurse has given Annie her meds and says she will go get the discharge papers. Why does everything feel like it moves in slow motion in a hospital? I go to the pharmacy and pick up her newest medications. They put them all in a grocery sack. Even the pharmacist comments, "That's a lot of medicine." And it doesn't even count the IV meds that will be delivered later to the store house. This round can't be put on a twelve-hour schedule like the last ones. Some are every six hours, some every eight and some every twelve. One of the meds she takes every eight hours causes an allergic reaction, so she gets

Benadryl thirty minutes before taking it. The schedule is so confusing, I make another spreadsheet so I can keep it all straight. Fortunately, I love a good spreadsheet.

Finally released and back at the store house, I make spaghetti for dinner, but Annie says it tastes funny and eats a couple pieces of heavily buttered toast instead. She follows up with a bowl of ice cream. I am just happy she is eating. The hospital delivers her IV meds and she watches TV while the IV drips. About 10:30, she says she is cold. I think it is probably just from the ice cream and IV. But she is wearing a sweater and has two blankets. Her cheeks are flushed. To make sure she's okay, I take her temp. 101.4. I can't catch a break.

I call the hospital hoping they will say just to give her some Tylenol. What could she possibly have come into contact with? We just left! But of course they want us back at the hospital. We are admitted to St. Jude once again at about midnight. At 1:00 a.m., she is settled in and I go back to the store house. Just as I have drifted into that comatose sleep, the phone rings. I knock my glasses off in the floor trying to find the phone. It is Annie's nurse. She asks me what medications I gave her at 10:00. I thought we had been all through this. I answer her (at least I think I answer her) and she repeats the question. I answer her again (at least I think I answer her again) and she laughs and says "I will figure it out. Go back to sleep." Something tells me the words coming out of my mouth were not as coherent as I thought they were. I fall back asleep exhausted.

DAY 96 – Monday, January 19, 2015

I wake up to the alarm I set for 7:15. I am bone tired. I get ready for work and call Captain Awesome to get an update on his week's schedule. I get an e-mail from an accountant that she is running late. She e-mails me her update. I pack up and head for the hospital. It feels like a Saturday. Hardly anyone is at the hospital. Then I realize it is Martin Luther King Day and they have not scheduled regular appointments today. Unfortunately, Annie's fever doesn't give us a holiday. But it is a beautiful day and there is plenty of available parking. The day is looking up.

Annie is sound asleep when I arrive. I put her quilt on her bed and creep back out of the room. I start working from The Kennel. The doctors come into her room mid-morning. They take some swab samples to test for infection. They tell me it will be at least 36 hours before culture results come back. I plan on staying a while.

I have both my laptop and my second monitor, but working without a desk is driving me crazy. I also forgot the plug-in piece of my wireless mouse in Oklahoma. At noon, I decide to go buy another wireless mouse and go back to the store house to get my foldable table. I get as far as the elevators when I realize I don't have my car key. Back to the room. I drive to Target and get the wireless mouse. As I am leaving, I see there is fresh Target popcorn just coming out of the popper. Unexpected bonus! I get my Target popcorn lunch and head for the store house. I am almost there when I remember my room key is still in The Kennel. Ugh! I drive back to the hospital, park and go up to The

Kennel, retrieve the key and drive back to the store house to pick up the folding table.

The hubs has told me the table is really easy to fold. He has always done it for me, but surely I can figure this out. I push and pull and try to bend metal. I will not call him. I can figure this out. I turn the table over on the bed and look at the places that bend. The legs are too long. There is no way this should fold, but I know it can be done. How did he do this? I have a college degree. And, I am smarter than the hubs (if he ever reads this I am in trouble!). Surely I can fold this "easy-to-fold" table. Finally, I see metal buttons on the legs. If they are both pushed in, the legs will collapse. But I need three hands – two to push the buttons and another to push down on the bar connecting the legs. I push both buttons while pushing the bar down with my chin. I am really glad no one is watching. Mission accomplished. Table now folds up easily like the hubs said. I find the handle on the side that he mentioned. Then I proceed to lug the table back to the car, into the hospital, in and out of the elevator and into the Kennel without banging my legs the entire way. Not an easy feat. This is the most I have exercised in months. I miss the hubs.

I get my office all set up in The Kennel and work until mid-afternoon when I see Annie is awake. I try to get her to eat something. She will not order from the cafeteria. She says all the food stinks. So much for free food at St. Jude. I go down to the cafeteria and call her with all the snack choices. She orders a fruit roll-up, peanut butter crackers and a Blue Bell fudge bar. I get a Blue Bell fudge bar for myself too. We eat our snacks and I go back to work. She visits with the nurses and seems to be feeling better. I work until dinner. She orders fruit roll ups and I think we will eat together. But she doesn't like the smell of my food from the cafeteria, so I am sent back to The Kennel to eat alone.

After dinner, I go sit with her until after 9:00 when she says I can go back to the store house. I think I am being dismissed. She will likely visit with the nurses all night. I go back to the store house, tack some towels over the window to try to block the light, try not to kill myself in the process, and read for a while. I am still trying to finish Condi's book (yes we are on nickname basis), *No Higher Honor*. But it is rather boring, so once again I am drifting off to sleep. I fall asleep exhausted.

DAY 97 – Tuesday, January 20, 2015

I have set the alarm for 6:30, but I lay in bed for another fifteen minutes before dragging myself into the kitchen to make the coffee. Seems like it should be Friday already. I get a text from work a few minutes before 8:00. And so it begins.

I call the office on my way to St. Jude and we start going over the day. Unlike yesterday, parking is practically non-existent today. I finally find a spot and go check on Annie. She is sleeping. The nurse says she was up all night. She is also complaining of headaches...likely from the morphine. If it isn't one thing, it's another.

I go into The Kennel to begin my workday. I take calls all morning while trying to accommodate the requests of auditors, bankers and tax preparers. Everyone at work is feeling the year-end pressure.

Everyone seems a little grumpy. Falling oil prices are not helping. I work until noon when I have a training session on new software. I am frustrated because I can't hear well on the speakerphone and have trouble following the training.

The doctors come in to check on Annie. She will not respond to them. She wants to sleep. Annoying! She hasn't pooped in three days. Plumbing problems were what started all her other issues with pain and sickness. I tell them to get her on double doses of Mirolax. We need results today.

I go back into work until 4:30 when Annie says over the intercom that she is ready to go to the bathroom. I haven't gotten this excited over bathroom visits since she was a toddler. My mother-in-law (whose job it was to potty train all my children) had Annie completely potty trained. Then Red Bull came along, and I was too weary to remind Annie a million times a day that we had a toilet. Much to my mother-in-law's dismay, I put Annie back in diapers. My sweet mother-in-law came back a second time to re-train. We hadn't had plumbing issues since. Now here I am writing her bathroom business on the marker board in her hospital room with a smiley face next to the activity time. The pain and suffering this time was less intense. I think she is on the mend.

Her primary care doctor comes by and we share the news. He says we can go "home" tomorrow. He talks to Annie about plans to take a break when her ANC comes back up. She doesn't want to go home to Oklahoma until she can stay home for good. But she talks of going to a restaurant, the mall, the zoo and, of course, I bring up Graceland. She rolls her eyes, but I will get her there. Yes, I will get us all to Graceland. With any luck, the counts will come up soon.

I ask Annie what she wants for dinner. Funyuns and fruit roll-ups. I get her random selections and get some Funyuns for myself to go with my shrimp etouffee from the cafeteria. I go back in The Kennel to eat so she doesn't have to smell my dinner. I switch between working and checking on Annie until nearly 9:00. She has asked me to shut off the intercom because she is talking to the boyfriend. They have been talking for hours. When I check on her the last time, she gives me permission to go back to the store house. I finish writing in my journal, go back to the store house and go to bed dreading tomorrow.

DAY 98 – Wednesday, January 21, 2015

The alarm goes off at 6:30. Red Bull hasn't called to complain that I am not waking her at 5:30. I miss her sweet voice in the morning, but am glad for the extra hour. I made coffee last night, so I just have to push the button. If I were really thinking, I would have set the timer. But at 10:00 at night after a full day at the hospital, I was not thinking of everything. I get ready and make my way to the hospital. Annie is still sleeping. I go to The Kennel to start my work day.

The doctors come in mid-morning and we talk about leaving later in the day. The cultures were all negative and she hasn't had fever since Sunday night. He says he will check on us later, but everything is looking good. Annie is not responding because she is still half-asleep. The nurses say she was up most of the night. She is getting on a nocturnal schedule.

I have a conference call at 10:30 that lasts over an hour and when I check on Annie again she is up and awake. I try to get her to eat. She orders cereal and milk. Wow. Normal food for a change. Never mind that it's Lucky Charms and Cinnamon Toast Crunch. I am just happy to get her to eat something. She follows up with fruit roll-ups and a Sprite. Nice.

I work through lunch and into the afternoon checking on Annie now and then. She doesn't want to watch TV, she doesn't read, she doesn't do much of anything but sleep. The doctors come back around and discuss taking her off some of her pain and nausea medications that she has been on, since she is feeling better. We decide to wait another day before leaving to see how she does with the new routine.

Late afternoon, Annie begins texting and calling friends and asks me to turn off the intercom in The Kennel so she can have some privacy. Clearly, signs that she is feeling better. I work until dinner. She snacks on her fruit roll-ups for dinner and I go back to the cafeteria. When I order the Bacon Cheddar Burger, the cook tells me they are out of burgers. I really want bacon. She tells me she will cook me a quesadilla instead and put bacon on it for me. I tell her I'll give it a try. She says I can't go wrong with bacon. I am liking this cook. She speaks my language. And she is right. The quesadilla is yummy!

Back at Annie's room, she doesn't want to smell my food and wants privacy. So I go back to The Kennel and work until nearly 10:00 when I hear her discussing something with the nurse. I go back in and the nurse tells me she is running a fever. Crap! She takes it again a little later and it has gone back to normal. She is feeling better and talking with the nurse. I decide to go back to the store house. I go to bed and read a little more Condi. I fall asleep wondering about tomorrow's schedule.

DAY 99 – Thursday, January 22, 2015

I wake up at 6:00 and start looking at Facebook. I waste 45 minutes before I decide I need to get up and get ready. I forgot to make the coffee last night. Rats! A few extra minutes before I can gulp it down. I get ready and head to the hospital. Annie is still sleeping. I go in The Kennel and start my work day.

I have several projects going and get frustrated when everyone starts calling at once. The doctors come in and tell us they are not letting Annie go home since she ran a fever the night before. Better safe than sorry.

It is easier to work from the hospital, but I worry about her just lying there for days on end. I try to get her to eat and she says she doesn't feel good. I am a little crabby with her – trying to get her to wake up, but finally I just go back to The Kennel to work some more.

Before I know it, it is lunch time and Annie is still sleeping. I go in, and once again, try to get her to eat. She wants me to order fruit roll-ups again. When I call room service, they know which room before I tell them. They ask me if she wants a Sprite to go with it. I hope they don't send the nutritionist up.

Annie says she doesn't feel like eating and I go back to The Kennel. In a short time, she is yelling for me. She needs to go to the bathroom, and on her way she gets very sick and starts throwing up. I grab the barf bag and help her make it to the bathroom. When did this become second-nature? When the nurse comes back and takes her temperature, she is running a fever again. Now I feel bad for being so crabby to her while trying to get her to eat. I don't have to wonder about the schedule anymore. We are going to be here awhile.

I work off and on while intermittently helping her to the bathroom or rearranging her blankets. She goes from being too hot to too cold. She is sick and irritable. I am tired and cranky. Not a good combination. She has been too sick to even ask me to turn off the intercom. During the commotion, I forgot to go down and get dinner in the cafeteria. I have missed dinner. I eat some cheese crackers that I had brought for Annie.

At about 9:00, she asks me to come sit in her room…in the dark…in the quiet. I ask if she minds me getting my computer. She says the sound of the clicking keys comforts her. Strange. But works for me. I write while she sleeps. At 11:00, I can't hold my eyes open anymore. She says she doesn't mind if I go back to the store house. I will see her in the morning.

I get back to the store house and all of a sudden start feeling very sick. I go to bed, but can't fall asleep. I ache from head to toe and break out in a sweat. I don't even feel like reading. I just lay there thinking I am going to die. I also think about how Annie has felt like this most of the time since October. I make a mental note to quit letting her crankiness make me cranky. Then I pray I will not get sick. I can't get sick. I fall asleep worrying that I will be too sick to get out of bed in the morning.

DAY 100 – Friday, January 23, 2015

I wake up at 6:30 when the alarm goes off. My pajamas are soaked from sweating most of the night. I need to get up. At 7:02, I crawl out of bed. I actually feel better. I make the coffee. Coffee always helps. I get ready and make it to the hospital by 8:15, but this morning I need more coffee. I go down to the cafeteria where they have better coffee than what they make on the floor. I smell the bacon before I see it. I really feel better now. The Hot Food counter is serving eggs, bacon, sausage, pancakes, biscuits and gravy. Why did I not know this was available before? I cannot resist. I get in line. I carry my biscuit and gravy with double order of bacon and, of course, coffee back up to The Kennel and start another workday off right.

Annie sleeps until the doctors come by mid-morning. They tell her she needs to get up and moving. They are planning on sending a physical therapist to show her exercises so she doesn't get too weak from lying in bed for weeks. She doesn't look happy. But they tell her if she doesn't run a fever, she can go home tomorrow. I try to get her to eat. She says she isn't hungry but needs to go to the bathroom. Just as we return, she says "What is that smell?" Every once in a while, there is a smell in the rooms that smells like something burning. I think it is a faint smell, but her sense of smell has been on overdrive for quite some time. As soon as I smell it too, she asks for the barf bag. She gets really sick and I know I will not talk her into eating anything any time soon.

Later, her child-life specialist comes in and loans her a noise maker to listen to different sounds while she sleeps. She stays and talks for a while with Annie about the different books they are reading. Annie is happy for some company besides her mother. I am happy to see Annie up and talking.

After a while, Annie lays back down and I go back to The Kennel and work until she yells for my help over the intercom. She has another episode of sickness where she barely makes it to the bathroom. But she starts to feel better and wants to sit in the recliner instead of lying in the bed. Progress. She gets out her laptop and is up for several hours. One of the nurses comes by and tells more funny stories about happenings around the hospital. The nurse has us laughing.

We hear screaming coming from the next room. The nurse asks if we are doing okay with all the commotion. I figure Annie has done enough of her own screaming. How can we complain? They tell us the little boy next door only speaks German so they cannot understand what he wants. He also won't speak to his parents, so they are having a difficult time. We know all about difficult times.

Dr. Rubnitz comes by for a visit. He says since it's been five weeks from her chemo (they count from the beginning) they may go ahead and do a bone marrow test next week just to make sure everything looks okay. Annie does not look happy about that. I try not to get too much anxiety. I don't think I can take any bad news. He stays and chats with Annie until he says he has to get home to feed his dogs. He never should have mentioned his pets around Annie. Being an animal lover, she wants to know all about his dogs and he has trouble making it out of the room.

After a couple more hours, Annie asks me to help her get back in her bed. When she gets up, she gets sick again. Ugh! I feel so sorry for her and so helpless. All I can do is watch her barf and tell her how sorry I am. I go ask the nurse to bring her more nausea medicine and Annie tries to sleep. About thirty minutes after the nausea medicine, she finally goes to sleep. I slip out and go back to the store house. I am so thankful she is old enough to spend the nights without a parent in the room. I cannot imagine the exhaustion of the parents with a toddler in the hospital!

Since the cafeteria closes at 7:00, I wasn't paying attention and missed getting dinner again at the hospital. I eat the leftover spaghetti from Sunday night. I have no idea if it's still safe, but it tastes good and I am starving, so a say a little prayer to fend off food poisoning. I watch a little of David Letterman before going to bed. I fall asleep looking forward to seeing the hubs tomorrow.

DAY 101 – Saturday, January 24, 2015

I wake up at 6:15 and can't go back to sleep. I read a little and drag out of bed at 7:00 to start getting ready. I have no clean underwear. Need to do laundry. I grab my clothes and the sheets off the bed and head for the laundry room in my pajamas without even combing my wild hair. The Hispanic lady that I cannot communicate with is back in the laundry room. I think she must do laundry every day. She is always smiling and trying to say something to me. She nods when she talks and smiles and even talks louder and slower. Doesn't matter. The slower rate and higher volume have no effect on this non-Spanish speaking Okie. I smile and say thank you. I am likely missing out on great laundry secrets.

I eat a couple of Eggo waffles and read my Bible while the laundry finishes. I make it to the hospital a little after 9:00. There is a band coming into the hospital as we are arriving. They speak Spanish. I saw a sign in the store house elevator where a band was coming to the store house at 1:15. It must be the same band. But the sign was written mostly in Spanish. So once again, I am left wondering.

When I get upstairs, the nurse tells me Annie had a really good night. But when I go into her room, Annie tells me she barely slept all night. As I sit on the vinyl couch and look at Facebook, she starts moaning and crying. For the first time, she tells me she doesn't think she can do this anymore. She doesn't want to live. My heart breaks. It is the worst moment since this began. I need to be strong and I'm going to be sick.

I stay strong and tell her she has no choice. She has to keep fighting. She starts to cry. When the nurse walks in, she is silent. After the nurse leaves, I tell her she needs to quit acting fine when the nurses are present and saving all the moaning for me. If she doesn't feel good, tell them. The next time the nurse comes in, Annie asks for a barf bag and starts violently puking. I guess she got the message.

About thirty minutes later, she starts to feel better. I open the blinds and turn on a small bedside light. She cringes. I tell her unless she is training to be a vampire, she needs to see some daylight. We are still hoping they will release her, as it is a beautiful day today. The doctors come in all draped in gowns, masks and gloves. They tell us that the cultures they have taken are now positive for VRE (a bacteria that is resistant to the antibiotic she has been getting). They explain that the infectious disease doctor will be by later. Not what we needed. Another complication.

The infectious disease doctor comes by. He tells us that it means Annie is at a much higher risk for infection. When she is in the hospital, she will be in isolation. Since the bacteria is contagious, she must be kept away from the other patients. Even though it is contagious, it is not particularly harmful to those of us with normal immune systems. But for those with weakened immune systems, the VRE can turn into something much worse...like sepsis or pneumonia. Since she is getting better, he is still planning on releasing us from the hospital this afternoon. Good news with that at least.

Just as I get in my car at St. Jude, the hubs texts "landed." Rats! I'm going to be late. I get to the airport, park and start to walk in. But the hubs is already on his way out. No movie-style hugs in the airport today. And I don't have a yummy drink waiting in the car for him either. Oh well. He is still glad to see me. We drive back to the store house for him to unpack. We make it back to the hospital in time for Annie to be discharged. As the hubs brings the car around, the nurse escorts Annie and me through the isolation ward. Our attire resembles the latest in hasmat fashion. We drive back to the store house feeling like lepers, but glad to be out of the hospital. I am hoping it lasts longer than a few hours this time.

When we get back to the store house, Annie is tired and goes to her room to take a nap. The hubs and

I eat a ten-minute skillet meal (my specialty) and watch TV. Afterward, I go back to my spreadsheet for medications and he starts loading the meds on the app on his phone. A couple of hours and a of couple arguments later, we have it all figured out. Basically, she gets medication around the clock. And it is time for the next round. He wakes Annie and encourages her to come watch TV with us and try to eat something. She stays up to eat some ice cream with us and we all go to bed exhausted.

DAY 102 – Sunday, January 25, 2015

I wake up at 3:15 and can't go back to sleep. I feel really sick. I think I ate more for dinner than I have eaten in a week. Bad idea. I get up, take a Benadryl and read *American Sniper* (my latest purchase) until 4:30. Finally, I am sleepy enough to go back to bed. At 5:00, the first alarm of the day goes off signaling to take

Annie's meds out of the fridge. I decide I will take care of the morning meds and let the hubs sleep. I take out the meds, but when the 6:00 alarm goes off to start the IV, I cannot move. The hubs gets up and starts her medication for the day. At 8:00, when the next alarm goes off, he gets up again. This time he stays up. I hear the TV going. Later, I smell coffee. Love that man! I get up and join him on the couch.

The sun is shining and we decide we will encourage Annie to go to the airport with us later, just to get her out of the apartment. Annie sleeps all morning. I watch TV with the hubs and read my book. After a while, I start to pack. I'm starting to hate Sundays. One of us is always leaving.

It starts to get cloudy outside and by the time we need to leave, it is pouring down rain outside. Annie says she doesn't want to go and we don't argue. Not crazy about her getting out in a rainstorm. I say my goodbyes and the hubs drives me back to the airport. We arrive early (of course we do). I get through security in record time. I read more of my book and have an uneventful flight to DFW. Getting off the plane at DFW, I see a Taco Bell. Yum! I haven't had their crunchy tacos in months. I sit down to eat a few tacos while I wait for my next flight.

At the gate, I spot the brother of a friend of mine. He boards before I have a chance to speak. He is a pastor in Russia and a well-known Bible teacher. When we arrive in Tulsa, I catch up with him at the baggage claim. I am nervous to meet him and feel like a stalker, but he is very kind when I interrupt his family reunion to introduce myself. My friend had told him about Annie, and he says a quick prayer for her healing, right in the baggage claim in the airport. Then I let him return to his family. An unexpected blessing!

On my drive home, the twenty-year-old calls and asks if I will bring home something to eat. In a word – "No." I get home and find everyone alive and not starving. They are eating macaroni and cheese. A staple of the poor. I hear my adorable grandson crying and go retrieve him from his crib. The twenty-year-olds will not be happy, but I can't resist him. I play with him for a while and visit with Red Bull before I go to bed exhausted.

DAY 103 – Monday, January 26, 2015

I wake up at 6:00 when my alarm goes off. Red Bull is not up. I go to her bedroom and ask if she is oversleeping. She assures me she is not. We both get ready and leave at the same time. After running by the dry cleaners, I make it back into the office after being out for the week in Memphis. The smiles on everyone's faces are always a nice welcome. The e-mails and voice mails waiting on me aren't quite so welcome – though I suppose they are job security.

I get a text from the hubs that Annie's blood labs today showed she was dangerously low on potassium and platelets. When they gave her the platelets, Annie had an allergic reaction. Since she is still sick most of the time and unable to eat, the doctors switch up her nausea medication. It is going to be a long day for them as they await the second blood test results.

I work on getting information to our auditors who are in our offices this week for the annual audit. This is also the week 1099's need to go out. Amid the fire drills, I am summoned to a meeting for over an hour that has no real point except it is scheduled every week. But if it is on the calendar, we have to meet. Otherwise, we may be arrested by the calendar police. I am re-thinking my decision to stay.

I leave work by 5:30 and call Red Bull. She has gone to a basketball game and wants to be picked up later. I get home by 6:15 and a friend of mine comes by with dinner. We eat dinner and visit. There are so many leftovers, I don't have to worry about dinner the next night either. Love her! When Red Bull calls, I go pick her up. We make it home and I am in bed by 9:30. I finish reading *American Sniper*, hoping the movie is better than the book. I fall asleep and dream about dodging bullets.

Annie and the hubs end up spending all day at A clinic and make it back to the store house in the evening. They are exhausted and Annie is still not eating. The hubs gives Annie her first dose of Phenergan to help her nausea. I do not see the text from him at 11:53 that says she had an allergic reaction to the medicine and they are back at the hospital.

DAY 104 – Tuesday, January 27, 2015

I wake up at 6:00 and see the text from the hubs. I decide he is probably sleeping, so I will wait to call until later to find out what happened. I get ready for work and call the hubs on the way in. He tells me when he went to check on Annie the night before at about 11:00, she was sitting up in her bed. He had expected her to be asleep, so he asked if everything was okay. She was wild-eyed and breathing fast. Her whole body seemed to be twitching. At first, he thought she might be having a seizure. But she started to talk. She told him she couldn't breathe – she had bricks on her chest. He tried to call the hospital, but his cell phone went dead, so he called the store house's front desk from our room's phone. They immediately called 911. When the paramedics came, they said her oxygen level was good. But she was saying there were spiders all over her. She also thought the room was flooding and she was drowning. Because of her needing a sterile environment, the ambulance driver suggested it would be safer for the hubs to drive her to St. Jude. They loaded her in our car and the hubs drove her to St. Jude. That's where they told him she was having an allergic reaction to the Phenergan. After two doses of IV Benadryl, she went to sleep, but her body still twitched until the time-released medication was out of her system.

The hubs tells me all this as I am driving. Though it sounds mean, I am so glad he was with her and not me. I do not think I would have handled all that as well as he did. He said they made it back to the store house about 3:00 in the morning. They have appointments later back at the hospital. He will keep me updated.

I am very stressed as I make it into the office. I try hard to immerse myself in my work so I do not lose it as I think about Annie. I just want all this to be over. I want to return to normal. I tell people at work what is going on with Annie. But it seems like they just want me to get through my saga so they can get back to the business at hand. Maybe that is just their way of coping. No one likes to talk about bad news.

I work until lunchtime when Captain Awesome suggests a lunch somewhere outdoors. It is an unusually warm and sunny day for January in Tulsa. I agree. The sun will do me good. After thinking about all the patio restaurants in the vicinity, we end up at the only one close by with tables in the sun. Panera Bread. I have never eaten at this particular one. After spending $10.50 for a small bowl of pasta and an even smaller bowl of soup with a small cup of water to drink, I remember why I don't eat at Panera Bread. But the sunshine makes me feel better, and I go back to work feeling better.

The afternoon goes quickly as there are people literally lined up at my door with questions. I want to get one of those rotating machines with numbers to pull. "Now serving number 17!" I leave at 6:30 and talk to the hubs on the way home. The doctors want to do another bone marrow biopsy on Annie tomorrow. They are trying to see if there is anything abnormal to explain why she is not yet rebuilding blood cells on her own. The hubs asks them if anyone has ever opted out of the fourth round of chemo. If the third round has been this awful and the fourth round is supposedly worse, can she even survive? Will she ever start making her own blood? The doctor says it has happened three times that he knows. In all three cases where the patients took longer than normal to start making blood again, they didn't do the fourth round of chemo and they are still in remission. The doctor is optimistic. We will know more after tomorrow's bone marrow test results. The waiting is brutal.

I make it home and eat yesterday's leftovers with my adorable grandson. The twenty-year-olds tell me they have found a house for rent and want to move out. They show me their budget (which I think will never work) and tell me they will still help out with the house and with Red Bull until we come home with Annie. I see they cannot be talked out of it. They just want a small loan until they get their income tax refund. Of course they do. Being the gullible, enabling parent I am, but also envisioning having the guest room and room over my garage back, I write the check. I will also fill out their tax returns myself and keep a close eye on the refund status.

After giving the hubs the updates of the day and kissing my adorable grandson and Red Bull goodnight, I go to bed lonely.

DAY 105 – Wednesday, January 28, 2015

I lay in bed waiting for the alarm to go off. I toss and turn enjoying a few more minutes of sleep. I hear Red Bull getting ready. Wait. I have been getting up before her. What time is it? 6:35. Rats! I've overslept. I drag into the bathroom and start getting ready. I get ready fast and can make it to work on time. As I am driving down the road, I see all the neighbor's trash cans out at the curb. Did I see ours out? No. I turn around, go back to the house and put the trash out. I am going to be late.

I work all day and have conversations with various people as we talk about the fate of the oil companies. Oil prices have dropped again. Oil companies are laying off employees. Am I staying too long? Should I leave the oil industry and go back to public accounting?

Annie has her "procedures" today. She has a bone marrow biopsy at noon. I go to lunch with the accounting department. I stuff myself on Mexican food…rather the chips and salsa that are served before the meal. Afterward, I am sleepy, but anxiously wondering how the tests went. Even though it was for a routine procedure, I still get nervous knowing Annie is being put under anesthesia. I try to not think about it as I work through the afternoon.

It is late in the afternoon, when the hubs calls and says all went well. We should have test results tomorrow. Annie has been so sick and has not eaten in so long, the doctors decide to try Marinol – medical marijuana in pill form. They are trying it as a last resort for the nausea, pain and lack of appetite. I tease the hubs that I will be taking a close inventory of the pills. He tells me he gave Annie her first one, but so far all she has done is sleep.

I start to leave work at 6:00, when a co-worker comes in that I haven't seen in a while. His wife just had twin girls. I want to hear all about them. We start talking about babies and work. Before I know it, thirty minutes have passed and I need to get home. Another friend invites me for drinks after work, but I feel guilty for not spending more time with Red Bull and head home. I call the hubs on the way home and he tells me Annie has the munchies. He caught her coming from the kitchen with a plate full of crackers and cheese. The first time she has voluntarily eaten in weeks. The hubs asked the doctor why Marinol is the last resort. "Because it's controversial." I feel like fighting with anyone who would deny my daughter anything that would make her feel better while she battles cancer.

When I get home, Red Bull is sleeping in her room. I wake her and tell her to come downstairs so she can tell me about her day. A co-worker has written a book and, thinking I am an expert since I am keeping a journal, I tell him I will help edit it. The twenty-year-olds have made fish sticks. After the Mexican food at lunch, I am not one bit hungry, but still munch on fish sticks as I read. By the time Red Bull comes downstairs, I am engrossed in marking up the friend's story with my red pen. Red Bull gets frustrated that I am not paying enough attention to her and stomps off to her room. I am tired and go to bed feeling like a failure.

DAY 106 – Thursday, January 29, 2015

I wake up to the 6:00 alarm and my right eye is sealed shut. Wearing contacts means I frequently have my fingers in my eyes and I get conjunctivitis about twice a year. Ugh!! I stumble to the bathroom and look for my prescription "miracle" eye drops. I can't find them. I remember the eighteen-year-old asking about my drops a few months ago. I text him to see where they are. No reply. I find some over the counter "pink eye relief" and drop it in my eyes. I see some leftover Ciproflaxin in the medicine cabinet. An antibiotic Annie didn't finish. I look online to see what it is good for. Bacterial infections including eye infections. Thank you God. I take a pill prescribed for someone else. I am hoping the pill police don't find out. Not sure an Oklahoma prison will be much better than a Mississippi prison. But I can't get sick. I have to take care of Annie next week.

I finish getting ready for work, but text Captain Awesome to say "I am gonna be late." When I get to work, an annoying co-worker tells me she may be coming down with something, so she needs to stay away from me. She doesn't want to risk making me sick before I go back to Memphis. Darn. She calls it a low-grade fever. I call it answered prayer.

I get a call from the hubs. Annie's test results are in. Good news. Her bone marrow doesn't show any sign of leukemia. Bad news. Her bone marrow doesn't show any improvement since finishing her chemo treatments 37 days ago. There is nothing more to do but wait. When she finally produces blood on her own again – and the doctors feel confident she will – we can discuss whether or not to complete chemo Round Four.

I get travel vouchers in the mail plus a one-hundred-dollar bill from a family in a nearby town who wants to help with our transportation costs. I get an e-mail from a friend who has a friend who has a friend and that friend's parents live in Memphis and their church wants to bring us meals. I am so grateful for all the people who want to help us. And I am tired from trying to come up with ways we need help.

I tell the friend of the friend of the friend's parents that Annie cannot eat anything prepared by someone else, but thank you. "Well, what do you need? Can you send a specific grocery list?" I send her a very specific grocery list. Not specific enough. She e-mails back with questions like "sour pickles?" and "creamy or crunchy peanut butter?" At this point, it's tiring to make even a decision about peanut butter, but I am once again overwhelmed at the kindness of random people. I vow once again to be nicer.

The hubs texts Red Bull. He tells her to tell me to "go get snacks for the Super Bowl." In a word – "No." He texts with a list, and texts her to "tell your mother I said NOW." Before she can finish telling me, he has texted again. She is laughing. His text is "Just kidding. Do NOT tell your mother that!" He knows me too well. There is no way I am going to do his Super Bowl snack shopping for him. He and Red Bull will likely end up at Buffalo Wild Wings if he wants to watch the game with good snacks.

A former neighbor that I haven't seen in a long time comes over. Annie and her daughter used to be very good friends. She has made a scrapbook page for Annie with sweet pictures of the girls and their friends. We visit until 9:30 and I go to bed feeling grateful.

DAY 107 – Friday, January 30, 2015

I wake up a few minutes before the alarm goes off and lay there wishing I was independently wealthy. Red Bull is in my bathroom rummaging for shampoo. We have no less than 17 bottles at the store house, but we are sharing one here at home base. I check out Facebook and drag out of bed to start my day. Today my right eye is better, but my left eye feels yucky. I have to get better. I cannot be sick when I go to Memphis. I continue to take my contraband prescription medicine.

I start getting texts from Annie. She says I am the only one she knows who is up at this ungodly hour, so she will text me. She is planning her "Make a Wish." Her St. Jude social worker has told her that all the patients receiving long-term treatment at St. Jude get to make a wish. Annie has been thinking about what she wants to do ever since. She has also found a swimsuit for me on Pinterest. I like it and ask her where I can get it and how much it costs. Nordstrom's and $130. I text her "Yikes!" She texts that she will look for it on Wanelo and order it for me. Not sure how she knows my size or how to place these orders, but hope I will look good in my next swimsuit.

I get to work only a few minutes past 8:00 and dive in to wrap up the week. I am already dreading being in Memphis next week. Though I actually get more work done in Memphis without the interruptions, it is hard feeling like I am not a part of what is going on. And, nerdy as we are, we still have fun together in the accounting department.

I get a call from the hubs that Annie is feeling better. A little high, but doing well. She had blood transfusions yesterday, and will get platelets today. Nothing new there. We just wait for her to make her own blood. I can tell he is ready to switch places and come home.

The whole accounting department – except for me – is busy getting the 1099's out the door. I e-mail them all asking them to join me for happy hour. I only get a few takers, but I invite others in the office and the auditors as well. At 5:00, about a dozen of us meet across the street. It is a good ending to a long week. Driving home, I remember we have no alcohol. Captain Awesome told me earlier in the week that I should get some from him that he will never drink. I text him and ask if I can drop by and pick up the beer he doesn't want. He asks me how much I have already had. He has become the alcohol police. I assure him that I have only had two – not past my limit. Besides, Oklahoma beer is very weak. He doesn't text back. Nice.

The hubs calls. In my quest to find alcohol, I have forgotten to give him my nightly call on my way home from work. He is a little ticked. I try to tell him I have a lot on my mind. I think he is just feeling lonely.

Red Bull has spent the night with a friend. So when I get home, I play with my adorable grandson, eat some potato chips for dinner, do some laundry and begin to pack for tomorrow. I go to bed feeling lonely.

DAY 108 – Saturday, January 31, 2015

I wake up at 7:30 thinking I have plenty of time since my flight doesn't leave until 10:45. Then it dawns on me. I need to leave the house by 9:00. I still need to pack. I get that feeling of panic that makes me instantly awake and I get up and start getting ready. I get a text from the eighteen-year-old. "I don't know where they are." What? Oh yeah. Thursday's text asking him about my eye drops. Timely.

I get to the airport in plenty of time. I get my ticket and go to the gate to read *Unbroken*. Soon they start the announcement to board the plane. Boarding all Gold, Platinum, Advantage, Admiral Club, First Class, Superstar, and Beautiful People. I wait my turn. Now boarding the peasant class. My turn. Should I bow as I walk down the aisle tripping over the royalty? At least I am in Group 1. I would never want to be that low class of Group 4. Really? Why do we even let them on the plane?

I don't understand how it is a privilege to board first. Everyone is looking at you, breathing on you, tripping over you, and waiting on you to be seated. Seems to me we should board from the back of the plane first. Wouldn't that make more sense? But they don't ask for my opinion.

I get to DFW with a couple of hours to spare and eat at TGIFridays. Not very hungry, but feeling like if I am taking up a seat, I should order. I get an appetizer. Warm pretzels with beer-cheese for dipping. Yum! But their cloudy ice tea leaves me hoping I won't get sick. One of the things Annie cannot have with her low bacteria diet is tea. In any form. Too much bacteria in any tea leaves. I love tea. But this glass has me thinking about the bacteria.

I get to Memphis. The hubs is waiting on-time (of course he is) and we do our usual movie-worthy hug at the airport. He has four different choices of yummy beverages in the car to choose from. A mobile liquor store. I choose the apple Crown and we are off to the store house.

Annie is up and in a good mood. We catch up and watch *Maleficent*. Annie has been trying to get me to watch this for months. For some reason I thought it was animated. When I mention this, the hubs reminds me that even though it is not animated, the fairies aren't real. Nice. The hubs does some laundry and cooks dinner. He makes us a cheese and cracker appetizer while we wait on dinner. Too soon, I am really, really tired and go to bed. Knowing I like it completely void of light when I sleep, the hubs has bought curtains to block the light. It is almost dark enough for me to sleep. I make a mental note to be nicer to the hubs and go to sleep content.

Groundhog Month

The alarm goes off to take Annie's meds out of the fridge at 7:00. I haven't slept well and tell the hubs I will take care of it. I come back to bed, but he gets up to make coffee. He has to pack and be at the airport by 9:00. He told me he got an earlier flight because he wants to spend more time with Red Bull on Sunday evening. Then I remember it's Super Bowl Sunday. Nice excuse Family Man.

It's raining again. Seems it's always raining when I take him to the airport. Matches my mood. I hang onto him in the drop-off lane so long that he peels me off and tells me not to cry. I can't promise him that. I decide as I drive away from the airport that I am not going to use Google Map to get me back to the store house. I have made this trip half a dozen times. I can do this. But I get confused coming out of the airport and go west instead of east on Winchester. I knew I wanted to go north. Where was any sign that said "North?" How can I not know the way back? How can my navigational compass be so far out of alignment? I drive for a minute trying to figure out where I am. I give up, turn Google Map on and my phone immediately says "Make a U-turn." Oh well, I'll try again next week.

I come back to the apartment and start to clean. Love the hubs, but his housekeeping skills are akin to my navigational skills. I get it all picked up and start more laundry. (The Mexican woman is back in the laundry room. Does she live in the laundry room?) The hubs texts that he is sitting in a row on the plane with two guys his size. He says he can barely text and would order a drink, but they would all have to share because there is not enough room for three drinks. LOL! It's a rough life riding in the peasant class.

Later, Annie and I turn on the Super Bowl, but we aren't too interested until half-time. Annie loves Katy Perry and I must admit the show is pretty good. We occupy ourselves doing other things until the last few minutes of the game. I am for the Patriots because I like their name (very patriotic and much better than a Seahawk) and their helmets are really cool too. They win and I think how many people are either really happy or sad over that game. People probably even prayed about its outcome. Given, its insignificance in the whole scheme of things, I go to sleep wondering what God thinks about the Super Bowl.

DAY 110 – Monday, February 2, 2015 –
Groundhog Day

I feel like every day since October has been Groundhog Day. When can I wake up, it's a new day, and we move on from cancer? I am dreading my weekly Monday morning work call. I get up at 7:00 and start to get ready for the workday. I get a call from an accountant that she is sick. I get an e-mail from Captain Awesome telling me his agenda for the week. He has way too much to do. Need to keep him happy or I'm in trouble. I have 14 e-mails by 9:00. After my Monday morning call, my computer isn't working right and I spend another incredible amount of time on the phone with the IT department trying to get the problem fixed. It's a Monday!

The phone rings. It's someone with Target House. Since Annie has a contagious infection, the woman tells me we need to move into the other Target House. Today! I tell her I am the only one here to move everything. I ask "Why the rush?" She answers they have been trying to get ahold of us since Thursday. Huh? Except when we were at the hospital, someone has been in the room the entire time. And haven't I walked past the front desk at least a half-dozen times a day? And, by the way, have they heard of sticky notes? They attach to doors. I live upstairs – right above the front desk. Another loser at hide and seek. She tells me she will send Maintenance with some boxes and they can carry our things over when I am ready. She says they can tell me more at the front desk. I call the hubs in tears. He tells me I can just load up shopping carts and move our things myself. He makes it sound simple. But he is not here, is he?

I go to the front desk to ask them about our new room, keys, parking, etc. The fire alarm starts going off. The lady at the front desk looks at me and says, "You'll have to go to the desk at Target House 1" and then she goes to take care of the fire alarm. The fire alarm is loud and I can barely hear myself think. It is not a false alarm and they are dispatching the fire department. I frantically look for the stairs. I should know the escape routes. Why did I not study those maps on the back of our door? Would it have done any good since I am directionally challenged anyway?

Someone points me to the stairs so I can go back upstairs and get Annie. She was still sleeping when I left. I picture her frantically crying out for her mother. I find the stairs and go racing up. I see Annie in the hallway. I yell out to her, "Thank God! I made it back to you as fast as I could!" She rolls her eyes and walks past me for the stairs. Maybe I have overemphasized my own importance.

We go downstairs and they tell us to exit the building. It is freezing cold. Annie and I are both in slippers. Neither of us have a coat. She tells me we should get in my car and turn on the heater. Great plan. Except I don't have my car keys…or my cell phone…or anything that will help us as we stand outside in the cold. Annie is giving me a look that asks the question, "Are you really my caregiver?" Someone from the store house brings around blankets as the fire department appears. They go into the non-smoke-filled building. Several minutes and several frozen toes and fingers later, we get the "All Clear." Annie and I go back into the building and wait our turn at the elevators to go back upstairs. It's definitely a Monday!

After our morning's adventure, I work through the rest of the morning until time to take Annie to her appointments at noon. We are late. Shocker that. She goes in through the isolation entrance (for lepers such as us) and I look for a place to park. I find one not too far away and make the trek back. We are there for three hours while they take blood, we wait for the results and then talk to the doctor. He tells us the fourth round of chemo for Annie is no longer an option. She is taking too long to recover from round three. Her blood is still not rebuilding. Her ANC is still at zero. She is excited about the possibility of going home. I am not excited about going home with her having no immune system and not finishing the protocol treatment for her type/risk of AML.

We go back to the store house and start packing for our move to our new apartment. Annie is taking her time, carefully folding everything in her room. I am wildly throwing things into the shopping cart. We set out for the first trip to Target House 1 with overloaded shopping carts full of our stuff. We haven't even made a dent in moving our things. How did we accumulate so much junk in 3 ½ months? The trip down the sidewalk is downhill. The carts start to move faster than we are. We lose a table that I had stowed underneath. I get it back in the cart. We make it down the hill, around the corner, in the doors, up the elevator and to our new room at the end of the hall. It is remarkably similar to our old room.

We unpack the first loads and Annie gets in bed. I try to convince her she needs to help, but she says her back aches and she is too tired. I tell her I am old and tired too. She says I don't know what recovering from chemo feels like. I tell her she doesn't know what being nearly fifty-years-old feels like. But I give her a pass. Chemo trumps being fifty. The last thing I need is for her to have a setback. I go back to our old apartment and finish the rest of the move on my own. Seven trips later I am finished. I am so tired I think I will be sick. But I am determined to get everything unpacked and put away tonight. Everything is in its place. Except Annie's room – she doesn't have a dresser in her room. The front desk tells me it is still on its way. We are also missing a couple of cabinets in the kitchen. I set things out on the counter. Everything is similar – but smaller – compared to our last apartment. When I sit on the toilet, I keep hitting my arm on the toilet paper holder. I feel like we have entered the land of the little people. But it is free. And clean. I am grateful.

I give Annie her nighttime meds, try to get her to eat – and fail. Did the groundhog see its shadow? I have no idea. I go to bed exhausted.

DAY 111 – Tuesday, February 3, 2015

I wake up at 4:30 to Annie saying she is sick and cannot sleep. She is throwing up. I get her green barf bag and some anti-nausea medicine. I stay up with her long enough to make sure she goes back to sleep. It is 5:30. Should I go back to bed or just get up for the day? I go back to bed because it is warm. This new apartment is cold all the time. I put the electric blanket on the bed and don't even think I am sleeping when the alarm goes off. It is 7:00. Time to get ready for work.

I get up and get to my desk (two steps away) by 8:00. I get an e-mail from a co-worker. He makes me smile with an e-mail that says he is in a good mood today. He is a good friend, but we have been at odds off and on lately. Today gets off to a good start.

I answer e-mails and put out the usual fires until time to take Annie to her appointments. We do the drop-off in the isolation entrance. I see a parking spot in front. But just as I am racing for it – as fast as appropriate in a hospital parking lot – another car comes from the other direction and nabs my spot. I think about using the valet, but it takes so long, I circle around one more time. Success. I find a spot. I make the trek back to the isolation entrance just as a car is pulling out of a spot right in front of the door. Figures.

I find Annie inside and we go into the room where we will be for the next few hours. Because she is in isolation, everyone comes to her. They test her blood and we wait. As we wait, I take calls and answer e-mails from work. Annie puts on her headphones so she won't have to listen to me. The doctor eventually comes in. The story is the same as yesterday. Blood counts still not recovered. But today her labs are not looking as good. And, she has lost more weight. They hook her up to IV fluids and send us home until tomorrow – when she will likely need platelets.

Back at the store house, I work until 6:00. Then I fix us a yummy ten-minute skillet meal. Annie wants to eat and watch TV in her room. I try to be a good mom and talk to her some, but she is not interested. She is Facebooking, Instagramming, and whatever elsing that she does. I am in her room talking to her when we hear a loud pop. We cannot figure out what it was. Annie thinks our new apartment is haunted.

I have a glass (or two) of wine and update the Annie's Army Facebook page. The hubs calls. He is on his way to pick up Red Bull at a basketball game. He has hired the eighteen-year-old (who is currently unemployed) to put down flooring in Annie's room. Since she may be coming home soon, we want to get her crappy, nasty carpet removed. In the process, he tells me the house is a mess. I am glad I am not there to see it. My sweet cleaning lady texts. The one that is still not charging me. I tell her she might as well wait until the house gets back in order. Later…in the spring?

The hubs tells me he doesn't yet have his plane tickets for the weekend. I get online and try to work out travel arrangements. Annie yells and says wants an ice cream sandwich for dessert. I am happy she is hungry. I give her the ice cream and forget what I am supposed to be doing online. I go to my room to get ready for bed and notice glass is all over the nightstand, all over the floor and all over the bed. What?? Then I remember the "pop" we heard. The lightbulb in the lamp on my nightstand has exploded into a million pieces. Are you kidding me? What next? I wipe and sweep glass trying not to cut myself until I think I have it all. I tell Annie not to even come in my room. I am sure I will be finding tiny glass fragments for a long time. I go to bed exhausted.

DAY 112 – Wednesday, February 4, 2015

I wake up at 2:30 a.m. to Annie saying she doesn't feel good. At this hour, neither do I. Since she is already up, I tell her to take a Benadryl. She can't find it. I am not very nice when I drag myself to the medicine cabinet and hand her the Benadryl. I want to be nicer. But at 2:30 a.m., I just can't. We both go back to bed. I wake up again just before the alarm goes off at 7:00. Surprisingly, I feel like I got a good night's sleep. I get up and start getting ready for work. I only have five e-mails by 8:00 and three of them don't require a response. Maybe it will be a slow day.

At 10:30, I take a break and look up the day's schedule at St. Jude for Annie. I thought the first appointment was at 12:30, but when I look, I see we were supposed to be there at 10:00. Rats! Annie is still in bed. I call A Clinic and they reschedule her appointment for 11:30. I get Annie up and start nagging her to hurry. I look at the clock as we are pulling out of the parking lot of the store house. It is 11:26. We are going to be late.

After dropping her off, I nab a fairly decent parking spot and join her in isolation. I work and take calls while Annie gets blood drawn for labs. She shushes me more than once. Annie has worn a wig today. She has braided her reddish blond wig and it looks cute on her. The nurses love it. She harasses one of the doctors that his clothes don't match. This is an ongoing discussion between the two of them. I am so grateful Annie enjoys the doctors and nurses at St. Jude. As expected, she needs platelets so we are moved to another room. She also gets hooked up to IV fluids which will have to be carried with her for 24 hours. We stay at the hospital finishing up until 3:00. Back at the store house, Annie gets on the phone with friends and is showing them our new digs while I finish up the workday.

Maintenance comes by to fix my light and reprograms the thermostat so it will be warmer too. The front desk calls and asks if I would like to have dinner brought up. Yes, yes I would. It isn't low bacteria, so Annie can't eat it. I make her some taquitos. She has a honeybun and ice cream sandwich for dessert. I am glad she feels like eating. My dinner arrives. A sandwich with goldfish crackers. Oh well.

At 7:00, I remember the hubs asked me to book his flights for the next two weekends. Some friends of friends that are very kind people that I don't even know have given us eVouchers from American Airlines. I get online to book the flights. I get to the payment info, but there is no place to input the eVoucher. I think maybe I wasn't supposed to use his

AAdvantage number. I start over. I book the flights again...go through everything again. Many screens later I am at the payment screen once again. And once again, there is no place to input the eVoucher. I call the customer service number and wait on hold for twenty minutes. Finally a woman picks up. When I explain my problem, she says, "Hold on." No, no, no, please don't put me on hold. I am back on hold. After a long while another woman picks up. She tells me I cannot reserve specific seats and use the eVoucher. Good to know. We get off the phone. I start over. I get to the payment information and it takes the eVoucher, but will not take my credit card. I call customer service. I am on hold for a few minutes when a woman picks up. In no time, I discover she is very bored to be dealing with a reservation illiterate such as myself. She tells me to close my browser. We will start over. I go back through all the screens. I have no idea what is different this time, but now the eVoucher and my credit card are accepted. I complete the reservation. She tells me after I get an e-mail confirming the flight, I can go back in and reserve specific seats. It is over an hour later. It is not easy to use eVouchers. The hubs has no idea how much he owes me.

After the reservation fiasco, I try to engage Annie in a meaningful conversation. At least watch TV together. But she is Facetiming a friend. Not interested in real facetime with mom. I get my Kindle and read *Unbroken*. Thankfully, I cannot relate to being starved or beaten, but I totally get having to submit to someone for whom I have no respect. I do it for work every day. Then I remember, I have a two-day reprieve from this person. Yes! I go to bed not dreading my workday.

DAY 113 – Thursday, February 5, 2015

I wake up at 12:30 to Annie texting she is sick and might be running a fever. I text back for her to find the thermometer. I don't hear back and figure she must be fine. I cannot make myself go check. She has become nocturnal and I cannot stay up all night.

I wake up again when the alarm goes off at 7:00. I lay in bed looking at Facebook until I get a calendar reminder that I have a webinar in fifteen minutes. Crap! I hurry to the bathroom to brush my teeth, but will have to show up for my workday in my jammies. Fortunately, no one will know…or care. I attend the webinar, then start my workday. After about an hour, I can't stand it. I take a break and go take a shower. I get ready and do my two-step commute for the second time this morning.

Annie has a day off today. I give her the meds at 8:00 and try to talk her into getting up. No success. But no fever after all. At noon, I go to wake her and give her the noon meds. She sits up and gets on her computer. Progress. A little later, the Marinol has made her hungry and she wants a honeybun. I'll take what I can get. I bring her the honeybun and some Skittles. The breakfast of post-chemo. I have two small, microwavable sausage biscuits for myself. Yum!

I work through the quiet afternoon, enjoying a small break from calls and e-mails. Annie's schedule at the hospital starts at 8:00 a.m. tomorrow. Ugh! I get a call from a co-worker that the OKC Thunder has been at St. Jude. Did we see them? No. Annie is in isolation. We are lepers. No contact with the other patients allowed. Brad Paisley better not show up now.

After work, the twenty-year-old calls. He has all his W2's and wants me to prepare his tax return. Knowing he will get money back, and he owes me money, I acquiesce. He puts my adorable grandson on the phone. Of course, I only hear heavy breathing, but I can imagine his sweet smiles. I miss them all. The daughter-in-law turned twenty-one today. I see the pictures of the alcohol she has bought on Facebook. Nice. I am hoping no one at DHS has Facebook. To help celebrate, I get some Lindt dark chocolate the hubs bought for me and mix it with a glass of merlot (also compliments of the hubs – he is forgiven for not helping me move). Ready to prepare the tax return.

I get everything input online except for banking information when I realize that this free return is not going to be free after all. Huh? If anyone qualifies for a free return, they do. I put the return away until tomorrow wishing I had used TurboTax. Annie and the twenty-year-old are Skyping. I see my adorable grandson. He is all smiles and apparently trying to grab the camera. So nice to be able to still see the outside world while in isolation. I finish *Unbroken* and purchase *The Giver* on my Kindle. I go to bed and start reading. A short while later, I cannot hold my eyes open and go to sleep dreading having to be at the hospital by 8:00.

DAY 114 – Friday, February 6, 2015

I wake up at 7:00 and start looking at Facebook. At 7:15, I remember we are supposed to be at the hospital by 8:00. We are going to be late. I get up, start the coffee and wake up Annie. I start getting ready as quickly as I can and at 7:38, it's not looking too bad.

The phone rings. It's the hospital. Our nurse says she just saw the schedule and since they are only doing labs, there is no reason we have to be there that early. We can come whenever we want. Oh well. Annie is out of bed before noon. But our progress slows dramatically. At 9:00, we finally make it out the door.

Annie has on another wig today. This one is darker – more her natural hair color. The nurse tells her she likes the lighter one better. The visits have become a fashion discussion. I work from my laptop while they draw her labs and she visits with the nurses. One of the nurses starts talking about babysitting, then about how fast her children are growing up, then about a Golden Book she loves to read called *Where Did the Baby Go?* I get all teary. The nurse says she didn't mean to make me cry. I tell her it's easy to do these days. Especially when I miss when my kids were little. I miss playing with them all day. I miss when they thought I was the smartest person on earth. I miss controlling where they go, who they are with, and what they eat! I can't even get Annie to drink water. Where did the baby go indeed?!

After the labs come back, the nurse says Annie will need to be hooked up to fluids all weekend (since she will not drink enough water). It will take a while to get the fluid bags sent over from the Medicine Room, so we decide to come back to the hospital later. Back at the store house, Annie gets online to decide where she wants to go for her Make a Wish. Since, we have been split up as a family for four months already, her wish is to take a trip with us altogether in a fun place. (At least this is what I convince her that her wish should be.) We talk about Australia (she has been told to dream big!), but the flight time is an entire day and when it is summer here – and our likely time to travel – it is winter there. Though it isn't cold, it would probably not be warm enough to get in the ocean. We talk about Europe. But she thinks we will just look at things, so Europe sounds way too educational to her. We talk about other places. She lands on Hawaii. (Also a wish of mine. Imagine!) With snorkeling, fishing, volcanoes, Pearl Harbor and, for her dad, a luau with a big roasted pig to eat, Hawaii sounds perfect.

I work on my computer while she reads about each island. She decides on Maui. I decide I am liking this Make a Wish thing. At 3:00, I call the clinic. The fluids are ready. Annie ditches the wig and puts on a top hat instead. She looks very stylish. I take a picture as we are walking out of the store house. When I post it on the Annie's Army page, she thinks she looks like Michael Jackson. I am glad she is still smiling.

Annie gets hooked up to her fluids. We get instructions on changing out the bags and resetting the pump. More nurse's training for me. I really lament that I cannot handle seeing someone in pain. Otherwise, I think I would have made a great nurse. Well, except for in the middle of the night, or when fire alarms go off, or when things are on a strictly timed schedule. Okay, so maybe not.

As we are leaving, I get a text from work that they are having a small party to celebrate the close of a sale. I miss the party. Foiled again. But I am glad to hear the company will stay afloat a while longer. Annie and I go back to the store house and I respond to a few e-mails. Calling it a day, I make chicken strips and Arby's fries for dinner. I have finished off all the adult beverages in the house this week, so I have a glass of milk with my dark chocolate for dessert. Annie is eating well, and with the fluids going, she is feeling better. When I give Annie her meds, I take a Benadryl for myself. My nose is runny. Not good. I have been taking Airborne all week too. My eyes have gotten better. I cannot get sick.

I read a little more of *The Giver* while we watch LSU gymnasts on TV. We judge them. Considering we never graduated from cartwheels, we give them good marks. But like the old lady that Annie calls me, I am so tired I can't hold my eyes open. I go to bed at 9:00 feeling appreciative that Annie and I have had a good day together.

DAY 115, Saturday – February 7, 2015

I wake up early and lay there a while before looking at the clock. It's 1:15. Huh? The Benadryl didn't last long. I cannot fall back asleep. Knowing I don't have to get up early, I reach for my Kindle and read the rest of *The Giver*. It puts me in a funk. I start having philosophical thoughts like, "What's life all about?" and "Am I doing what I'm supposed to be doing?" and "Does my life make a difference…does anyone's?" I start praying that I am doing the right things…making the right choices.

Then I start doubting. "Does God really care about us?" Then I go deeper. "Is there really a place where God is?" "What really comes after I die?" "Is God really caring for my grandparents that have passed away?" Then I go shallower. "Do dogs go to heaven?" "If they do, will they be able to talk?" "What language will we speak in heaven?" "Does God know that it needs to be English for the Americans?"

I get a text at 3:59. It says "Great news. OK state has accepted your return." The twenty-year-old should get his refund. If I had been asleep, I am not so sure I would think it was great enough news to wake me at 4:00 a.m. Someone should re-think the timing for deliverance of their great news. Timing is everything.

I fall back asleep sometime after 4:00. Sometime after I have asked God to forgive my doubt. Sometime after I have thought about Jesus and what I have always told myself. Jesus is the only one to have not only raised some friends from the dead, but also raised himself from the dead. And surely since he didn't say he was just joking about being equal with God and just make wine for weddings, but instead he allowed himself to be beaten and nailed to a cross, he cares. His closest friends told his story. I believe them. And since Jesus is the only one to have conquered death, he is my ticket to eternal life. All he asks me to do is love God. Got it! And love people. Ugh! There's the rub. But I put away my doubting.

I fall asleep sometime in the middle of my self-pep-talk. I wake up again at 8:28 when I get a reply to a text from a friend. Glad for the early text, because I have missed giving Annie her 8:00 meds. I get up and give her the pills. She goes back to sleep. I make the coffee. It's the last of the coffee. I will have to go to Kroger. Can't survive without coffee. I come into the living room and see my Benadryl on the end table. That explains my lack of sleep. I never took the pill. Oh well. At least I didn't have to get up early.

I get a text from the hubs. Our Pikepass isn't working. Our credit card numbers have been highjacked a couple of times while we have been in Memphis. I forgot to change the Pikepass over to the new card. I try to do it online, but get locked out when I can't get password right. I try to call, but their offices won't be open until Monday morning. Ugh! One more thing. The upside is some of the random automatic charges that I have tried in vain to stop will also go away. Like those magazine subscriptions that I got "free." I never did get the charges reversed and still get several magazines I never read. Now, they will stop.

I get a text from Red Bull asking when I will be home tomorrow. Since the twenty-year-olds have moved out, I ask her who is staying with her tonight. She says she is staying home alone. I am more nervous about it than she is. She tells me, "I got this, mom."

The hubs will be here around 3:30. At noon, I decide to get dressed. Today is a dressing change for Annie. It should have been yesterday, but she talked me into waiting. I gladly agreed, since I hate to change her dressings. The hubs always has a neat little package when he is finished. I always have a jumbled up pile of tape that I hope will last another couple of days. Her bag of fluids is out. A good time to disconnect her and let her shower. After her shower, I start the dressing change. As usual, it is all crooked and unless I run the lines across her entire chest, they will be too kinked to run the fluids through. Annie rolls her eyes. She has told me no less than ten times how "Daddy does it this way." Now I roll my eyes. I can do this. I get out the Remove and start over. My second pass is much better. The line makes a J, then each lumen makes a perfect heart over her heart. I top it off with a nice square of Hypafix and she is good for a few more days. I get out the next bag of fluids and Annie helps me change the bag out of the motor. My phone beeps. A text from the hubs, "landed." I text "on my way!" But I am still helping Annie get the new bag of fluids going. I am going to be late. But the last time I arrived at the airport, the hubs had time to drive all the way there and park before my bag came out.

It is a beautiful day out, unusually warm, and I roll the back window down as I drive to the airport. The hubs texts that he is already at the curb. His bag came right away. Of course it did. But he is in a good mood and says he doesn't mind waiting. I see him at the curb when I drive up. All smiles. How I miss that man! We drive back to the store house to check on Annie, then leave to run errands. We have prescriptions to pick up at St. Jude and Annie has a list from Target including a fedora hat and false eyelashes. (Her eyelashes have completely fallen out. In fact, she has no hair anywhere on her body. Why was I worried about buying disposable razors?) The hubs and I go to Target. I stop off for Target popcorn, and we pick up the items on Annie's list plus of few other things. Over $100 later, we are headed back to the store house.

We spend the evening watching TV. The hubs and Annie watch the first *Harry Potter*. Do they ever get tired of that movie? I read through some of the magazines that have stacked up. The hubs makes dinner and I do laundry to get ready for my return home tomorrow. It is a nice evening. I go to bed and fall asleep wondering when we can go home for good.

DAY 116, Sunday – February 8, 2015

I wake up all during the night. Several times my own snoring has disturbed me. I am also not used to someone in the bed and the hubs' tossing and turning wakes me. I finally get up and make coffee around 8:00. I go to put in my contacts and my eyes are extremely swollen. Good grief. What does this mean? I find one of Annie's eye icepacks and strap it on. I give Annie her meds and join the hubs to watch the American Bible Challenge on TV with Jeff Foxworthy. It's as close to church as we can get. A St. Jude commercial comes on. I don't think I can watch those commercials any more. Watching scenes of our everyday life at St. Jude on the TV makes us both cry. Then we watch *Evan Almighty*. It gets to the scene where God (aka Morgan Freeman) is talking to Evan's wife in a restaurant about how God answers prayer. "If someone prays for their family to be closer, do you think God's answer is warm, fuzzy feelings? Or does he give them opportunities to love each other?" Wow. Why have I never noticed that scene? I am crying again. The swollen eyes aren't going away soon.

I start packing to go back to Tulsa via Atlanta – flying Delta this time. Another bittersweet trip. Looking forward to being back home and seeing Red Bull. Not looking forward to missing the hubs and Annie. After saying goodbye to Annie, the hubs gets me to the airport early. Of course he does. I get checked in with Delta and try to figure out what to read next. I buy *Looking for Alaska*, but am too tired to read. I get on the plane and stare into space until we arrive in Atlanta. We arrive on time, but I only have 45 minutes until my next flight leaves…15 minutes until boarding. I take the train to my gate and get there just in time for peasant-class boarding. Perfect. Delta serves free peanuts and pretzels with a drink. No such snacks on American. Bonus. With my coke and snack, I wake up a little and start reading *Looking for Alaska*. I had thought this would be about traveling north. Instead Alaska is the name of a girl. But the book isn't bad.

We land a little early in Tulsa. I get my luggage and head to the parking garage. The remote won't work for the car. I can't make the horn honk. I can't find the car. I call the hubs. He gives me directions. He has parked in the same general location we always do. He tells me to go down the main aisle as always and go to the left. I wander and wander, griping at him, sure that he is mixed up on where he parked. Then I realize when I came down the main aisle, I turned right not left. How can I not remember my right from my left? As soon as I go back the opposite direction, past the main aisle, I find the car right where he was saying. I'll keep that little secret to myself. I huff and say, "I finally found it. Will you please get this remote fixed?" He apologizes and says he will. He sounds eager to get off the phone. After I get on the road, I call him back to say I'm sorry. Before I do, I hear voices in the background. I ask him where he is. He sheepishly replies, "The Bass Pro Shop." I hang on to my apology and ask him to please not spend too much. He assures me he is under control.

Back at home, Red Bull gets the door for me. As soon as I walk in, she says, "Mom what gives with all the soup?" She walks in the kitchen and opens the refrigerator door. Huh? It has gallons of different kinds of soup. She says she has been told that we LOVE soup. I tell her someone asked if we liked soup and I assured them that yes, we loved whatever they bring. Soup or anything as long as I don't have to cook. Red Bull says all they heard was that we loved soup. We heat up two big bowls and have our dinner.

The twenty-somethings moved out over the weekend. They have a new rent house they will never be able to afford. I go up to see the damage the twenty-something's left behind when they moved out. As I suspected, their former room is a wreck. Red Bull and I get trash bags and rubber gloves and clean up the mess. Since Red Bull is riding with her teacher tomorrow and has to be at her teacher's house by 6:30, we get to bed early. I read a little about Alaska – the girl not the state – and have no trouble falling asleep in my own bed.

DAY 117 – Monday, February 9, 2015

The alarm goes off at 5:30 and I have to get up and get ready. I don't want to make someone late when they are doing us a favor. Red Bull and I grab a YooHoo for breakfast and make it to her teacher's house on time. It's going to be a good day. I make it to work by 7:00, and I am the first one in the parking garage. That's when it dawns on me that I forgot my keys to get into the building and into my office. It's a Monday!

I don't have to wait long until one of my co-workers arrives and I walk in with him. But since I can't get into my office until Captain Awesome arrives (he has my spare office key), I visit with all the other earlybirds and cause them to be as unproductive as I am. Soon he arrives, my office is open and the workday begins. I have a meeting first thing with the auditors that runs over and causes me to miss my weekly staff meeting. I hope the calendar police don't arrest me. I have two more meetings with the last meeting scheduled at 11:30. It's a morning full of meetings. Productivity at zero.

I get a call from the hubs midday. Annie needs a platelet transfusion. No surprise. Still no ANC. Disappointing. The waiting is brutal. I am hopeful she will build up her ANC soon, and we can go home. Her teacher at St. Jude has visited and her school lessons are back on track. He will be keeping up with her progress during the week. Something normal. Normal is good.

I have invited the twenty-somethings and eighteen-year-olds over to belatedly celebrate the twenty-one year-old's birthday. I stop off at Walmart to pick up a cake and ice cream. Red Bull calls. Someone has brought dinner. Guess what's for dinner? Soup. When I get home, my adorable grandson is there. He has taken his first steps this week and is doing the Frankenstein walk. Another friend brought over a casserole. We eat the soup (which is actually a yummy stew) and the casserole, sing happy birthday and everyone goes home happy. Red Bull and I clean the kitchen and go to bed exhausted.

DAY 118 – Tuesday, February 10, 2015

The alarm goes off at 5:30, but I lay there for another fifteen minutes. Red Bull doesn't have to be at her teacher's house until 6:45. I finally drag myself out of bed and get Red Bull to her teacher's house on time again. I am setting some kind of record. I make it to work by 7:15 with keys in hand and have a calendar request to reschedule yesterday's staff meeting. Bummer. At 9:00, I have another hour-long meeting that is basically a repeat of our last hour-long meeting. These meetings make me think of the movie *Groundhog Day*. I put on my best attitude and get through it.

At noon, I go to get my nails done. I find out Tom, my usual manicurist, has quit. I go to Becky instead. Becky tells me that Tom left without giving notice and has left her in a bind. She is nine months pregnant...due to have her baby any day. But she tells me she is only taking off for two weeks and should be back to do my nails next time. Two weeks? At two weeks after giving birth, I was still in a sleep-deprived fog, begging for narcotics. She is making American women look bad. She leaves my thumbnail a bit crooked, but when I tell her, she says something I don't understand, files it a second more and says "Okay now?" as she nods. She tells me she is much better than Tom. She says my fingernails are beautiful now. She nods the whole time. I find myself nodding and agreeing though the thumbnail is still crooked. Then she speaks something in Vietnamese to all her friends. They all laugh. She tells me they are just talking about her baby. Sure they are. I get up, wash my hands and pay knowing I'll be back in a few weeks. I think Becky practices hypnosis on me as she does my nails.

I get a call from the hubs. Annie is feeling better. She has the day off today. They are hanging out at the store house while she plays with her new false eyelashes and orders new things from Amazon. They even make a trip to Hobby Lobby to get supplies for some crafts to do to pass the time. I am wondering how much more money is spent when the hubs is in Memphis versus when I am.

Back at work, my face starts feeling really warm. It feels like I have been wind burned, though I haven't been out in the wind. Just when my swollen eyes are doing better, my face has big red patches on it. Did I get some weird fingernail dust on me? It's always something. The CEO comes by to see how I am doing. Has news of my red-splotched face gotten out? He sits in my office and tells me of upcoming plans for the company. He tells me he wants me to let him know if I am having any more problems. I have no idea why he is being so nice. I figure it is to get me through the audit and tax season. But I appreciate the effort. It is working. I find myself thinking this job is not so bad after all. Maybe Becky has called to let him in on her hypnosis secrets.

I work until 5:15 when I remember my Bible Study group is coming over at 6:00. Red Bull is supposed to pick the house up. I call her to make sure. She doesn't answer. I text her to please make tea. She calls back. She tells me she has already picked up the house and is already making tea. Love that girl! One of my friends arrives early and helps her get dinner ready. Red Bull is serving soup!

Our Bible Study is really eighty percent visiting and talking about all our problems and twenty percent Bible study. We eat our soup and catch each other up on all our troubles. Everybody has something. We watch a video about how to not compare yourself to other people. Good advice. Hard to do. It's time for them to leave too soon. We hear coyotes off in the distance as they are walking to their cars. Spooky. I check on Red Bull and we both go to bed. I go to sleep grateful for good friends.

DAY 119 – Wednesday, February 11, 2015

I wake up to the sound of coyotes. They are loud. They must be close. The alarm goes off at 5:30, but I am taking Red Bull to school this morning. She cannot be there until 7:30, which means we don't need to leave until 7:00. We get up and get ready, take our time drinking our YooHoos and leave at 7:20. I text Captain Awesome that I am going to be late. I take Red Bull to school and make it to work by 8:45. People with questions are lined up at my door. Job security.

Red Bull's school has early release today and she goes home with a friend. The hubs calls and reports that Annie needs two pints of blood. But her ANC has gone up to 200. The first time it's been above 100 in 55 days. We are trying to not get too excited, yet we both want to do the happy dance. Things are looking up.

I tell the hubs about hearing the coyotes. I tell him I am sure they are probably farther away than they sound. He says he would tell me something, but I wouldn't want to hear it. Why do people say things like that? No one ever replied, "Okay then, you'd better not tell me." Instead, I must know what he's not telling me. I tell him to quit being ridiculous and tell me. So he says he has seen where the coyotes are digging around our fence. I ask why they would do that. To get to some food, of course. He was right. I did not want to hear that.

After work, the accounting department goes to happy hour across the street. We get caught up and have a few laughs before I need to make the trek to pick up Red Bull at her friend's house. After picking her up, I see Red Bull isn't wearing a coat. She tells me she doesn't have one. I could swear that I pick up and hang up no less than a half dozen jackets and coats throughout our house every day, but I offer to take her shopping anyway. As we go into the light, she comments that my face looks better. It is only red on my left cheek now. I still have no idea what caused the weird rash.

The little town we are in has only four possibilities for finding a coat; Hibbett Sports, Stage, Maurice's and Walmart. Red Bull cannot find any coats or jackets she likes at the first three, and she will not take me up on my offer to go to Walmart. All I end up buying her is a T-shirt. We stop by Sonic and get M&M blasts for dinner. Glad Red Bull doesn't get visits from Annie's nutritionist. We drive home and both go to bed full of yummy treats. I fall asleep listening to the yipping of coyotes…not too far away.

DAY 120 – Thursday, February 12, 2015

The alarm goes off at 5:30 and I get up. My red splotchy face is much better. Maybe I can look normal for a change. We need to be at Red Bull's teacher's house at 6:45. We get ready and make it there on time.

Red Bull's teacher cannot bring her home today. I asked the twenty-one year-old yesterday if she could pick Red Bull up from school and take her home. She said the only problem was that she needs gas money. Of course she does.

This morning, I drop by the new rent house to deliver my debit card for gas. My adorable grandson is lying on the bed. He climbs down and crawls to me when he sees me. I pick him up and he hugs me. Worth the trip! I look around the little house. Not bad, but makes no sense to me to give up a big house that's free for this. But I appreciate their desire to be independent. I just wish I didn't have this eerie feeling that I'll be paying for this soon. I play with my adorable grandson as long as I can before leaving for work, and I hope that his mom remembers to pick up Red Bull.

The auditors are still in the offices and everyone is getting tense. We work all day filling requests and trying to get them to wrap it up. I wrap up my work by 6:00 and head home. Red Bull calls. Someone has brought dinner. Lasagna. A hallelujah moment!

I call the hubs on the way home. Annie had the day off again today. They hung out at the store house. He tried to get her to drink more since they removed her IV fluids yesterday. But she was gulping down water and threw it all up. Two steps forward, one step back. He felt bad that she had thrown up. I told him she threw up every day I was there so she is doing better. He felt better.

The twenty-one year-old and my adorable grandson have stayed for dinner. The eighteen-year-olds show up also. Red Bull has put the lasagna in the oven and they all watch *Supernatural* while we wait. I go pay a few bills and start doing laundry that has piled up. I have been invited to my nurse friend's house for dinner tomorrow, so I won't be able to do my laundry then. When dinner is ready, we all eat together and play with my adorable grandson. The lasagna and cheesy bread are from the Amish. I have never eaten anything bad that the Amish have made. Is there some kind of cooking test to be Amish? If so, I could never be Amish. While there are many other reasons I could never be Amish, I'll just stick with it's because I can't cook. I eat so much that I feel sick. Before they leave, the eighteen-year-olds ask if they can borrow my debit card to get supplies from Walmart. I loan them the card, but stay up until they return with it. When they get back, I load them up with the leftovers and remind the eighteen-year-old that his dad wants his help over the weekend with some projects around our house. He tells me he just remembered some things he had to do over the weekend. Of course he did. I need to go to Enablers Anonymous.

Red Bull goes to bed early. I finish the laundry and go to bed exhausted.

DAY 121 – Friday, February 13, 2015

I wake up when the 5:30 alarm goes off. Friday the 13th. I lay in bed until the last possible minute and rush around to make it to Red Bull's teacher's house by 6:48. I make it into work by 7:20 and run into a co-worker on the way in. I start my workday lamenting that Captain Awesome has taken the day off.

I spend the day putting out the normal fires. The joint interest billings have posted incorrectly, the revenue distribution has problems, and the auditors are still there with questions. Once again, job security. I eat almonds and Skittles for lunch and actually feel productive by the day's end. I pack up everything I can think of and plan for next week in Memphis. It would be really nice if next week is the last week in Memphis.

I get a call from the hubs. Annie's ANC is still at 200, but we are excited that it has not dropped. Her platelets actually went up a point with transfusions. We are hopeful. The boyfriend wants to see her for Valentine's Day, so I make plans to fly with the boyfriend and his dad on their plane. I haven't ridden on the little four-seater yet. I have never flown on anything but a commercial flight and am hoping my stomach will hold out.

Red Bull calls. She wants to go to a pizza party with her soccer team tonight. I tell her I am supposed to have dinner at my nurse friend's house. But I can hear the disappointment in her voice, so I agree to take her to the pizza party and afterward we will go to my friend's. She also wants to fly with us tomorrow. Her daddy gets her a commercial flight to come back on Sunday with him. It looks like a fun weekend is in store. I get another text from the hubs. "Clinic probably thinks I'm a pothead." I text, "Why?" He texts "I had to get a refill on Marinol cause I spilled them in the sink. Cabinet too crowded for my big hands. Sink was not clean...so I was afraid to give to Annie." I text, "Sure. Likely story!" He texts, "I offered to bring in the old ones. They gave me refill." Priceless.

I make it home from work by 6:00, pick up Red Bull and we head to Pizza Hut. Her soccer team has a room reserved and the one waitress assigned to the room is overwhelmed. I talk to the other soccer parents. The soccer cult is really the hubs' arena – not mine. But they did a fundraiser for Annie, and Red Bull really likes her coach. There are some new parents that I visit with. They find out that I am Annie's mom. The Annie from Annie's Army? Yes. They tell me they have kept up on Facebook with us and have been praying for us. They ask questions and I once again tell the story of how it all started. I always get weepy telling about when the doctor first came in to tell us Annie had leukemia. They are really understanding. They are moms. Red Bull and I are the last ones to get our pizza. After an hour and a half, we get our thin crust pepperoni. Pizza Hut does not disappoint. The other moms are already leaving, but one of them slips me a check. Says she wants to help with our gas money. It is super sweet. I am weepy once again. Should I tell her that it is mostly going for commercial airline tickets – not gas – because I am too spoiled to drive? I don't. I gratefully accept the donation. I am still amazed at how random people have been so good to us. Once again, I make a mental note to be nicer.

While we were eating, two more large groups came in to Pizza Hut. I feel sorry for the kids who are working. I have never seen this place so busy. They are scrambling to keep up. We go to the counter to pay and there are two women being really rude to the workers because their pizza was so slow in coming. They are having a really good time complaining. I ask Red Bull if I should explain to them that their life is really quite good if their biggest problem is slow service...at a pizza place...on a Friday night...in America...where it has only been a few hours since their last meal...and, by the way, all of the kids with them look very well-fed. Red Bull encourages me to let it go. I take her advice.

After Pizza Hut, we go to my nurse friend's house. As usual, she offers a glass of wine. Her mother is there and they have eaten hamburgers. I tell her we have already eaten, but her mother insists I try her cheesy potatoes and her garlic dip. I am not one bit hungry, but my friend has the kindest mother on earth. I would walk on hot coals for her. I certainly will eat whatever she wants me to eat. The potatoes and dip do not disappoint. Now I am thoroughly stuffed. My nurse friend tells me about another friend trying to figure out what causes cancer. Her friend believes it is because of all the unhealthy food we eat. Since everyone loves a know-it-all, maybe her friend should tell that theory to the Amish at St. Jude.

Too soon, it is time to go. Red Bull and I have to be at the airport at 7:30 to meet up with Annie's boyfriend and his dad for our Memphis trip. We say our goodbyes and go home. I finish up some laundry while Red Bull goes out on the back deck with a spotlight and tries to see coyotes. She is her father's daughter. But she doesn't have any luck and she is letting the cold air in. I tell her to give it up. We go to bed listening to the yipping of hungry coyotes...sounding closer.

DAY 122 – Saturday, February 14, 2015

I set my alarm for the normal 5:30. We don't want to keep the boyfriend's dad waiting. It's Valentine's Day. I have three blocks of wood with an "i" on one, the shape of a heart on one, and a "u" on one. They have clothespins on the back to hold pictures. A friend of mine gave this to Annie. She will never know. I pack it along with the only picture of the hubs and me that I can find. One from a Valentine's banquet we went to that was three years ago. The picture was still on our fridge. Now I have a gift for the hubs. I am congratulating myself on my resourcefulness. He will be surprised. He called me earlier in the week to ask if I wanted the usual flowers. But since I was coming back to Memphis and would only appreciate them for a day, I told him to just take me out to dinner in Memphis. He agreed.

Early in our marriage, he used to buy expensive gifts. I was usually unappreciative and complained about the cost. Then the book *The 5 Love Languages* became all the rage. I read it to keep up with my fellow Christians. That's when I discovered the hubs' love language was gift giving. Mine was acts of slavery. (I think that's what it was called?) So I began to understand his need to give me gifts. After nearly 27 years of marriage, he is still trying to give me gifts and I am still trying to turn him into a slave.

Red Bull and I arrive at the airport. It's 7:33. Not bad. We are only three minutes late. The boyfriend's dad takes us to the hangar and we see the airplane. It looks like a toy. I am thinking the worst. He asks us our weight. (He actually guesses mine – I'm thinking he could always get a job at a weight-guessing booth at the fair.) He has to arrange the bodies and bags just right so the plane can take off. This does not calm my nerves. We load up and take off. It is smoother than I imagined. It is extremely loud, but we each have headphones and can talk to each other through their attached microphones. I feel so high-tech. We listen as the boyfriend's dad talks to the air traffic controllers. I understand about as much of what is being said as I do of my Vietnamese manicurists. It is really fun and soon the flight becomes boring. Boring is good on a four-seater plane.

We land two hours later at a small airport in Memphis. Instead of the long, lonely walk to baggage claim, we are greeted by a man on a golf cart who invites us into the office for coffee and doughnuts while he gets the courtesy car. If I ever have extra money, I am buying an airplane. This is the way to go!

I haven't had any coffee all morning for fear of having to go to the bathroom on the trip. I get my first cup and attempt to sip it down. The hubs has always laughed at my inability to sip. He says I only know how to gulp. I usually put an ice cube in my cup so I don't burn my mouth on hot drinks. But there is no ice and I am dying for a drink of the steaming coffee. I carefully get my first sip. I suck it down wrong and it hits the back of my throat. I begin coughing and choking and slop coffee all over myself. After making a scene, Red Bull informs the other people in the office that sneezing will be next. She knows me well. Several sneezes later, the other people in the office can once again carry on their conversations. I embarrassingly eat my doughnuts and drink my coffee (and yes, I scorch my tongue). Fortunately, the courtesy car arrives soon and we are off to the store house.

Back at the store house, Annie greets us in the lobby and, of course, runs to give the boyfriend a big hug. We go up to the apartment, and the hubs is waiting to give me a big hug. I try not to cry at being back. While I am happy to see Annie again, this place is really starting to get to me. I am dreading another week in Memphis. I can't imagine what it must be like for Annie to see people come and go week after week and be stuck here…hoping to get well enough to go home. The boyfriend's dad leaves for Tulsa (the boyfriend is staying over until Monday), and after lunch, Red Bull and I take a nap while the hubs watches TV.

The hubs wakes me and we catch up for a while before deciding to go to dinner. He feels like Mexican food, so once again we decide to go to On the Border. Red Bull stays with Annie and the boyfriend. They are watching a movie. We get to dinner early, so there is only a fifteen-minute wait. We eat and stuff ourselves, even though neither of us were that hungry. Afterward, we go to the Bass Pro Shop and get a gun case that we can check at the airport. The case we get for my gun turns out to be too small and will need to be returned. I think the hubs did that on purpose so he can keep coming back to his favorite store.

We pick up McDonald's for Red Bull and get back to the store house early. Red Bull and her daddy start their usual teasing and wrestling and are loud and obnoxious. I go into the bedroom to have some peace. The thin walls make it impossible and I find a good white noise app on my phone. I play some Sudoku and soon Red Bull comes in, takes my puzzle book and starts working them herself. Soon, I am too sleepy to hold my eyes open and I go to bed dreading Red Bull and the hubs leaving tomorrow.

DAY 123 – Sunday, February 15, 2015

I wake up at 7:30 when the alarm goes off to take the hubs and Red Bull to the airport. He is holding onto me and warm in the bed. I don't want to get up, but don't want him to miss his flight. We get ready and they say their goodbyes to Annie. It is freezing outside. The hubs runs ahead of me to the car to open the door. I lament that I won't have someone to open doors for another week. I drop them off at the airport and drive away trying not to cry. I set my GPS for the Sheridan downtown where I pick up the boyfriend. He is staying at the store house with us tonight, since it is back to just Annie and me.

I pick the boyfriend up and we come back to the store house. We wake Annie. Fortunately, her daddy has gotten her out of her nocturnal lifestyle and she gets up and dressed right away. While watching *Groundhog Day* together (how fitting is that?), Annie makes a grocery list. I text the hubs to ask him where the Kroger card is. He texts back "In my wallet. Sorry." I decide to go to Target. Annie and the boyfriend decide to go too.

The boyfriend gets a text from his mom with the Scripture from the Sunday sermon. I mute the TV while he reads the passage to us. I say an Amen at the end. Our Sunday service is completed, and we leave for Target. After getting Target popcorn for lunch, I set out to get the items on Annie's list. Annie and the boyfriend set out to see what random stuff they can find that they don't need. We meet up in the checkout line where Annie puts the movie, *Divergent*, in my cart. She checks out through another line so she can talk to her friend, Aaron, who works there. When we very first came to Memphis, Aaron was working in our checkout lane at this Target. Every time since, Annie has found him and he wants to know how she is doing and tells her he is still praying for her. He always makes her smile. When she smiles, I smile.

We get back to the store house, I get some laundry going, and I go lie down to take a nap. I get an electric blanket, turn on the noise maker app on my phone and could sleep forever. But after a while, Annie and the boyfriend wake me up to ask about switching around the laundry, so I get up and finish the laundry.

We talk about the sleeping arrangements. Even though she is sick and hooked up to IV fluids, I still don't think I want them to share a room all night. The boyfriend will sleep in my room and I will sleep in the other twin bed in Annie's room. We make popcorn chicken for dinner, I write in my journal, and I go to bed in Annie's room hoping I can sleep in another strange bed and dreading trying to work tomorrow.

Baby, It's Cold Outside

DAY 124 – Monday, February 16, 2015

I wake up to the sound of Annie crinkling paper. What is she doing? I look over at her and she is sound asleep in her bed. The noise is coming from the window. I peek out the blinds and see sleet hitting the window. Yuck. Not looking forward to getting out in that. I go back to sleep and get up when the alarm goes off at 7:00. I get ready for work and make it to my desk by 8:00. I get texts from Captain Awesome. The weather is bad in Oklahoma too. Those with more than the two-step commute are going to be late.

The boyfriend gets up a little later and tells me he just got a call that his flight has been cancelled. I work until 11:00 and keep getting calls from the boyfriend's parents as they try to arrange for him to get home. Annie has appointments at the hospital at noon. The boyfriend goes and starts my car, scrapes off all the sleet and ice, warms it up and drives it around by the door for us. I am not too anxious for him to get a flight out of Memphis.

I drive down the narrow lanes of the street of Memphis. Driving in Memphis is not easy under normal conditions. The lanes are too narrow with no room to roam. And since lots of drivers have problems with roaming out of their narrow lane, there are plenty of accidents. Today, I am nervous about driving. Especially when I realize it's a free-for-all because the lines marking the lanes can't be seen. But I act like I have it all under control because I'm the mom and

262

that's what moms do. We make it to the hospital, and I drop off Annie and the boyfriend at the isolation entrance and pull into valet parking. No way am I going to hunt for a parking spot and make the trek back in the sleet. I don't bring my computer bag because I don't want to risk slipping on the ice with a heavy bag, and for once I am bored while they take Annie's blood and we wait for test results. Finally, the nurse comes in and reports that Annie's ANC has gone up to 400. A hallelujah moment! I see visions of leaving Memphis!

We make the drive back to the store house without incident and I start back to work. I have my weekly staff meeting call at 3:00. It lasts the usual hour. It's a *Groundhog Day* meeting. Afterward, I get a call from the boyfriend's dad. The boyfriend's early morning flight for tomorrow has also been cancelled and now he won't be leaving until tomorrow evening. Since school is out anyway, he doesn't care and Annie is very happy. When she is happy, I am happy. I also don't feel guilty about working because he is keeping her entertained. They watch all the *Home Alone* movies for the hundredth time while I work. The boyfriend makes chicken fajitas for dinner. I could get used to this. The boyfriend gives me some Melatonin to help me sleep (of course he does) and they begin watching *Liar, Liar* as I go to bed. I fall asleep wondering if I should be a better chaperone.

DAY 125 – Tuesday, February 17, 2015

I wake up sometime in the wee hours and realize Annie is not in her bed. I really don't want to get out of my warm electric blanketed bed, so I text her to come to bed. No response. I go into the other room and find the TV running with both Annie and the boyfriend sound asleep. Annie awakens with a start, hops up and goes to her bed. I think she is probably sleep-walking, as once she lays down, she doesn't even move. I get back in my cozy bed and fall asleep until the sound of my own snoring wakes me up. I roll over and wake up again when the alarm goes off at 7:00. Surprisingly, I feel like I have had a good night's sleep.

I get ready for work and make the two-step commute. I start answering e-mails and try to reconcile a few accounts. I can't get anything to tie-out. I feel like I have taken stupid pills. I repent of all the times I have criticized others for being dumb, because I am feeling really dumb that I can't figure some things out. Captain Awesome is irritated with me – and for good reason. We finally decide to switch projects. I make a little progress.

A maintenance man knocks on the door and says he is here to fix the TV in our bedroom. I look at him questioningly. He asks if it is working okay. Knowing that Annie and the boyfriend watched movies on it until the wee hours of the morning, I tell him there is nothing wrong with the TV. Smiling, he tells me he will mark that repair order off the list. Annie and the boyfriend make s'mores brownies for lunch. I eat one and feel better. I make more progress until time to take the boyfriend to the airport. I will miss him!

Annie has had a day off from appointments, so we have not been out. I am a little apprehensive about driving after all the sleet and snow, but we make it to the airport without incident. As we are pulling into the drop-off lane, the boyfriend gets a call that his flight has been delayed for three hours. Yikes. If I were more confident of my driving on the ice (and if I had more energy), I would offer to take him back to the store house and bring him back later. As it is, I ask him if he has money to buy a book to read. He says he does. He acts anxious to get out of Memphis. I feel bad that he will arrive so late back in Tulsa, but we say our goodbyes and Annie and I return to the store house.

I had forgotten my phone and follow-up on a few calls from work. I ask Annie what she wants for dinner, but she is in a funk. I am sad the boyfriend/butler has left too. I tell her to think about what she wants for dinner (the snack food choices are plentiful) as I finish up my workday. We are hopeful tomorrow's test results will show even more improvement in Annie's ANC and we can get out of Memphis soon.

Annie wants fish sticks for dinner and she preheats the oven. Not one to complain about junk food, I finish up work and pay some bills. I try to figure out the medical bills that are still rolling in from Annie's week in the hospital in Tulsa. But I am not educated enough. I need to call the insurance company to figure out which ones we owe and which ones I need to dispute. One more thing to do. When the fish sticks are ready, I make us both a plate. I get our dipping sauces. Ketchup for me, honey mustard for Annie (yuck!). Annie does not want to join me in on the couch, so I watch *The Middle* and play Sudoku and Text Twist all evening while she Facebooks and texts the boyfriend...who is still stuck at the airport. He finally gets a flight out at 9:05 and ends up spending the night in Dallas with friends of the family. I hope the visit was worth it for him. I enjoyed his acts of slavery. He spoke my love language.

Finally, I go to bed and read a little until I can't hold my eyes open anymore. I fall asleep hoping for better test results tomorrow.

DAY 126, Wednesday, February 18, 2015

I wake up before the alarm goes off at 7:00. I look at Facebook until time to get up. I get ready, give Annie her 8:00 meds and do the two-step commute. It is a slow work morning. A few random texts from work, but I am able to work on a few projects without interruption until it is time to take Annie to her 9:30 appointments.

It is still frigid outside. Thankfully, I remembered my battery-operated heated gloves this week and my Raynaud's doesn't have a chance to make me miserable. There is a new dusting of snow on everything. I would think it was really nice, if I weren't afraid of driving on slick roads. But the roads are mostly dry and we make it to the isolation entrance without incident. There is even a parking spot close to the door – the first time since we have been in isolation. We park and walk in. The wind is brutal. I forget my phone and go back to get it, but I can't find it and it is too cold to hunt for it. I go back into the hospital and start working from my laptop.

We wait for over an hour when the doctor comes in to report that Annie's labs show all her counts have dropped. Her ANC is down from Monday to 300. I feel like I have been sucker-punched once again. Annie looks like she might cry. But the doctor is optimistic and we still are hopeful we can leave Memphis next week. He says once her ANC gets up to 500 and is stable, we can go home. Once a week visits for labs in Tulsa should be good enough. They can transfuse, if needed, from there. When her blood counts recover to normal, we will come back to St. Jude for another bone marrow biopsy. Sounds like a plan to me. Since Annie's kidney function was okay, they didn't hook her back up to IV fluids, but she promises she will drink like a camel. I am thinking a battle is in store.

Back at the store house, she drinks one water bottle, but then falls asleep. After getting my phone back, I find I missed quite a few calls and I work all afternoon. I get a call from the office. Two of the accounting staff have announcements. One guy is getting married, another woman is becoming a grandma. I am happy for both of them. Happier still to have company in the grandma category...though I prefer to be called Nana.

I go to wake Annie after a short while, but she is out so soundly that her mouth has fallen open. I don't have the heart to wake her. I finish up working – actually get quite a bit accomplished – and finally wake Annie at 5:30. I don't want her to be awake all night. She decides on PF Chang's Chicken Fried Rice for dinner (another ten-minute skillet meal) and we eat our rice and watch the movie *Divergent* together. I actually watch the entire movie – except when I am cleaning up the kitchen, and sorting laundry, and texting. I text the hubs to ask if one of my friends brought dinner over. He replies "Yes...delish!" I watch the movie a little more. The main guy in it is really hot. I text my Texas friend to see if she has seen the movie. No, but she is watching *Sons of Anarchy* which has an equally hot guy. We laugh about how we are old enough to be the moms of the guys in these movies. Wishing the hubs were with me, I send him a lewd text. I get a prompt reply. "This is Red Bull. Let's keep this G rated please. DAD IS DRIVING!" Yikes! He needs to give me a code word when the kids have the phone!

The movie finishes. I clean the kitchen, write in my journal and go to bed. I fall asleep wishing today's test results had been better.

DAY 127, Thursday, February 19, 2015

I wake up at 5:40 and don't feel good. I go to the bathroom, get back in bed and hope for more sleep. I toss and turn and wake myself talking in my sleep. Finally, at 7:00 the alarm wakes me out of a deep sleep. I lay there until 7:30, then drag myself back to the bathroom to get ready. After Annie's 8:00 meds, I start my workday at my computer. Annie has the day off today. I settle in.

I wake Annie at 9:00 to give her another glass of water. I have started logging her water intake. She is not happy. I get several work e-mails from co-workers making mountains of molehills. I once again think about what I want to do when I grow up.

I get a call from a nice lady at Make A Wish. She asks all kinds of questions about Annie and tells me they will be in touch. I get a call from another lady who lives in Memphis. She is the friend of a friend of a friend and has heard about us and wants to bring some "goodies" by. A Good Samaritan. Fine with me. We arrange for her to come later in the day.

I get a call from the hubs. He says the eighteen-year-old cannot pay his rent and bills. Now that the twenty-year-olds have moved out, he wants to move home. The hubs says he will talk to him.

I get more random calls and e-mails from work. Lots of fires to put out today. A variance analysis that doesn't make sense, unexpected banking issues and cranky vendors. Job security, but quitting time comes none too soon.

The friend of a friend of a friend calls. She will also bring me dinner. Nice. Good Sam arrives around 7:00 with the supplies and my dinner. I make Annie come downstairs to meet her. Annie is all masked up. I take Good Sam back to where the Target shopping carts are stored and she takes a cart back to her car to load the supplies. I would go with her but it is freezing, and I'm not wearing a jacket.

She comes back inside with her daughter and introduces her. It's an awkward moment. What is protocol for acknowledging someone's generosity? Annie gives them both a hug. Thank goodness she is such a sweet girl. Do I invite them up? Do I show them around the store house? They seem eager to leave. Good Sam volunteers to run errands or get us anything else we need. I can think of several things: good test results, a new job, something to stop my gray hair from sprouting. But, unfortunately, nothing with which she can help.

We awkwardly say our goodbyes and I bring our stash of goodies upstairs. Dinner is delicious and she has brought all our favorites: Captain Crunch (with crunch berries), Capri Suns, Fruit Snacks and lots of loofahs for Annie. I should put her on speed-dial.

The hubs calls again. Isn't someone supposed to bringing him dinner? The meal train has been bringing dinner to our house every Monday and Thursday. We never asked for meals, but now that they have been scheduled for weeks, we kick back two nights a week and depend on someone else to feed us. What is protocol when the meal doesn't show? How long do you wait? Do you call someone on the meal train? I text a friend who I know has been hounding people to bring us dinner. (I am sure the whole community will be glad for the break when we return home.) Turns out it was her night. She is mortified that she forgot. I tell her the hubs will order pizza…but she owes me.

Annie finishes her third water bottle of the day. Not great intake, but the best I could force her to drink. I can only imagine the stories of waterboarding torture she is telling the boyfriend. We do some laundry, take out the trash and call it a night. I go to bed hoping for good test results tomorrow.

DAY 128 – Friday, February 20, 2015

I get a good night's sleep for a change. I wake for the first time when the alarm goes off at 7:00. I think I was snoring, but if there is no one there to hear, does it count? I look at Facebook for a while and get in the shower at 7:30. Then I remember Annie has labs at 8:30. Crap! I storm into her room and wake her at 7:45. I tell her she has thirty minutes. Hurry up! She moans and rolls over. We're not going to make it on time. I give her the 8:00 meds and finish getting ready. Why did they schedule a teenager so early? I don my heated gloves, Annie bundles up and we head for St. Jude.

We are only a few minutes late and of course there is no parking. I drop her off at the isolation entrance and drive to the valet parking. It is so cold, for the first time the man taking my keys asks me to step inside to keep warm while he writes down my information. I walk through the Chili's Care Center to isolation instead of taking the shorter route outside. It's been a while since I have been through the halls. Looking at all the bald, sick kid's faces and the tired, weary parent's faces always makes me sad. I find Annie in isolation and we settle in to our little room. I pull out my laptop and start working. She rolls her eyes and tries to ignore me.

After a couple of hours where Annie visits with the nurses and takes a short nap, we get the lab results from our nurse. ANC is back to 400, but hemo has dropped. Not the results we need to go home. No transfusions today though. They want to hold off as long as we can to try to give Annie's body a chance to make its own blood. Annie is in a funk. I go back to the valet to get the car and call the hubs. I tell him he can go ahead and make our usual flight plans for the next two weekends. He pays extra for the insurance on the tickets – just in case.

As I am getting in the car it starts to sprinkle. Right after Annie gets in the car, it starts to rain. The rain is freezing on the sidewalks. By the time we get back to the store house, it is blowing a hard rain and even colder than when we left. Now I am grateful for the early morning appointment. I get to avoid driving on slick streets again. We come back up to our apartment and I crank up the heat. We settle in and I start back to work.

The front desk calls. Annie has a package. A friend of Annie's that moved to Louisiana has sent a "Get Well" banner signed by a bunch of Louisiana gals. It cheers Annie up. When Annie is cheered, I am cheered.

I make Ramen noodles for lunch at Annie's request and get back to work. I work all afternoon and into the evening. I lose track of time. Every time I think I will finish just one more thing, the "one more thing" takes longer than expected. I heat up fish sticks and Arby's fries for dinner. Annie is in her room all evening on Facebook, listening to music, and working on some crafts projects.

Finally, at 9:00, I quit working and eat. Then I remember that I didn't give Annie her 8:00 meds. Rats! So much for my nursing skills.

I take her meds to her, make sure she still has plenty to drink and tease her about all the glitter that is everywhere. She was doing a craft with glitter and somehow managed to get the glitter everywhere. The way glitter multiplies, I can imagine future store house occupants sweeping it up for years to come. It is mostly gold glitter, and it sparkles nicely on Annie's bald head.

I get a text from the hubs. He is excited about our conjugal visit tomorrow. I am already in a funk about seeing him less than twenty-four hours for a whole week again. It has only been four months and I feel like we have been doing this for years. I go to bed at midnight and fall asleep looking forward to seeing the hubs.

DAY 129 – Saturday, February 21, 2015

I wake up to the sound of someone knocking on the window. Now they are shaking and rattling the window. I am wide awake with my heart pounding wondering how they made it up to the second floor window. I hear footsteps outside my door. I'm surrounded. Then my foggy brain realizes it is storming outside. The wind is beating the rain against the window. It is Saturday. I may have slept in, but others are up in the store house and though it sounds like they are in the next room, they are really just walking down the hall. Crisis averted.

I get up and make strong coffee. I don't feel good. I may have had too many adult beverages last night. The hubs will have to go back to the liquor store. I don't do liquor stores. Unless they are the big fancy kind with shopping carts and all of the beverages displayed in wide aisles by type, brand and cost. Then it is technically a department store, not a liquor store, and I can shop there. Also, if I am in Missouri with my best friends and have no responsibilities whatsoever for an entire weekend, I may enter any kind of establishment in search of alcohol, even in flip-flops and without wearing makeup. But I am not in Missouri, not with my BFFs and NOT responsibility-free. So I can't be seen at a liquor store. The hubs will have to go out in the rain.

I give Annie her meds at 8:00. She has been in a funk since yesterday. I try to get her to get up out of bed. She rolls her eyes and moans that it's Saturday. I'm not sure what difference that makes since every day is the same for her since we have been in Memphis. I try to get her to drink some water. She reminds me she threw up last night. I had forgotten that after I went to bed I heard her stumbling around. She came into my room to show me the green barf bag full of puke that she was throwing in the trash. Her way of saying, "Thanks, mom, for making me drink so much water that it made me sick." Foiled again.

I read my Bible for a change. I used to be an every-day sort of gal, but since being in Memphis, I haven't had any sort of routine. I quit trying to keep up with my Sunday night study group, since I haven't been to study since October. But I pick up the workbook where I last read. The readings are all about faith. The faith of Abel. The faith of Abraham. The faith of Moses. The faith of Rack, Shack and Benny (thanks, *Veggie Tales*). Do I still have faith? Faith that can move the mountain of cancer from our lives. Faith that I can still enjoy my job. Faith that my sons will make good decisions. Faith that the hubs and I will stay strong through the battles. I think on it for a while and I pray. I decide. Yes, yes I still have faith. Even so, Lord increase my faith!

The hubs texts that he was given the shake-down by the Gestapo at the airport in Tulsa. Though his gun is in a locked case in the bag he is checking, apparently (at least in Tulsa) they prefer you have a special TSA lock on your gun case. This was not in the requirements online. They finally let him go through security, but he will likely be on a terrorist watch list.

I do some laundry and ask Annie if she is hungry. She wants Ramen noodles, so I make us lunch. After weeks with no appetite, I have been really hungry lately. I see some leftover cake on the counter. When

Annie made cupcakes a couple of weeks ago, she froze the leftover batter. Two nights ago, she made it into the most delicious cake topped with the most delicious butter cream icing I think I have ever eaten. Annie isn't supposed to eat food left sitting out for more than an hour. But I notice there is a hole in the middle of the leftover cake. She says she dug into the middle of the cake so she could have a piece that had not been exposed to air. That's desperation. I give her a pass. I eat a little of the mutilated cake and put the rest in a baggie. No cake left behind.

Annie had made a cake instead of cupcakes because when we moved, I didn't get all of our bakeware or utensils out of the cabinets. Among other things, I left the muffin tin behind. Since she was with her dad when they bought all the extras for the kitchen, I didn't realize that a lot of the stuff in our kitchen didn't come with the store house. It belonged to us. I left it in the other apartment. They have both given me a hard time about it. But did either of them help me move? No, they did not. Besides, I consider it my gift to future residents. (But I hope they will not be telling their next-door neighbors about the assortment of bakeware and utensils in their apartment and their neighbors call the front desk to complain because they are missing their muffin tins and fancy stirring spoons and spatulas.) I have also learned how to think outside the box. Who needs a long plastic spoon to stir the drink mix in a pitcher when you can use a long-handled cheese grater just as easily? Multi-purposing. I think I am Martha Stewart.

The hubs texts. His plane has landed. I leave for the airport. It is pouring down rain and cold. I call the hubs when I get to the airport to say I will not be coming inside. I will park in the garage and wait. It's too cold for a movie style welcome. He finds me in the garage. While he is loading his bags in the car, I pour him a shot of apple Crown. I am good wife. I drive us back to the airport while he tells funny stories about his week. I am laughing so hard, I can barely drive. How I've missed this man!

Annie is up and in a talkative mood. I should have changed her dressing and claves yesterday. But the last time I did, Annie told me it was the best dressing change yet. I want to leave on a high note, so I get the hubs to change the dressing. I am his assistant, opening packages and throwing the trash away. Since Annie is telling her daddy all about the movie *Divergent*, we decide to watch it again. I watch the parts I missed the first time. It is actually a good movie when you put it all together. After the movie, Annie goes back to her bedroom to Facetime and likely to keep up with the Kardashians. The hubs and I go to bed early. I fall asleep dreading the trip home tomorrow.

DAY 130 – Sunday, February 22, 2015

I wake up early. The hubs has pushed me over in the too-small bed all night. I am pressed up against him to keep from falling off the edge. He is warm. My own personal electric blanket. I pretend we are in our own bed at home and it's just another normal day. I snuggle in more and warm my feet on him. He mumbles something that sounds like "That makes me love you more." But he is talking through his Frankenstein mask (also called a Cpap machine), so I ask him "What?" to get him to repeat his declaration of love. He answers, "That's NOT very COMFORTABLE!" Oh. I move my feet back. I reach for my phone to look at the time. It is a long reach. I am not on the edge of the bed as I had thought. In fact, I have pressed up against him so he is the one on the edge. Oops! It's 6:00 a.m. Too early to get up on a Saturday. But I feel bad for tossing and turning and, apparently making the hubs uncomfortable, so I get up and make the coffee.

I get ready and pack the suitcase along with my gun. Every trip back and forth I have this constant recurring thought, "What am I forgetting?" This morning is no exception. I don't know why I should worry about it. By this time, I have two sets of everything. Mostly I'm carrying my work stuff and books back and forth. This is the first time to take a gun. My stomach is a little upset. The hubs tells me I am being ridiculous. He tells me all I need to say at the check-in counter is, "I have an unloaded firearm in a locked case." I repeat my mantra over and over so I will get it right. I don't want to be slammed to the ground and strip searched at the airport.

The hubs drops me off at the curb and we do our usual goodbyes that leave me in a funk. I walk inside. When it's my turn at the counter, the lady asks me my destination. I reply a little too loudly, "I HAVE AN UNLOADED FIREARM IN A LOCKED CASE!" She gives me an incredulous look and tries another method. "Are you flying to Dallas?" "Yes. I mean, no...Tulsa." "Via Dallas?" she asks. "Yes." She looks at the lady next to her and says, "I don't even know what to do with this one." Does she mean me? Or my suitcase? My gun?

Or what? The other lady gives me a paper to fill out that says "Unloaded Firearm" and tells me to put it inside my suitcase. I put it in the outside zippered pocket. She tells me it has to be with the gun inside the suitcase. I move the paper to the right place, hands shaking. She hands me my boarding pass, and as I continue to stand there, preparing for the harsh terrorist interrogation to begin, she looks past me and yells, "Next please!"

The hubs calls to tell me he stopped to give cash to a one-legged black man we saw on the way to the airport. The hubs never judges, and usually gives to people asking for money. The hubs tells me when he handed the man the money, the man was rambling incoherently. The only words he understood the man say was "Thank you." But when the hubs started to drive off, he swears the man said as plain as day "She's going to get out this week." Taken aback, the hubs looked at him and said "What?" But the man was already rambling again. The hubs thinks it was a word from the Lord that Annie will be well enough to go home this week. I asked him if the man looked like Morgan Freeman. He did not appreciate my humor at his word from the Lord. We are both praying the man was a prophet.

The flight back is uneventful. I begin reading *The Girl You Left Behind* on my Kindle. When I get back, I follow the herd to the baggage claim. And wait and wait and wait. After 45 minutes, our luggage comes out. My suitcase is wet and a wheel is broken off. Wow. Welcome home. I should complain, but there is a long line of people in the same situation, and I just want to get home. I drag the suitcase out to the parking garage and quickly find the car. Thank goodness because it is 26 degrees and I packed my heated gloves in my suitcase. When I open the suitcase at home, the tag I had put inside to declare my firearm is gone. Did they take my gun out for target practice and shoot the wheel off? As I unpack, I hear Red Bull wants to take a trip to the mall. Apparently, Victoria Secret has "Pink" apparel that "everyone" is wearing. But at $50 for a sweatshirt, I talk her into being an individual, not following the crowd, and of course, wearing cheaper clothes. She orders a jacket online to get out of her shopping urge. I get out of going back into the cold.

We decide to watch *The Sandlot* for the tenth time, but then Red Bull figures out it's Academy Awards night, so we switch the channel and watch it instead. We only recognize a couple of the movies (our favorites like *The Hobbit*, *Maleficent* and *Captain America* didn't make it). But we watch until the end at 11:00 and go to bed exhausted. I fall asleep grateful to be in my own bed and for a good night with Red Bull.

DAY 131 – Monday, February 23, 2015

I wake up at 5:30 when the alarm goes off. I know this is a hair-washing day for Red Bull and I don't see her light on. I get up and go into her pitch black room. I turn on her closet light and ask if she is oversleeping. She says, "Huh?" I ask again if she is oversleeping. She says, "No", but quickly hops up and runs to take a shower. I am so sleepy I think I can make it if I just lie down for ten more minutes. So I do. I get up and start getting ready quickly. Red Bull's teacher is taking her to school and we don't want to keep her waiting. We make it only two minutes late and I get to work by 7:20.

Being the first one in accounting, I unload the dishwasher, make the coffee and pat myself on the back for being such a servant. The staff starts trickling in and I visit with everyone before getting things ready for my Monday morning staff meeting. I go to my meeting and we set a new record. One hour and 40 minutes of re-hashing things talked about week after week. Having endured my *Groundhog Day* meeting, I make it back upstairs and begin to work.

It snows on and off all day. I sit through two other boring meetings with low-productivity, but do manage to call my insurance company on my lunch break and get a few of Annie's medical bills figured out (those from St. Francis that were still unpaid). The hubs calls. Annie's ANC has reached 500 – the magic number to go home. It's a hallelujah moment! She has another appointment on Thursday. If her counts stay up, we can go home – for good!! Do I dare get excited?

At 4:00, the snow is coming down steadily and I can see cars slipping around on the slick roads outside. I send an e-mail to the staff telling them they can leave and be on the honor system with their time this week. (Because that's the kind of good boss that I am.) I leave at 4:20 nervous about driving on the slick roads. But I don't slip and slide too much, and the farther north I get, the better the road conditions. I make it home by 5:10. Very early for me. Red Bull is home by herself and tells me someone is bringing dinner over. A pasta-chicken-cheese casserole with bread sticks and salad. Yum! The bar has been set so high, I will never be able to cook for the family again.   Red Bull and I eat together and the eighteen-year-olds say they will be over later.

After dinner, Red Bull works on her algebra while I pay bills. She has found a website where she can check her answers. I am impressed 1) that she found this website that does the algebra and 2) that she really is doing the work and not just copying down answers. Maybe my fourth child will make me feel better about my parenting skills.

The hubs calls and says he is making potato soup for Annie for dinner and she is making cupcakes for dessert. It sounds like they are having a good time together. He bought another muffin tin so they are both happy, and I am forgiven for leaving the bakeware behind in the move. He says they took Annie off all her antibiotics in the hope that her blood counts would recover faster. I am willing to try anything.

After staying up late last night, Red Bull and I go to bed early. I read a little more of my book and fall asleep hoping Annie can come home this week.

DAY 132 – Tuesday, February 24, 2015

I wake up with the alarm at 5:30 and wake up Red Bull. We both get ready early and are on her way to her teacher's house ahead of schedule. That's when we see the railroad crossing lights come on and the bar come down. So much for being early. We arrive five minutes late instead. Oh well. I get to work by 7:20 and find someone set the timer on the coffee pot and it is ready and waiting. Love this staff!

I go back to my office and work until my co-workers start trickling in at 8:00. I respond to countless e-mails, but manage to avoid morning meetings and conference calls. Quite an accomplishment. Captain Awesome and I have a lunch meeting with a recruiter for a potential new hire for our accounting department. I enjoy the free lunch.

On the way back to the office, I turn down the wrong street. What is wrong with my navigational skills? I am losing it. Captain Awesome gets a big laugh out of it.

After lunch, I find I have several texts from the hubs and finally an e-mail that says "Call me" gets my attention. I call the hubs and he says he has been worried something was wrong when I didn't respond to him all morning. What is with the sudden paternal instincts? He tells me Annie's teacher came by and the hubs is all caught up on her lesson plans for school. He is getting in touch with the homebound teacher at the high school so she can finish out the year when we get home.

He also tells me he has gotten a rental mini-van for the weekend. I can pick it up at the airport when I get there. We can pack it up as well as our small car to bring all of our belongings home. He says he is going to tell the store house we are leaving. Whoa! I tell him to slow down. If Annie's counts drop we won't be able to leave, and I don't want our room at the store house to be given away. I let some of the air out of his sails.

His sails lose more air when he calls the airlines to ask about cancelling his return trip. We bought insurance on the last set of round trip tickets, anticipating that they might not get used. He is told that insurance doesn't mean the tickets are refunded. It means that you can file a claim and state the reason for your cancelled flight. If it falls in one of their permissible reasons, you can get refunded in ninety days. Guess we didn't read that fine print too well. Medical reasons are permissible for cancelling, but we will have to read more fine print to see what type of medical reasons apply. Something tells me that cancelling because your daughter gets to go home early isn't going to get us a refund. So much for flight insurance.

I work all afternoon and come home looking forward to eating the leftover casserole from last night. But the eighteen-year-olds beat me to it. There is nothing left but the empty pan on the counter. Plan B is popcorn. Red Bull has Ramen noodles. Red Bull joins me in the dining room and brings her algebra book.

With four kids, I have done so much algebra, I should be able to work the problems in my sleep. But because factoring equations doesn't come in handy in my day-to-day world, it takes me a minute to remember. Then, like riding a bike, it all comes back to me. I show her a short-cut method I learned back in the day. She rolls her eyes and says that's not how they taught them to do it. But I tell her, my way is faster. But she gets frustrated and says she is following the way her teacher showed her at school. So much for my help. I am old school. I go back to my popcorn and she goes back to being frustrated.

Annie sends a text of a recorded Skype. She has been skyping with the twenty-somethings and my adorable grandson. She is in Memphis and seeing more of him than I am since they moved out. I miss my adorable grandson. The eighteen-year-olds are moving in soon, so I won't get to feel lonely too long. I am suddenly feeling as old as my algebra techniques. I go to bed and soon fall asleep wondering how long before I have to start coloring my hair to hide the gray.

DAY 133 – Wednesday, February 25, 2015

I wake up at 5:30 when the alarm goes off. I wake up Red Bull and we start the morning routine. We get ready and on the way to her teacher's house, I try to make small talk. Red Bull isn't much of a morning talker. I try to make her laugh by saying silly stuff. She rolls her eyes and tells me I am not funny. I yell at her, "Oh yes, I am VERY, VERY FUNNY!" She is still not laughing. I continue to be obnoxious the entire ride. We finally arrive right on time at 6:45. I point to the clock in the car and yell "We are PUNCTUAL!" She gets out of the car and as she is closing the door, she sticks her head back in and says, "You are DYSFUNCTIONAL!" Then she blows me a kiss before getting in the car with her teacher. Mission accomplished.

I get to work by 7:20 and try to get a little work in before everyone else arrives. I work on answering all the e-mails that I didn't get to yesterday. As everyone else arrives, Captain Awesome announces that he is getting married. He jokes so much no one believes him. He has to call me in for verification. (I have never made a good liar!) So now there are two getting married in our department. I like to think it is my constant state of matrimonial bliss that has encouraged them to walk the aisle.

Almost lunch time, and someone has brought large chocolate chip cookies. I eat the cookies and work through lunch. I text the hubs and Annie that they need to make a scrapbook page to put on the wall of the store house. Everyone who stays at Target House gets to "leave their mark" by making a scrapbook page, which they display on the walls in the hallway. The hubs calls several times asking me about how to do it. I tell him to pick out pictures and send them to the Walgreen one-hour photo lab. Meantime, go to Hobby Lobby and tell Annie to look in the scrapbook aisle for paper and page decorations. He tells me this is really stressing him out. He has handled everything really well until now. And now after everything we have gone through, the scrapbook page is what is really stressing him out? They follow my instructions and get the supplies. He calls and tells me they spent $30 at Hobby Lobby. On one scrapbook page? I am glad it stresses him out. If this were his hobby, we would be broke for sure.

On my way home from work I call Red Bull and ask what she wants for dinner. She says Whataburger. Sounds good to me. After last night's popcorn dinner and today's cookie lunch, I am really hungry. I pick her up and ask if she will pump gas in my car. Having recently learned how, she wants to try again. Hating to pump my own gas, I am happy she enjoys doing it. We go get gas and then go get our burgers. On the way back, my car is so dirty we pull into a carwash. The attendant is just putting a cone in front of the entrance when he sees me pull up. He removes the cone and motions me to drive up. He tells me he will have to reboot the computer, but it will just take a second. He probably feels sorry for me since my car is such a mess. What a nice guy. I will get the detailed car wash. As we are waiting for it to reboot, he is making small talk. I ask him what the weather is supposed to do. He says the weatherman is calling for more rain and sleet on Thursday night. After the computer reboots, I insert my card and select one of the cheaper washes. Red Bull gives me a knowing look. Yes, I tell her, knowing bad weather will be back tomorrow, I just chose the cheap wash. While the attendant excels in customer service, he really needs to take some lessons in sales.

We go home and eat our burgers and go to bed early. I look at Facebook and read personal e-mails until I can't hold my eyes open. I go to sleep praying for good test results tomorrow.

DAY 134 – Thursday, February 24, 2015

The alarm goes off at 5:30, but Red Bull's morning schedule is different for the next two days so her eighteen-year-old brother (who just moved back in our house) is taking her. I can sleep a few more minutes. At 6:00, I get up and get her up. She hops out of bed and rushes past me in a huff. It is a hair washing day and I didn't wake her early. Who knew? Her brother comes upstairs before she is ready. He is ready to go. He is rushing her. Like father, like son. At least he is up and ready and seems to be in a good mood. He is very talkative, and knowing how she is not a morning person, I am hoping she will be civil to him on the ride to school. I need him tomorrow morning too.

I get to work and find a co-worker scrambling to get things ready for a big meeting. I offer to help, but think he is best served if I keep out of the way. The advantage of coming in before everyone else is having a few minutes to get settled in slowly before everyone else arrives. But I am not that early this morning. Everyone is asking me questions and needing something before I can get down the hall and back with my first cup of coffee. Need. Coffee.

I get anxious for test results and call the hubs in the afternoon. Nothing yet. Labs have been taken, but they are still waiting. Then I get a text with lab results. Annie's hemoglobin and white blood cells have dropped, but her platelets are up a little and her ANC has held at 500. I call the hubs, but he immediately says he's with the doctors and will have to call me back. When he finally calls me back, he practically yells, "We're going HOME!" I am sitting at my desk and want to scream or cry or something, but I keep still and say "Hallelujah!"

Then begins the scramble to talk to our hometown doctor and find out about getting records transferred, the place where she can get labs and transfusions, and how to navigate the next few weeks. I have a mini-anxiety attack as I think about everything returning to "normal" again. I haven't been home with the hubs at the same time in quite some time. I have enjoyed people bringing food twice a week that lasts a good part of the week. And I will have to start paying my sweet cleaning lady again! All the changes back to normal are worth it to have Annie coming home and cancer-free.

Red Bull calls and says someone is outside in a car. The eighteen-year-old says he heard the doorbell ring but didn't go to the door. Red Bull says it's a woman in a car. I tell her to open the door. It is probably someone bringing dinner. She says she opened the door, but the woman is on the phone and not looking. I tell her to go to the car. It is probably someone bringing dinner. She says it's too cold outside. I tell her, "OPEN THE DOOR, THEY ARE PROBABLY BRINGING DINNER." I hang up on her and call the eighteen-year-old and scream at him "OPEN THE DOOR! DON'T MAKE IT HARD FOR SOMEONE TO BRING US DINNER!" He says his dad is on the phone with Red Bull. He has told her to open the door. Someone is there with dinner. When did my children become incapable of communicating with the outside world?

Turns out it was a dear friend of mine, who happens to be a great cook. I tell them I am on my way home and they better save me some dinner after all the trouble it took to get it in the house. They ask me to stop at the store and get drinks and cat food. I tell them I will go through the drive-thru and get drinks, but it is too cold to get the cat food. I leave work, get three cokes at McDonalds, and make it home to find enchiladas and chocolate cake. Yum!

We eat dinner and Red Bull tells me about her day. Annie has finished her scrapbook page and put it on Facebook. The hubs is getting boxes to start packing. The eighteen-year-old is moving his dresser back upstairs. I go to bed thinking about life returning to normal.

DAY 135 – Friday, February 27, 2015

I wake up at 4:00. I can't sleep. My stomach hurts. Why did I eat so much yesterday? I lay there until 5:30 when I feel it is a sane time to get out of bed. I start getting ready and try to find a phone charger. Mine is at 31%. Someone has stolen my charger from my room. Since Red Bull has a charger, that leaves the eighteen-year-old. Ugh! This is a recurring problem. Do all families misplace phone chargers like ours?

The eighteen-year-old is taking Red Bull to school, so I leave for work at 7:00 when they leave. There is no traffic. I wonder where everyone is. I use the time to think and pray.

I pray Annie would be completely well and we would never worry about cancer again. I pray my boys would find their purpose in life and start living up to their potential. I pray for the hubs and I to get along okay after we have spent four and a half months separated. I pray that if I am in the job I am supposed to be that it will be fun and rewarding again. I pray for all my extended family, my friend's children and children of my friends. I pray for all my co-workers and their children. Even the co-workers that I don't like.

I think about all those with babies at work. Seems the baby fever is going around among the young couples. I encourage them to bring the babies to work because I love to hold them. We all stand around and say "Look at those eyes. Aren't they a content baby! Look at those little feet and their sweet expressions." I think we should bring our thirteen-year-olds to the office. We could stand around and say, "Look how they roll those eyes. Aren't they moody! Look at those trendy and overpriced shoes on their feet and their totally-bored-with-you expressions." No one prepares you for that at the childbirth classes.

I make it to work and it is bitter cold. With my car in the garage at home, I don't really get a feel for how cold it is. But the parking garage at work is open on the sides and the wind is brutal. I make it into work and turn on my space heater. I get it so warm in my office that no one wants to come in. A great way to avoid disturbances. I get a lot of work done and the big sale also gets done. The CEO sends an announcement that we will celebrate the close of the sale on Monday and also the return of Annie Lindsey. My heart is warmed that he would want to celebrate Annie's return alongside such a big company event.

About 4:10, the CEO sends another message that we better get home if we are going to be safe. It has been snowing all afternoon, and Tulsa doesn't do snow well. I can see cars sliding in the parking lot. I pack up quickly and go downstairs with everyone else in the exodus. My drive home takes twice as long as normal. Just when I am turning on the county road to my house, the car in front of me spins around and lands in the ditch. The driver motions me past. I creep down the county road to my house. It is 5:20 and the school bus is still dropping off by my street. Finally, I coast down into the garage. The eighteen-year-old is going out to play on the four-wheeler in the snow. He agrees to take me to the airport in the morning.

The hubs texts to tell me Red Bull went home with a friend and needs to be picked up. She will have to spend the night. I am not going back out. He has also bought boxes and given notice at the store house. I hope the roads don't get too bad for us to drive home on Sunday. The hubs will drive no matter what. He wants desperately to come home. And I'm with him.

I check on my flight for tomorrow. Cancelled. Ugh! I call American Airlines. The wait time is over two hours. I leave my name and number. I eat some popcorn for dinner, change into my jammies and wait for the phone call. I finish reading a book that Red Bull said I would like called *One for the Murphys*. She is right. It's pretty good. I finally can't hold my eyes open, and I fall asleep hoping I make it to Memphis tomorrow.

The phone rings. It's a very nice lady from American Airlines. The problem is with the flight to Dallas. They are having issues. She gets me on a Delta flight to Memphis via Atlanta for tomorrow afternoon. I am wide awake and have trouble falling back asleep. I text the hubs to give him the news. I finally fall asleep praying for better weather.

DAY 136 – Saturday, February 28, 2015

I wake at 7:00 when the alarm goes off. Today is the hubs birthday. Sort of. He is a leap year baby, so technically he doesn't have a birthday this year. I will wish him a happy birthday anyway. (Because that's the kind of wife I am.)

I look outside. It's snowing. I can't even see where my driveway ends and the yard begins. Not good. I get up and do some laundry. I check my new afternoon flight to make sure it hasn't been cancelled. It's still a go, so I wake the eighteen-year-old and ask him to drive me to the airport. He starts his little SUV, which is a four-wheel drive, and he clears all the snow off of it. We make it to the airport without any problems and I am very early. I eat a Quizno's sandwich and start reading *1000 White Women*. Another good recommendation from my Texas friend. We board the plane on time and then sit and sit and sit on the runway. It takes them over an hour to de-ice the plane. I text the hubs that there is no way I am going to make my connecting flight in Atlanta. Bummer.

I try to make small talk with the man sitting next to me. But he puts on his headphones and acts like he doesn't speak English. Maybe not an act. I have snubbed many people on these plane rides, but it is the first time I have been snubbed. I don't think I like it. I would much rather be the snubber instead of the snubbee.

Finally, the plane takes off and, just as I feared, by the time we land, my connecting flight is leaving Atlanta. They book me on another plane and I go to TGIFriday's to wait for my flight two and a half hours later. I sit at the bar and read my book. I visit with people coming and going. The woman next to me has missed the last flight out to Springfield for the evening. She is trying to get a hotel and not very happy. Just as I am finally leaving to catch my plane, she asks where I am headed and I tell her St. Jude and about Annie's diagnosis with AML. She says her ex-husband had AML ten years ago. I sit back down and listen to her story. I sit there too long. By the time I make it to the gate, it is five minutes from take-off and all the other passengers have boarded. I almost missed the last flight out from Atlanta. What was I thinking?

I am so tired and looking forward to a quiet ride to Memphis. I sit next to a woman on the plane who is from California and who cannot stop talking. I go from being snubbed to being held hostage. I listen and try to nod occasionally. She is very nice and when I manage to tell her why I am headed to Memphis, she pauses in her chatter for just a moment while she thinks. Then she tells me she has a good feeling about Annie. She is going to be fine. I'll go with that. Then she resumes telling me every detail of her life.

We finally arrive in Memphis and when I get to baggage claim, the hubs and Annie are waiting and all smiles. Ahhh...what a sight for sore eyes! I give both of them movie style hugs. The hubs grabs my bags and we take off for the store house. Annie is feeling good and is talkative the whole way. I love to see her in such good spirits. Everyone is so excited about getting out of Memphis tomorrow that it takes us a long time to unwind and go to bed. I go to sleep with nightmares about missing flights.

DAY 137 – Sunday, March 1, 2015

I wake up when I notice the sun is up. I have tossed and turned all night. I am still upset that I nearly missed my flight. I need to let it go. All is well. We all get up and start packing the remaining things. We have an SUV we have rented. We had reserved a mini-van a week ago, but when the hubs went to pick it up, there were no mini-vans available. We laugh how it is like the *Seinfeld* episode where he goes to pick up his rental car. Like Seinfeld says, "They know how to "take" a reservation, but they don't know how to "hold" a reservation. And really the "hold" is the most important part. Anyone can just "take" them."

We have to check out with the front desk. They do the room inspection, we carry out the last of our belongings and the hubs is in tears. I think I am still in shock. This whole experience has seemed so surreal that I wonder when everything will finally hit me. The hubs drives the SUV, I drive my little red car, and we drive out of the store house for the last time. Annie takes a picture of St. Jude from the car as we drive by on our way out of Memphis. I try to hold it together. We are headed home.

The drive between Memphis and Little Rock is brutal. The highway is terrible and it is raining. There are so many semis on the road, it looks like railroad cars going down the highway. Driving next to them brings visibility to zero when the wind sprays the rain all over the car. Annie chatters for the first hour, but then falls asleep so soundly her head falls back and her mouth falls open. At Little Rock, the rain clears for a while and the highway is smoother. We stop in Conway for lunch and get a couple of hours normal driving until we turn off I-40 and head north in Oklahoma. Then the blowing rain continues off and on until we get back home. The eighteen-year-old texts when we are close and asks if we are bringing dinner because there is nothing to eat in the house. Some things never change.

Finally, we pull up in the driveway. We sit there a minute. It's been four and a half months since Annie's daddy took her to the ER and our nightmare began. Four and a half months that I would never have dreamed I could have survived. Four and a half months that have made us stronger.

I look over at Annie and say, "Welcome Home!"

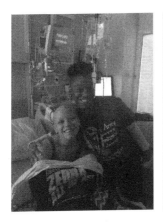
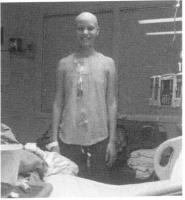

EPILOGUE

Sunday, July 12, 2015

Going back. I woke up at 8:00 with that in my head. We are going back to Memphis today. It will be our second trip back since leaving on March 1. We went back two weeks later to remove Annie's Hickman. That was a great day. We also used that trip to go to Graceland. After all the time we spent in Memphis, I finally got to visit Graceland. Red Bull became an instant fan. Annie, not so much.

But now it has been nearly four months since we have been back. Today is Sunday. We talked about going to church as usual, but nothing seems usual about this day. Everyone is a little apprehensive. We haven't been back since March. Four months of normal. Other than Annie's weekly trips for blood testing – which indicate nothing out of the ordinary – everything has been normal. Normal enough for Annie to get her driver's license. Normal enough for Annie to get her first speeding ticket. Normal enough for Annie to have her first fender-bender. Yes it has been normal.

After sleeping too late to attend the blue jean service with the Methodists (our normal), I get up and get in the shower. Afterward, I wake up Annie and Red Bull and tell them to start getting ready for the trip to Memphis. Red Bull comes and throws herself on our bed. She loves irritating her daddy. Today is no exception. She yells at him to wake up while I finish getting ready. The hubs moans and Red Bull laughs. Irritating, but normal. I can do normal.

We leave for Memphis around noon in Annie's car. She has named her car Carlos. I can't remember why, but it has stuck. Red Bull wants to take the hubs' new truck, but since Carlos gets better gas mileage and Red Bull isn't buying the gas, we head off to Memphis in Carlos.

Everyone is hungry. Hungry and apprehensive is not a good combination. We don't make it past the next town before stopping for gas and snacks. With promises of Mikey D's on the turnpike, Red Bull selects grapes as a healthy snack to go with our cokes. Now we are ready to travel.

A six-hour drive is not fun no matter what good parents you try to be. I quickly tire of singing along to their music. When I change the station to country, the girl's earbuds are inserted. I can still hear the beating of the bass coming from Annie's iPhone, but with all she is going through this weekend, a little hearing loss is the least of my worries.

The hubs is the official road trip driver, but I am responsible for entertainment. I pull out my Kindle. I have been reading chapters of James Herriot's *All Creatures Great and Small*. I read four chapters and after the Mickey D's stop and another bathroom break on the interstate, we are coming into Little Rock. I dread the remaining couple of hours knowing the road gets considerably worse. The last time we drove this route, I feared my car wouldn't make it. I have been told this is a "trucking route", meaning "due to heavy loads that were only meant for the railroad, this highway is full of giant pot holes that swallow small cars." We are pleasantly surprised when a good portion of the highway has been repaired and we are able to carry on a conversation at normal decibels with much less gasping noises until we are about an hour outside of Memphis.

Driving across the Mississippi River quietens everyone. There is a sense of foreboding. All of us just stare until we see the "Welcome to Tennessee" sign and Annie says, "We're back!"

After checking into the Sheraton and much debate about where to eat dinner, we decide to walk a couple of blocks to a restaurant called Westy's. Walking in the evening in downtown Memphis is no small feat. I wonder if we have come this far only to be mugged and killed underneath a bridge. But the girls are fascinated with the cameras installed under the bridge and I think I make them feel safe by telling them, "Mama's packin' and her hand is on the trigger."
After a dinner that will take hours at the gym to work off, we take a late night swim at the Sheraton and I fall asleep exhausted. Being normal is hard.

Monday, July 13, 2015

I wake up early, but don't want to wake anyone else. We have a free day today before Annie's tests at St. Jude tomorrow and I am determined not to spoil it. Every other time we have been here, I have ruined the trip at some point by working. Not today. In May, I started a new job. A job where I can take a day off during the work-week and actually not work. A job where I am trusted and my work is respected. Normal. It feels like I have been released from prison.

I creep into the bathroom and get ready quietly. The hubs and I told the girls we would go to the zoo today. Red bull swears she has never been to the zoo. She just doesn't remember the wonderful mom I used to be...about seven years ago. I get ready and they are all still snoozing at 8:30. We were going to be at the zoo by nine. Obviously, not happening. I pull back the thick drapes bringing the blinding sunlight into the room and yell, "It's a beautiful day, the sun is shining, the tank is clean!" Right on cue, Annie sits up in bed and yells, "The tank is clean?!" The hubs, not exactly a first-responder, raises up looking a bit crazed and yells, "What...what, WHAT IS IT?" Red Bull never budges. Annie and I look at each other. She says, "Never mind!" If you have to explain your jokes, it's just not worth it.

We get to the zoo and take the obligatory picture at the front gate. We are all smiling. Of course we are. We haven't yet experienced the 100 degree temperature outside the smelly rhino cage. I have never been a zoo fan, but what kind of a parent doesn't take their kids to the zoo? Especially when Annie is an animal lover. She runs from exhibit to exhibit saying, "Oooohhh, this is my favorite animal!" I am careful to take the pictures...document the moment. Prove I can be a good mom.

After we sweat off a few pounds at the zoo, Annie says she wants to see her scrapbook page on the wall at the store house. She "left her mark" by making a scrapbook page which they mounted on the wall after we left and she wants to see it.

Driving in the gates is surreal. It is hard to go back. I feel like I am going back in time and it's all I can do to keep from getting sick. I try to think of only the positive. I can do this. We check in and go up to the second floor where we lived. There is her page on the wall. The hubs takes pictures and we look at some of the other recent pages. The little girl's page next to Annie's reads "AML and Down Syndrome." Geez! You have to be kidding! I tell the hubs I need to leave. He is more than willing to get out of there. Thank God for Target House, but I hope I don't ever have to go back.

After the zoo and store house, we go back to Tri Delta where we are staying for the night. The sorority house is also a bit hard to come back to, but Annie says it feels like home. I don't like admitting that I feel the same way.

We rest up and take off on the adventure the hubs has been waiting for. The new Bass Pro Shop in Memphis has opened at the Pyramid. The entire time we were living in Memphis, he was teased and tormented by advertisements announcing its future opening. The grand opening was right after we left. We can't come back without seeing what all the hubbub is about.

We get there early in the afternoon thinking it won't be crowded since it is a weekday. We are sadly mistaken. Though the parking lot is full, we find a spot that doesn't require the shuttle and make it inside before melting in the heat. It is a small city inside. We pay the ridiculous price to ride the elevator to the top of the pyramid and stroll around the "Top of the World." Well, at least the top of Memphis. From this height, we can pretend the inner city is a magical world. After spending another ridiculous amount of money on appetizers and drinks just to say we did, we go eat ice cream at Maggie Moos downtown.

By the time we get back to the sorority house, we are all literally sick from overeating. The clean room and soft bed make it easy to fall asleep early. I fall asleep thinking it was a good day and trying not to think about tomorrow.

Tuesday, July 14, 2015

I wake up at 5:00 and can't go back asleep. I refuse to get up this early on a vacation day. I check my work e-mail, but there is nothing. I only got a couple of e-mails yesterday and both were easy to answer. I can't get used to having a normal job. I keep waiting for the other shoe to drop. I decide to just enjoy the freedom and go back to sleep.

My alarm goes off at 7:00 and I need to get up. Annie has appointments at St. Jude beginning at 8:30. I creep to the bathroom, but Annie is already awake. Today is different. Everyone is anxious. No one is sleeping in. Everyone is crabby. The hubs takes a quick shower and goes down to the dining room for breakfast. Red Bull is quick to follow. Annie and I take our time, but we are ready when they return and say it's time to walk over to the hospital. I put on my game face and we take off.

Annie has labs first, so Red Bull and I sit in Registration and play Text Twist while Annie and her daddy go back to have her blood drawn. After a short time, they return and Annie has an IV line inserted in her arm in preparation for her later "procedure." We all go to the gift shop to kill time. We buy several T-shirts and other St. Jude logo items in our continued support of finding a cure.

While we are waiting for the lab results, Annie, Red Bull and I go up to the second floor where Annie spent so many weeks. As soon as the smiling nurses come up to give us a hug, I nearly have a breakdown. I don't think I can do this. I can't talk normally. They took care of us for months when I was at the absolute lowest point in my life. They deal with sick and dying children on a daily basis. I feel like they should be the ones crying. But, they are still smiling. I don't know how they do it. I let Annie do all the talking. She has no problem with that. Everyone loves Annie.

We make it back to A Clinic, and after just a few minutes of Text Twist, her name is called. We see the doctors who also love Annie and seem equally as happy to see us. They give us partial lab results – the numbers we recognize – hemo and WBC are slightly low, but platelets and ANC are within the normal range. Good news. Things continue to progress toward normal.

Finally, Red Bull is weary of waiting and wants to go back to the sorority house and take a nap. I go with her, but can't rest. I begin walking back to the hospital when the hubs texts that they are ready for Annie in "Procedures." I meet them walking with the nurse on their way and we go to kiss her goodnight.

The hubs and I walk to the cafeteria commenting on all the new pictures we see as if we are doing a home tour. Trying to keep upbeat. We decide to get a snack. The hubs picks sushi. I give it a try. As I suspected... Yuck! But I am starving and eat half of it anyway. We sit and talk for a while and when we start back to the waiting room, we get a call that Annie is waking up. She is in a bad mood. Her back hurts and she is nauseous. The nurse brings her some goldfish and we wait for her smile to return. After about an hour, when we decide her temperament is as good as it will get for the evening, we get her discharge papers and wheel her back over to the sorority house. We offer to spend another night for her to recover, but she wants to sleep in her own bed. I can relate. We check out of the sorority house and say goodbye to St. Jude for another four months. We pray for good test results as we begin the six-hour drive home.

Annie wants complete silence, so I am relieved of my entertainment duties. We stop after a short time so she can go into a restroom and puke. I offer to get a motel room for the night and tell her we can drive the rest of the way in the morning. She ignores me and goes back to the car.

We stop at Mickey D's (of course we do), load up on junk and begin the rest of the way home. The rest of the ride home is (thankfully) uneventful.

Thursday, July 16, 2015

I am at work when I get the call from the hubs. He has heard from St. Jude. Good news! No sign of cancer. Though we had prayed for it and expected it, the news is such a relief, I sit for a minute and cry and say thank you to God. Then I go share with my co-workers before texting everyone I know.

This will be our life for the foreseeable future. Trips to Memphis, tests and anxiously awaiting results. Cancer sucks.

My *Don't* List

1. Don't think you can plan everything. Life can change in a day – for better or worse.

2. Don't worry about tomorrow. God doesn't let us see tomorrow because we can't handle tomorrow. He gives us grace as we need it to get us through each day.

3. Don't second-guess the thoughtful decisions you made regarding your child's treatment. (Thanks, Dr. K!)

4. Don't see every problem as a curse. God can always turn what was meant for evil into good. (Thanks, Joseph!)

5. Don't judge the decisions of other parents. Each family is different. What works for you might not work for them.

6. Don't neglect to pray for spiritual health rather than just physical health. Sick souls can cause more grief than sick bodies.

7. Don't forget about the child (or children) left behind. They are healthy and not getting the attention (and presents) of the sick child.

8. Don't give medical advice unless you are a physician.

9. Don't expect thank-you cards when you give to someone who is sick, grieving or in need. Thanks are only necessary for celebratory gifts.

10. Don't be shy about asking for your dishes back when you take food to a friend...or else you will never get them back. We want to give them back. We truly cannot identify their owners.

Made in the
USA
Columbia, SC